Chinese Labour in the Global Economy

Chinese development is widely considered to be an example of successful developmental catch-up with double-digit growth rates year on year. Some even talk of an emerging power, which may in time replace the US as the global economy's hegemon. And yet there is a dark underside to this 'miracle' in the form of workers' long hours, low pay and lack of welfare benefits. Increasing levels of inequality have gone hand in hand with super exploitative working conditions. Nevertheless, Chinese workers have not simply accepted these conditions of super-exploitation; they have started to fight back.

Set against the background of China's integration into the global economy along uneven and combined development lines, this volume explores new forms of resistance by Chinese workers, be it through the state trade union All-China Federation of Trade Unions (ACFTU) or through informal labour NGOs. It also analyses the links between Chinese formal and informal labour organisations with labour organisations outside China.

This book was originally published as a special issue of the journal *Globalizations*.

Andreas Bieler is Professor of Political Economy and Fellow of the Centre for the Study of Social and Global Justice (CSSGJ) in the School of Politics and International Relations at the University of Nottingham, UK.

Chun-Yi Lee is Fellow of the Centre for the Study of Social and Global Justice (CSSGJ), deputy Director of China Policy Institute (CPI) and Director of Taiwan Studies Program (TSP).

Rethinking Globalizations

Edited by Barry K. Gills, University of Helsinki, Finland and Kevin Gray, University of Sussex, UK.

This series is designed to break new ground in the literature on globalization and its academic and popular understanding. Rather than perpetuating or simply reacting to the economic understanding of globalization, this series seeks to capture the term and broaden its meaning to encompass a wide range of issues and disciplines and convey a sense of alternative possibilities for the future.

The Redesign of the Global Financial Architecture
The Return of State Authority
Stuart P. M. Mackintosh

Markets and Development
Civil Society, Citizens and the Politics of Neoliberalism
Edited by Toby Carroll and Darryl S.L. Jarvis

Occupying Subjectivity
Being and Becoming Radical in the 21st Century
Edited by Chris Rossdale

Localization in Development Aid
How Global Institutions enter Local Lifeworlds
Edited by Thorsten Bonacker, Judith von Heusinger and Kerstin Zimmer

The New Global Politics
Global Social Movements in the Twenty-First Century
Edited by Harry E. Vanden, Peter N. Funke and Gary Prevos

The Politics of Food Sovereignty
Concept, Practice and Social Movements
Edited by Annie Shattuck, Christina Schiavoni and Zoe VanGelder

Time and Globalization
An interdisciplinary dialogue
Edited by Paul Huebener, Susie O'Brien, Tony Porter, Liam Stockdale and Rachel Yanqiu Zhou

From International Relations to World Civilizations
The contributions of Robert W. Cox
Edited by Shannon Brincat

Chinese Labour in the Global Economy
Capitalist Exploitation and Strategies of Resistance
Edited by Andreas Bieler and Chun-Yi Lee

Chinese Labour in the Global Economy

Capitalist Exploitation and Strategies of Resistance

Edited by

Andreas Bieler and Chun-Yi Lee

Routledge
Taylor & Francis Group
LONDON AND NEW YORK

First published 2017
by Routledge

2 Park Square, Milton Park, Abingdon, Oxfordshire OX14 4RN
52 Vanderbilt Avenue, New York, NY 10017

Routledge is an imprint of the Taylor & Francis Group, an informa business

First issued in paperback 2018

British Library Cataloguing in Publication Data
A catalogue record for this book is available from the British Library

ISBN13: 978-1-138-72660-4 (hbk)
ISBN13: 978-0-367-22047-1 (pbk)

Typeset in Times New Roman
by RefineCatch Limited, Bungay, Suffolk

Publisher's Note
The publisher accepts responsibility for any inconsistencies that may have arisen during the conversion of this book from journal articles to book chapters, namely the possible inclusion of journal terminology.

Contents

Citation Information

The chapters in this book were originally published in *Globalizations*, volume 14, issue 2 (February 2017). When citing this material, please use the information from the original files, as follows:

Chapter 1
Chinese Labour in the Global Economy: An Introduction
Andreas Bieler and Chun-Yi Lee
Globalizations, volume 14, issue 2 (February 2017) pp. 179–188

Chapter 2
China's Place in the Global Divisions of Labour: An Uneven and Combined Development Perspective
Jane Hardy
Globalizations, volume 14, issue 2 (February 2017) pp. 189–201

Chapter 3
Exploitation and Resistance: A Comparative Analysis of the Chinese Cheap Labour Electronics and High-Value Added IT Sectors
Andreas Bieler and Chun-Yi Lee
Globalizations, volume 14, issue 2 (February 2017) pp. 202–215

Chapter 4
Why the Foxconn Model Does Not Die: Production Networks and Labour Relations in the IT Industry in South China
Boy Lüthje and Florian Butollo
Globalizations, volume 14, issue 2 (February 2017) pp. 216–231

Chapter 5
Bringing Class Struggles Back: A Marxian Analysis of the State and Class Relations in China
Chris King-chi Chan and Elaine Sio-ieng Hui
Globalizations, volume 14, issue 2 (February 2017) pp. 232–244

Chapter 6
A Class Against Capital: Class and Collective Bargaining in Guangdong
Tim Pringle
Globalizations, volume 14, issue 2 (February 2017) pp. 245–258

Chapter 7
The Labour Politics of China's Rural Migrant Workers
Jenny Chan and Mark Selden
Globalizations, volume 14, issue 2 (February 2017) pp. 259–271

Chapter 8
Dockworkers' Resistance and Union Reform within China's Globalised Seaport Industry
Xuebing Cao and Quan Meng
Globalizations, volume 14, issue 2 (February 2017) pp. 272–284

Chapter 9
The Yue Yuen Strike: Industrial Transformation and Labour Unrest in the Pearl River Delta
Stefan Schmalz, Brandon Sommer and Hui Xu
Globalizations, volume 14, issue 2 (February 2017) pp. 285–297

Chapter 10
The Makings of Subaltern Subjects: Embodiment, Contradictory Consciousness and Re-hegemonization of the Diaosi in China
Ngai-Ling Sum
Globalizations, volume 14, issue 2 (February 2017) pp. 298–312

Chapter 11
The China Price: The All-China Federation of Trade Unions and the Repressed Question of International Labour Standards
Rob Lambert and Edward Webster
Globalizations, volume 14, issue 2 (February 2017) pp. 313–326

Chapter 12
What Future for Chinese Labour and Transnational Solidarity?
Andreas Bieler and Chun-Yi Lee
Globalizations, volume 14, issue 2 (February 2017) pp. 327–333

Notes on Contributors

Andreas Bieler is Professor of Political Economy and Fellow of the Centre for the Study of Social and Global Justice (CSSGJ) in the School of Politics and International Relations, University of Nottingham, UK. He is author of *The struggle for a social Europe: Trade unions and EMU in times of global restructuring* (Manchester University Press, 2006) and co-editor (with Bruno Ciccaglione, Ingemar Lindberg and John Hilary) of *Free trade and transnational labour* (Routledge, 2015).

Florian Butollo is Assistant Professor at the Department of Labour, Industrial and Economic Sociology at the University of Jena, Germany. He is author of *The end of cheap labour? Industrial transformation and 'social upgrading' in China* (Campus, 2014).

Xuebing Cao is Lecturer in Human Resource Management at Keele Management School, Keele University, UK. His research interests include health professionals' pay, the emerging issues of trade unionism and migrant workers in China.

Chris King-Chi Chan is Associate Professor in the Department of Applied Social Sciences at the City University of Hong Kong. He has published widely on Chinese labour, including the book *The challenge of labour in China* (Routledge, 2010) and articles in leading journals in China, labour and development studies.

Jenny Chan (PhD in 2014 is an Assistant Professor of Sociology at the Hong Kong Polytechnic University. Prior to joining PolyU, she was a Lecturer of Sociology and Contemporary China Studies at the School of Interdisciplinary Area Studies, and a Junior Research Fellow (2015–2018) of Kellogg College, University of Oxford. She also serves as a board member of the International Sociological Association's Research Committee on Labour Movements.

Jane Hardy is Professor of Political Economy at the University of Hertfordshire. She is the author of *Poland's new capitalism* (2009). She has researched extensively on the political economy of migration in Europe and the responses of organised labour, and has most recently published in the *European Journal of Industrial Relations*, *European Urban and Regional Studies* and *Transfer*.

Elaine Sio-ieng Hui is Assistant Professor at the School of Labor and Employment Relations, Pennsylvania State University, USA. Her research interests include critical state theories, legal theories, class consciousness, civil society, social welfare and labour relations in China. She has published in peer-reviewed journals, such as *British Journal of Industrial Relations*, *Journal of Contemporary Asia*, *Journal of Industrial Relations*, *China Quarterly* and *International Labor Review*.

Rob Lambert is a Winthrop Professor of Employment Relations at the University of Western Australia's Business School. He is also a founder of the Southern Initiative on Globalisation & Trade Union Rights (SIGTUR). Together with Andries Bezuidenhout and Eddie Webster, he is the author of the award-winning book, *Grounding globalization: Labour in the age of insecurity.*

Chun-Yi Lee is Fellow of the Centre for the Study of Social and Global Justice (CSSGJ), deputy Director of China Policy Institute (CPI) and Director of Taiwan Studies Program (TSP). She is author of *Taiwanese business or Chinese security asset?* (Routledge, 2012). Chun-Yi's constant involvement in research testifies to her enthusiasm for and commitment to the field of Chinese Studies, International Relations and Political Economy.

Boy Lüthje holds the Volkswagen Endowed Chair for Industrial Relations and Social Development at the School of Government of Sun Yat-Sen University, Guangzhou, China. His recent publications include *From Silicon Valley to Shenzhen: Global production and work in the IT industry* (Rowman & Littlefield, 2013) and *Beyond the iron rice bowl: Regimes of production and industrial relations in China* (Campus, 2013).

Tim Pringle is a Senior Lecturer in Labour, Social Movements and Development at SOAS with special reference to China. Tim entered academia at the age of 45 when he embarked on a PhD programme at the University of Warwick while simultaneously working as a co-investigator on a major research project examining trade union reform in Russia, China and Vietnam. He has published two books: *Trade unions in China: The challenge of labour unrest* (Routledge, 2011) and *The challenge of transition: Trade unions in Russia, China and Vietnam* (Palgrave, 2011) with Professor Simon Clarke.

Quan Meng is Lecturer in Employment Relations and Labour Study in the School of Labour Economics, Capital University of Economics and Business, China. His research focuses on Chinese workers' collective action, trade unions, government intervention in labour protests and theories of employment relations.

Stefan Schmalz is a Senior Lecturer in Sociology at Friedrich-Schiller-University Jena. His research centres on labour relations in Europe and China and global political economy. His most recent book is on strikes and changing labour relations in Germany.

Mark Selden is a Senior Research Associate at the Asian/Pacific/American Studies Institute at New York University, Professor Emeritus of Sociology and History at Binghamton University, and Editor of the *Asia-Pacific Journal*. He researches the modern and contemporary geopolitics, political economy and history of China, Japan and the Asia Pacific. His work ranges broadly across themes of war and revolution, inequality, development, regional and world social change, social movements and historical memory.

Brandon Sommer is a PhD candidate at the International Institute of Social Studies in The Hague. His research interests lie in the areas of industrial and labour transformation in newly industrialized zones as well as precarious work, especially in China.

Ngai-Ling Sum is Reader in Cultural Political Economy in the Politics, Philosophy and Religion Department and Co-Director (with Bob Jessop) of the Cultural Political Economy Research Centre at Lancaster University. She was awarded (with Bob Jessop) the Gunnar Myrdal Prize by the European Association of Evolutionary Political Economics (EAEPE) for their coauthored book *Beyond the regulation approach* (Edward Elgar, 2006).

Hui Xu is a PhD candidate at Friedrich-Schiller-University Jena. His research interests focus on industrial upgrading and labour relations in China.

Edward Webster is Research Professor in the Society, Work and Development Institute at the University of the Witwatersrand. Among his publications is *Grounding globalization: Labour in the age of insecurity*, written with Rob Lambert and Andries Bezuidenhout, winner of the 2008 Distinguished Scholarly Monograph Prize, awarded by the American Sociological Association Labor and Labor Movements Section.

Chinese Labour in the Global Economy: An Introduction

ANDREAS BIELER & CHUN-YI LEE

University of Nottingham, Nottingham, UK

ABSTRACT *This Introduction outlines the main purpose of this special issue volume: to analyse new forms of resistance by Chinese workers against conditions of super-exploitation. After an assessment of the new international division of labour, we provide an overview of Chinese production in the global economy, followed by an introduction of the contributions to this volume.*

China is generally regarded as the new economic powerhouse in the global political economy. Some even talk of an emerging power, which may in time replace the US as the global economy's hegemon. And yet, there is a dark underside to this 'miracle' in the form of workers' long hours, low pay, and lack of welfare benefits. Increasing levels of inequality have gone hand in hand with widespread working conditions characterised by super-exploitation.

Nevertheless, Chinese workers have not simply accepted these conditions of exploitation. They have started to fight back. The purpose of this volume is to analyse these various forms of resistance by Chinese workers and the way they are organised, be it through the official state trade union All-China Federation of Trade Unions (ACFTU), be it through informal labour NGOs, or indeed both. Considering the large number of workers in Chinese production, what happens in China does not only affect Chinese workers, but equally workers elsewhere. Hence, the findings of this special issue on Chinese labour in the global economy are not only confined to China. They are of relevance for the global economy as a whole.

In this Introduction, we will first analyse key developments in the global political economy to set the stage. Second, we will assess the location of Chinese production within this new international division of labour, before providing an overview of the contributions to this volume.

Global Restructuring: The New International Division of Labour

The post-Second World War years in industrialised countries were characterised by enormous growth rates and increasing wealth. National class compromises between capital and labour were the foundation of this post-war economic recovery. While labour accepted capital's prerogative over the means of production and the way production is organised, capital in turn agreed on workers participating in growing wealth through a steady increase in wages and improvement in working conditions. In tripartite relationships, the state supported this compromise through Keynesian, demand-led economic policies guaranteeing full employment in a system of mass employment and mass consumption. Additionally, the state supported the class compromise through an expanding welfare state establishing universal access to services such as health and education. Observers often speak of a golden capitalist age when commenting on the post-war period. Nevertheless, when the rate of profit started to decline, economic growth was no longer strong enough to ensure both, capitalist super-profits and rising wages for workers. The late 1960s and the early 1970s saw increasing levels of industrial conflict in Western industrialised countries.

In response, capital renounced the national class compromises. While they technologically innovated production at the high-value added end in industrialised countries, in a spatial fix labour-intensive parts of manufacturing such as the textile industry were transferred to cheap labour locations in the Global South (Silver, 2003, pp. 64–66). Transnational corporations (TNCs) became the dominant companies within the new, transnationalised social relations of production, and a transnational capitalist class emerged as the new key agent of global capital within what has been referred to as globalisation (Robinson, 2004).

The increasing transnationalisation of production is reflected in the drastic increase in FDI especially since the mid-1980s, establishing lasting production links across borders. Outflows of FDI rose from US$88 billion in 1986 to US$1187 billion in 2000 as peak year (Bieler, 2006, p. 50). A period of recession caused a decline in FDI flows from 2001 to 2003, but four years of consecutive growth led to a new all-time high of FDI outflows of US$1996.5 billion in 2007 (UNCTAD, 2008, p. 253). Overall, there were close to 80,000 TNCs with roughly the same number of foreign affiliates in 2007 (UNCTAD, 2008, p. 212). Unsurprisingly, FDI flows have again declined since the onset of the global financial crisis in 2008 (UNCTAD, 2015, p. 18), but even slightly lower levels contribute to the continuing build-up of FDI stocks over time, indicating the ever more important role played by TNCs. While outward FDI stocks had been US$2,253,944 million in 1990, they were US$7,298,188 million in 2000 and US$25,874,757 million in 2014 (UNCTAD, 2015, p. A7).

The increasing transnationalisation of production has gone hand in hand with greater decentralisation and fragmentation of the production process itself through processes of outsourcing along the production chain. Thus, transnational production, under the direction of TNCs, is increasingly organised in global commodity chains (GCCs) (Robinson, 2008, p. 27). In this process, TNCs 'began dividing the production process into ever finer segments, both vertical and horizontal, and locating the separate stages in two or more countries, creating cross-border production networks' (Hart-Landsberg, 2013, p. 91). In these networks, TNCs no longer own the various production sites along the GCC, but rely on 'independent contract manufacturers to procure the necessary parts and components and oversee their assembly into final products' (Hart-Landsberg, 2013, p. 92). In other words, TNCs are still in charge, but their strategy has significantly changed. From owning cross-border production structures, they have moved to co-ordinating GCCs. As confirmed by the UN, 'TNC-coordinated [GCCs] account for some 80 per cent of global trade. Patterns of value added trade in [GCCs] are shaped to a significant extent by the investment decisions of TNCs' (UNCTAD, 2013, p. xxii).

> Developing Asia occupies the leading position in the new international division of labour. The region's share in total world exports of manufacturers grew from 11.1 percent in 1996–1997 to 33.8 percent in 2009/2010. Its share of total third world exports of manufactures increased from 68 percent to 76 percent over the same period. (Hart-Landsberg, 2015, p. 4)

Within Asia, China mainly operates as the regional assembly platform.

> It is China's unique position as the region's production platform that enabled the country to increase its share of world exports of IT products from 3 percent in 1992 to 24 percent in 2006, and its share of electrical goods from 4 percent to 21 percent over the same period. (Hart-Landsberg, 2013, p. 34)

In turn, these products are mainly destined for markets in North America and Europe integrating East Asia tightly with the global economy, but also making it dependent on continuing demand in the Global North. In sum,

> since the region's trade activity largely involves an intraregional trade of parts and components culminating in China-based exports aimed primarily at the United States and the European Union, the reality is that Asia has become ever more tightly integrated and dependent on exporting to developed capitalist markets, especially the United States. (Hart-Landsberg, 2013, p. 36)

The idea of South–South trade and economic co-operation as an alternative growth model for developing countries has not materialised. Rather, while China is the assembly platform of global capital, Latin America and Africa have mainly been reduced to exporters of primary commodities, with China having become their main customer.

> While Latin American and sub-Saharan nations have long specialised in the export of primary commodities, developing Asia, especially China, has now replaced core capitalist countries as their main export market. China has surpassed the United States as the world's largest consumer of major metals and agricultural commodities. In 2011, it consumed approximately 20 percent of all nonrenewable energy resources, 23 percent of major agricultural crops, and 40 percent of base metals. (Hart-Landsberg, 2015, p. 6)

Importantly, as David Coates remarked, the increasing organisation of production across borders and the related possibility for capital to move labour-intensive production to cheap labour locations is not due to new technology, but the result of social developments. 'Capital is more geographically mobile than it was in the past because it now has more proletariats on which to land' (Coates, 2000, p. 255) and more proletariats to create. The integration of China, India, and the former Soviet Union during the 1980s and 1990s doubled the global workforce to almost three billion by 2000 (Freeman, 2010). In 2011, China's working-age population alone numbered over 1 billion (Economist, 2012). The increase in the global workforce has also fuelled the informalisation of production. This is especially the case in developing countries, which had never been in a position to establish a large industrial sector with permanent and secure employment.

> According to the most recent estimates, non-agricultural employment in the informal economy represents 82 per cent of total employment in South Asia, 66 per cent in sub-Saharan Africa, 65 per cent in East and South-East Asia (excluding China), 51 per cent in Latin America and 10 per cent in Eastern Europe and Central Asia. (ILO, 2014, p. 6)

Nevertheless, informalisation more and more also affects developed countries in the North, where employers are on the offensive and demand a flexibilisation of the labour market with the argument that it is necessary in order to retain competitiveness (Standing, 2011). 'Although affecting workers in all core countries, the trend has probably gone furthest in Japan. There, part-time workers, who make on average 38 percent less per hour than full-time workers, now account for approximately 40 percent of the workforce' (Hart-Landsberg, 2015, p. 9).

The implications for workers around the world are clear. In times of transnational production, national labour movements are increasingly put into competition with each other. If workers in one country do not accept the demands by capital, production is moved to other locations where workers are more amenable. While trade unions were able to organise workers well at the national level, they have struggled to avoid cross-border competition. Additionally, it has been very difficult to organise along GCCs as well as within the informal economy (Bieler, Lindberg, & Sauerborn, 2010).

Chinese Production in the Global Political Economy

As a result of the particular location of Chinese labour in the global political economy as outlined above, Chinese production is characterised by two key aspects. First, it is predominantly based on cheap labour, necessary for assembling the various parts into final products for export to North American and European markets. 'Chinese leaders have, like the leaders of most other countries, consciously pursued a low-wage growth strategy for some time' (Hart-Landsberg, 2015, p. 14). Second, Chinese exports are dominated by foreign TNCs. By 2003, foreign TNCs and joint ventures 'accounted for almost 80% of China's exports of industrial machinery, 90% of computers, components, and peripherals; and 71% of electronics and telecommunications equipment' (Panitch & Gindin, 2014, p. 152). This tendency has intensified further in recent years.

> TNCs produce approximately 85 percent of China's high technology exports. Moreover, the share of China's high technology exports produced by wholly owned TNCs continues to grow, from 55 percent in 2002 to 68 percent in 2009, suggesting a tightening of foreign control. (Hart-Landsberg, 2015, p. 5).

Unsurprisingly, it is these foreign TNCs that reap super-profits from exploiting Chinese workers. Foxconn, assembling products for Apple, is a clear example in this respect. 'Hon Hai [Foxconn] made $2.4 billion in profits in 2010, or $2400 per employee, compared to $263,000 in profits reaped by Apple for each of its 63,000 employees (43,000 of whom are in the United States)' (Smith, 2012).

As most export production is based on cheap labour, China must ensure a continuing supply of workers willing to work for low wages. This has been secured partly as a result of the privatisation of state-owned enterprises in the mid-1990s, which resulted in the redundancy of some 60 million workers, and partly due to the growing group of migrant workers, which amounted to 269 million workers by 2013, coming from the countryside to the new production power houses in the coastal areas (Chan & Selden, 2014, pp. 600–601). The power of workers decreased significantly as a result of increasing precarity and labour's share of GDP 'fell from approximately 53 percent of GDP in 1992 to below 40 percent in 2006. Private consumption as a percent of GDP also declined, falling from approximately 47 percent to 36 percent over the same period' (Hart-Landsberg, 2013, p. 50; see also Qi, 2014).

The agricultural sector has played a crucial role in ensuring the supply of cheap labour in that it provided a separate stream of income especially for the dependents of migrant workers left back at home. In turn, this facilitated the super-exploitation of migrant workers themselves. Agriculture is, thus, closely linked to industrial production in that

> agriculture and the rural society provide the conditions for the reproduction of labour power. For rural households, agriculture in most cases is merely one of their income sources. Rural households are semi-proletarianised as they are participating in both household-organised agricultural production and wage employment. (Qi, 2014)

Unsurprisingly, this development model has led to enormous levels of inequality. Capitalism in general is driven by dynamics of uneven and combined development and unevenness characterises the international situation between different countries, as well as the situation within countries. China is no exception in this respect (see the contribution by Jane Hardy in this volume). Internationally, despite Chinese development the gap between China and industrialised countries has remained large.

> In 2010 (even after the aftermath of the crisis and recession) China's GDP was $5.9 trillion—only 40 percent of the US's $14.6 trillion. Translated into GDP per head this gap is even starker: China's $4,260 was only 9 percent of the US's $47,240. (Hardy & Budd, 2012)

As Neil Davidson concludes, 'although China develops more dramatically than any of the countries, like India, with which it is usually bracketed, it is unlikely on any remotely foreseeable scenario, to "catch up" with the West in any overall sense' (Davidson, 2006, p. 226). Within China, inequality has increased too.

> Whereas inequality in China in 1980 was comparable to that of social democratic Germany (Gini coefficient = 0.25), by 2005 it was less equal than Russia (Gini coefficient = 0.45). The wealthiest 10 percent of the Chinese population earned seven times that of the poorest 10 percent in the 1980s but by 2005 that inequality had risen to a factor of 18. The richest 10 percent of the population now accounts for 45 percent of the country's wealth, the poorest 10 percent only 1.4 percent. (Smith, 2008, p. 256)

Hypermodern coastal regions are counterpoised to backward, inner rural areas.

> According to one estimate, the 'winners' of the economic reforms—the state administrators, managers, private entrepreneurs, professionals and technicians—amount to approximately 9 per cent of the entire population. The losers, on the other hand—the production workers, service workers, farmers, the unemployed and underemployed—amount to about 82 per cent of the population. (Gray, 2010, p. 460)

In response to the global financial crisis, China implemented a stimulus package of US$586 billion in 2008 and 2009. Highly praised at the international level and regarded as proof of the narrative of China as a lender able to lead the global economy out of crisis, the way it was structured had dramatic implications at the national level. Because local governments were asked to provide matching funds for central government investment, the result was an 'increasing commodification of land as a means to generate income' (Sum & Jessop, 2013, p. 457). In turn, this had social consequences. 'Land sales and property development became important investment and speculative activities with consequences such as a property bubble, forced displacement from land, peasant riots, state terror, dispossession of the already vulnerable (e.g. migrant children) and increasing inequalities' (Sum & Jessop, 2013, p. 463). Moreover, this stimulus package has not increased private consumption as a percentage of GDP. In 2012, it was still at 35% (Hart-Landsberg, 2015, p. 14).

And yet, importantly, workers are not only victims of capitalist exploitation. They have also got agency of resistance. As Chan and Selden indicate, labour disputes are on the rise, workers are fighting back:

> Official statistics show that in 1996, 48,121 labor disputes were accepted for arbitration, the total rising sharply to 120,191 in 1999, involving more than 470,000 aggrieved laborers as numbers soared in the context of massive layoffs of state sector workers. The upward trend continued from 2000, reflecting widespread incidences of rights violations as the private sector expanded. Labor cases further skyrocketed to 693,465 involving more than 1.2 million laborers nationwide in the economic crisis of 2008. These were disputes over wage and insurance payments, illegal layoffs, and inadequate compensation payments. (Chan & Selden, 2014, p. 607)

Demanding higher income, better working conditions, respect for their dignity, and social protection, Chinese workers are no longer prepared to work in conditions of super-exploitation. This volume is dedicated to a focus on workers' resistance and an assessment of the possibilities of Chinese workers to improve their situation.

Overview of Special Issue Structure

In her contribution, Jane Hardy analyses in detail how Chinese production is integrated into the global political economy along lines of uneven and combined development. While Chinese development is closely combined with global development, it is also extremely uneven between China and other countries as well as within China itself. Hardy further indicates how the stimulus package in 2008, with which the Chinese government attempted to avoid being dragged into the global recession, resulted in a huge crisis of overaccumulation. The official figure of US$586 billion needs to be complemented by the additional loans taken up by local governments across China, all in a desperate search for profitable investment opportunities. Ultimately, China's response to the global financial crisis is based on a fundamental contradiction. On the one hand, the government intends to boost domestic demand through higher wages to become less dependent on exports to North America and Europe; on the other, however, it needs to keep wages low to ensure increasing productivity and continuing competitiveness, on which large parts of Chinese exports are based. It is, therefore, not surprising that the results of the stimulus package are highly mixed and private consumption as a percentage of GDP has not increased (see above).

Andreas Bieler and Chun-Yi Lee, in turn, start their comparative analysis of resistance in the cheap labour, low value-added electronics sector in the Pearl River Delta (PRD) area and resistance in the higher-value added IT sector in the Yangtse River Delta (YRD) with an assessment of the different locations of these two production sectors in the global economy. Because the electronics sector is mainly based on cheap labour, there are higher levels of industrial conflict over pay and working conditions. By contrast, the higher-value added IT sector depends on a more skilled and stable workforce. Hence, it has to provide better pay and working conditions. Unsurprisingly, these different locations in the global political economy shape the forms of struggle in the two sectors. In the electronics industry, informal labour NGOs generally assist workers individually and collectively in securing their rights, often in open confrontation with management, while more formal labour NGOs in the IT sector focus on organising interesting after-work activities for workers. Does this indicate that general upgrading to more high-value added activities could be a more general path towards improved working conditions for workers?

Boy Lüthje and Florian Butollo's research casts doubts over this assumption. They investigate in more detail the electronics contract manufacturing (ECM) industry in China's Pearl River Delta (PRD). They identify technological upgrading and diversification of production, combined, however, with a continuation of super-exploitation of workers, based on extremely flexible mass production with a low-skilled workforce and a high turnover of personnel. There have been some continuing, modest wage increases due to a raising minimum wage, but base wages in general remain low and workers continue to depend on excessive overtime. In short, the linkage between industrial upgrading on the one hand and an upgrading of work and labour relations on the other is weak. Social innovation in the workplace is still missing. Interestingly, the PRD continues to be a major site of ECM production with new factories further inland complementing rather than replacing factories in the PRD.

How can we then understand the role of the Chinese state in industrial development and workers' struggles for their rights? In their chapter on class struggle and the Chinese state, Chan and Hui argue that neither the notion that the role of the state has been undermined by globalisation, nor the concept of the state as an autonomous, independent actor is adequate, when assessing the Chinese state. Rather, the state needs to be understood as a field and condensation of class struggle. Hence, during the economic crisis global capital pushed the Chinese state towards reducing the protection of workers. In the wake of economic recovery, however, workers started to re-assert themselves in a wave of strikes such as the strike at Honda in 2010 and at Yue Yuen in 2014. To ensure the overall continuation of capitalist accumulation the state had to intervene in their support in relation to demands around collective bargaining and company contributions to social insurance systems. In short, class struggle rather than technological upgrading is the way towards improved working conditions.

This conclusion is supported by Tim Pringle. In his contribution to this volume, he pursues a class against capital approach in his analysis of rising demands for collective bargaining by Chinese workers. Rather than drawing on the notions of 'class-in-itself' and 'class-for-itself', where especially the former is considered to be the result of workers' location within production and, thus, delinked from struggle, the notion of class against capital emphasises the centrality of class conflict. Pringle, thus, overcomes artificial notions of fragmented working classes, often imposed by capital and the state from above to undermine labour solidarity. Interestingly, in his analysis of class struggles in the southern province of Guangdong, he also investigates in detail the struggles of the highly precarious and fragmented sanitation workers in Guangzhou in addition to the more well-known strikes in the Honda-owned auto parts factory in Foshan, at the Yantian International Container Terminals and the Yue Yuen shoe manufacturer in Dongguan, examined by other contributions to this volume. Overall, he argues that labour has emerged as a class against capital in Guangdong changing the balance of class forces and pushing capital and state into forms of collective bargaining.

The article by Chan and Selden focuses specifically on the situation of China's migrant workforce. A new generation of migrant workers is emerging, they argue, which no longer intends to return to their homes in rural China, but wants to improve their lives in the cities, where they are working. Against the background of super-exploitation in companies such as Foxconn they adopt a variety of strategies to support their demands for better pay, better social benefits, and more human working hours. The state increasingly attempts to intervene in disputes also through the official ACFTU to mediate between workers and employers, but workers are continuing to push independently to secure their rights from employers. Considering the crucial location in GCCs and the fact that there is a decrease in the number of young workers, these workers enjoy considerable bargaining power vis-à-vis employers and the state. It is this bargaining power that ultimately ensures that class struggle results in gains for workers.

Xuebing Cao and Quan Meng analyse the strike by dockworkers at the Yantian International Container Terminals in 2013. They demonstrate how these workers were able to organise themselves towards strike activity in the absence of an active official union, which resulted in a pay increase of 30%. They could rely on a range of different sources of bargaining power, including, most importantly, workplace bargaining power. The introduction of new technology in ports had implied that the work carried out had become ever more specialised. Hence, when these workers went on strike, their company was unable to replace them.

In their contribution to this volume, Schmalz, Sommer and Xu analyse the underlying dynamics of the mass strike at the shoe factory Yue Yuen in Dongguan. Overall, three factors contributed to the strike. First, there has been increasing low wage competition by other regions in China and other countries putting downward pressure on shoe factories in southern China. Employers such as Yue Yuen attempted to cut costs by not paying social insurance contributions. Second, the Communist Party's anti-corruption campaign is creating new spaces for workers to demand that employers comply with their legal obligations. Third, social insurance payments and their vital importance for older workers close to retirement have increasingly become an important issue for industrial conflict. Interestingly, unlike Chan and Selden in this volume, they point out that it is not necessarily always younger migrant workers who take strike action. Middle-aged and older migrant workers too go on strike in order to defend their social protection such as pensions upon retirement. When it became apparent that their employer Yue Yuen had not paid the legally required social insurance payments, 40,000 workers took strike action concerned about their personal future.

Against the background of two closely related hope projects—the global hope project of China as an object driving global growth as well as the Chinese hope project based on building national strength and modernity—Ngai-Ling Sum traces the emergence of a new subaltern class in China, the so-called Diaosi. This new group, on the one hand, actively embraces its loser identity and marginality in Chinese society. At the same time, she also demonstrates that this development does not automatically imply that these Diaosi form a group of resistance to their exploitation. Many actions are also an expression of resignation. Capital, moreover, attempts to re-integrate the Diaosi into society by providing particular avenues of specific consumption for these people. It discovers the Diaosi as a potential market and thereby pacifies them. Finally, the state increasingly attempts to control their actions of resistance in the name of civility and social stability. In short, mounting resistance by Chinese workers against super-exploitation should not be taken for granted. It emerges in processes of class struggle, which also include moments of exploited workers' co-optation into the hegemonic Chinese modernisation project.

Globalisation has put different national labour movements in competition with each other. Hence, the level of exploitation of workers in China has direct consequences of exploitation levels of workers in other countries. Unsurprisingly, the global labour movement in its institutional expression of the International Trade Union Confederation and various Global Union Federations assesses its possibilities of engaging with Chinese labour organisations and workers' struggles and here in particular the ACFTU. With about 134 million members, it appears to be too powerful an organisation to be disregarded. And yet, in their contribution to this volume, Rob Lambert and Eddie Webster caution against a rush towards official contact. As they point out, the ACFTU is actually part of the Chinese labour regime. Being closely aligned with, and subordinated to, the Chinese Communist Party, the ACFTU has little room for independent manoeuvre. Most importantly, the ACFTU has not accepted the international labour standards of the ILO including, for example, the right to free association. It is, therefore, not a 'proper' trade union independent from the Chinese state and can, as a result, not fulfil the function of organising workers' resistance against exploitation. Rather than co-operating with the ACFTU, Lambert and Webster conclude, international labour organisations should support local workers and their struggles. Simultaneously, they should intensify their pressure on the ACFTU to accept international labour standards. In the Conclusion to this volume, we will pick up on the issue of how to support best Chinese workers in their struggles for social justice.

Acknowledgements

This special issue is the outcome of the workshop *Chinese Labour in the Global Economy*, held at the University of Nottingham/UK on 11 and 12 September, 2014. We thankfully acknowledge the grant of £275k by the Economic and Social Research Council (ESRC) for the project on 'Globalisation, national transformation and workers' rights: an analysis of Chinese labour within the global economy' (RES-062-23-2777). The workshop as well as this special issue are part of our outputs from this research project. Many thanks to the contributors to the special issue and Barry Gills for their comments on the Introduction and to Jon Mansel for his research assistance in editing this special issue.

Disclosure Statement

No potential conflict of interest was reported by the authors.

Funding

This work was supported by the Economic and Social Research Council (ESRC) [grant number RES-062-23-2777].

References

Bieler, A. (2006). *The struggle for a social Europe: Trade unions and EMU in times of global restructuring*. Manchester: Manchester University Press.

Bieler, A., Lindberg, I., & Sauerborn, W. (2010). After thirty years of deadlock: Labour's possible strategies in the new global order. *Globalizations*, *7*(1–2), 247–260.

Chan, J., & Selden, M. (2014). China's rural migrant workers, the state, and labor politics. *Critical Asian Studies*, *46*(4), 599–620.

Coates, D. (2000). *Models of capitalism: Growth and stagnation in the modern era*. Cambridge: Polity.

Davidson, N. (2006). China: Unevenness, combination, revolution? In H. Radice & B. Dunn (Eds.), *100 Years of permanent revolution: Results and prospects* (pp. 211–229). London: Pluto Press.

Economist. (2012, January 21). *China's labour forces: One billion workers*. Retrieved from http://www.economist.com/blogs/freeexchange/2012/01/chinas-labour-force; accessed 01/12/2015

Freeman, R. (2010). What really ails Europe (and America): The doubling of the global workforce. *The Globalist*. Retrieved from http://www.theglobalist.com/what-really-ails-europe-and-america-the-doubling-of-the-global-workforce/

Gray, K. (2010). Labour and the state in China's passive revolution. *Capital & Class*, *34*(3), 449–467.

Hardy, J., & Budd, A. (2012). China's capitalism and the crisis. *International Socialism: A Quarterly Journal of Socialist Theory*, *133*. Retrieved from http://www.isj.org.uk/?id=777

Hart-Landsberg, M. (2013). *Capitalist globalization: Consequences, resistance, and alternatives*. New York, NY: Monthly Review Press.

Hart-Landsberg, M. (2015). From the claw to the lion: A critical look at capitalist globalization. *Critical Asian Studies*. doi:10.1080/14672715.2015.997024

ILO. (2014). *Transitioning from the informal to the formal economy*. Geneva: Author. Retrieved December 16, 2014, from http://www.ilo.org/wcmsp5/groups/public/—ed_norm/—relconf/documents/meetingdocument/wcms_218128.pdf

Panitch, L., & Gindin, S. (2014). The integration of China into global capitalism. *International Critical Thought*, *3*(2), 146–158.

Qi, H. (2014). 'The labor share question in China'. *Monthly Review*, *65*(8). Retrieved from http://monthlyreview.org/2014/01/01/labor-share-question-china

Robinson, W. I. (2004). *A theory of global capitalism: Production, class, and state in a transnational world*. Baltimore, MD: John Hopkins University Press.

Robinson, W. I. (2008). *Latin America and global capitalism: A critical globalization perspective*. Baltimore, MD: Johns Hopkins University.

Silver, B. J. (2003). *Forces of labor: Workers' movements and globalization since 1870*. Cambridge: Cambridge University Press.

Smith, J. (2012). The GDP illusion: Value added versus value capture. *Monthly Review*, *64*(3), 86. Retrieved from http://monthlyreview.org/2012/07/01/the-gdp-illusion, accessed 08/11/2013

Smith, N. (2008). *Uneven development: Nature, capital, and the production of space* (3rd ed.). Athens: The University of Georgia Press.

Standing, G. (2011). *The precariat: The new dangerous class*. London: Bloomsbury Academic.

Sum, N.-L., & Jessop, B. (2013). *Towards a cultural political economy: Putting culture in its place in political economy*. Cheltenham: Edward Elgar.

UNCTAD. (2008). *World investment report 2008: Transnational corporations and the infrastructure challenge*. Geneva: UN. Retrieved from http://unctad.org/en/Docs/wir2008_en.pdf

UNCTAD. (2013). *World investment report 2013 – Global value chains: Investment and trade for development. World investment report 2013*. New York, NY: UN. Retrieved from http://unctad.org/en/PublicationsLibrary/wir2013_en.pdf

UNCTAD. (2015). *World investment report 2015: Reforming international investment governance*. Geneva: UN. Retrieved from http://unctad.org/en/PublicationsLibrary/wir2015_en.pdf

China's Place in the Global Divisions of Labour: An Uneven and Combined Development Perspective

JANE HARDY

University of Hertfordshire, Hatfield, UK

ABSTRACT *By examining the contradictions in China's model of growth and the shifting dynamics of its place in the global division of labour, the aim of this paper is to understand the tensions in the class relations that underpin the Chinese 'success story'. The theoretical lens will be that of uneven and combined development. The notion of 'combined' informs the way in which China's integration with global capitalism and global circuits of capital has been a major source of its meteoric growth, but has increased its economic vulnerability, particularly after the 2008 crisis. The element of unevenness explores the differentiation between and within sectors and regions, and the way that the inherent dynamics of equalisation and differentiation, and the role of labour within these processes, underpin the dynamics of China's insertion into the global divisions of labour.*

Introduction

After meteoric rates of growth, averaging nearly 10% for two decades, in 2015 China was officially declared to be the world's largest economy. It is the world's largest exporter and trader, accounts for 22% of global manufacturing, and dominates the production of a wide range of goods (Meckstroth, 2014; UNCTAD, 2014). However, the sustainability of this success story, predicated on low wages and high exports of goods and capital, is being increasingly questioned as a result of a slowdown in growth rates and the recognition of significant tensions and contradictions in China's model of accumulation. This model is based on a set of class relations that are being increasingly challenged by explosive protests and unprecedented levels of strikes by workers. Indeed Hung (2015) argues that not only is China a major source of global imbalances and crises, but that its boom is set to fade. The aim of this article is to contextualise these tensions in class relations in general, and labour relations in particular, by elaborating a political economy of China in the global division of labour in which an increasingly restive Chinese working class, which is the subject of this special issue, can be located.

The argument comprises two conceptual strands. First, drawing on political economy approaches, at a macro level emerging divisions of labour are placed and understood in wider processes of capitalist development and the integration of China with the global economy, and in particular the way in which significant sections of production are locked into the value chains of western transnational corporations (TNCs). It is argued that the mode of accumulation that is driving the economy is beset with contradictions; particularly salient is the need to raise domestic consumption at the same time as maintaining competitive advantage based on low wages. Second, drawing on insights from economic geography, at a micro-level, unevenness and emerging divisions of labour need to be underpinned by the law of value. Both of these elements are brought together in the theory of uneven and combined development (Anievas, 2010; Ashman, 2006, 2010; Dunn & Radice, 2006; van der Linden, 2007; Novack, 1972; Smith, 2006, 2008; Trotsky, 2008), which enables a dynamic and non-teleological account of contradictions in the regime of accumulation and exploration of the associated implications for sectors, regions, and labour.

The structure of the paper is as follows. The following section elaborates the analytical foundations of uneven and combined development from a political economy and economic geography perspective. Section three examines unevenness and tensions within China's regime of accumulation as it has increasingly integrated with the global economy, and how these have been exacerbated since the 2008 crisis. Section four focuses on China's capital in global divisions of labour. In particular, it explores how far it is making technological leaps to catch up with advanced capitalist countries and whether it can shift its comparative advantage from low wage production, based on foreign TNCs, to indigenous production that is moving up the value chain.

Conceptual Framework: The Macro and Micro Foundations of Uneven and Combined Development

Although the notion of uneven and combined development is conceptually integrated, drawing on Marxist ideas, political economy and economic geography posit different routes to understanding its significance, effects, and relevance for China. In the case of the former, the broadly macro perspective emphasises the role and development of states in a unified global market, while the micro foundations of economic geography enable an analysis of labour and spatial and sectoral specificities.

A Macro Political Approach

The starting point of the conceptual approach of uneven and combined development is the assumption that the world economy, rather than being a sum of national parts, is an independent reality, created by the international division of labour and the world market (Barker, 2006; Li, 2008). The general proposition that the development of one economy is, positively or negatively, a condition for the development in others is heightened in advanced capitalism. Unevenness implies difference and hierarchy, but also a totality in which unevenness can occur (Ashman, 2006, p. 93). Capitalism unifies the world into a single interactive productive system under the dominance of capital, where social entities are bound together into an interacting and interrelated whole and in that sense are combined. However, the world economy and nation states are not dichotomous entities, whereby the coercive laws of the value in the former unfold and are inflected in the latter. Rather they are mutually constitutive in a process where nation states are both constrained and shaped by the parameters of accumulation processes in the global economy, but at the same time the strategies of states and capital reshape these accumulation processes and forge a new set of parameters and dynamics.

However, although the global economy is unified into a single world market 'world society has *emphatically* not become a homogenous capitalist milieu' (van der Linden, 2007, p. 151). Within this unified system there are competing blocs, the economic, political, and military dynamics of which do not work in the same direction. Entangled within these blocs, as well as nation states, the competing logics of TNCs and different fractions of capital have to be included. Therefore uneven development is reflected in the structured inequality of the world system, and in addition to individual countries it is manifest in local and regional disparities and between different sectors and individual firms within them. The relationship between core capitalist and 'backward' economies is encapsulated in the following (oft used) quote:

> The laws of history have nothing in common with pedantic schematism. Unevenness, the most general law of the historic process, reveals itself most sharply and complexly in the destiny of backward countries. Under the whip of external necessity, their backward culture is compelled to make leaps. From the universal law of unevenness thus derives another law which, for lack of a better name, we may call the law of *combined development*—by which we mean a drawing together of different stages of the journey, a combining of the steps, an amalgam of archaic with more contemporary forms. A backward country assimilates the material and intellectual conquests of the advanced countries ... The privilege of historical backwardness ... compels the adoption of whatever is in advance of any specified date, skipping a whole series of intermediate stages. (Trotsky, 2008, pp. 4–5)

Further, in contrast to incrementalist accounts of development, uneven and combined development holds the possibility that beyond accelerated change and catch-up there is the potential for leapfrogging the technical innovations of core capitalist economies (Novack, 1972), albeit unevenly between firms, sectors, regions, and localities. While this summarises the elements of a broad political economy perspective on uneven and combined development geographers have advanced a theoretical understanding of its micro foundations.

The Micro Foundations of Unevenness, Spatiality, and Labour

An understanding of the 'whip of external necessity' (Trotsky, 2008, p. 4), which imposes competitive pressures on economies, has to be rooted in the inner workings of capitalism explained by Marx's law of value. The essential contradiction lies between a constant tendency for differentiation rooted in the division of labour and organisation of production and the opposite tendency towards universalisation reflected in the drive towards the equalisation of the rate of profit (Smith, 2006). This critical dynamic of capitalism has a spatial element and concrete outcomes as capital moves to specific places where higher profits can be obtained or falling profits restored. There is a contradiction between these two opposing tendencies; on the one hand there is radical differentiation and on the other competitive equalisation of the conditions of social production and reproduction.

> In practice, this contradiction, internal to the logic of capital accumulation, finds it resolution precisely in uneven geographical development, which established discrete places differentiated from each other and at the same time pressures these places, across borders into a single mould ... The

> levelling tendency of capitalism continually gnaws at the radical differentiation of the conditions for the exploitation of labour, and yet corrosive differentiation of labour also eternally frustrates this 'annihilation of space by time'. (Smith, 2006, p. 190)

Put another way the competition for markets between different firms in the same industry and the exit and entry of capital from less profitable to more profitable sectors leads to the formation of a general rate of profit. Competition is therefore a force for equalisation, but technological and institutional change, as well as contestation by workers, constantly produces a new unevenness. What emerges is the twin processes of equalisation and differentiation as each capital, by raising productivity and intensifying the exploitation of labour in its own unit aims to realise extra profit (Ashman, 2006).

Geographers, therefore, have elaborated in much greater detail how the inner workings or micro foundations of the system produce the spatial unevenness inherent to capitalism (Harvey, 2006; McGrath-Champ, Herod, & Rainnie, 2010; Smith, 2008). Others have looked at how unevenness is constructed through the intricacies of global value chains and how networks of embodied labour are embroiled spatially and in the workplace (Coe, Dicken, & Hess, 2008; Rainnie, Herod, & McGrath-Champ, 2013; Starosta, 2010).

The pivotal role of labour in understanding unevenness and spatiality needs to be understood at two broad levels. First, labour as the sole source of value, derived from the necessary labour time spent in producing a commodity, underpins the whole edifice of Marx's work. In competitive accumulation he argues that employers will seek to increase absolute and relative surplus value. 'The production of absolute surplus value turns exclusively upon the length of the working day; the production of relative surplus value, revolutionises out and out the technical processes of labour, and the composition of society' (Marx, 1976, p. 645). Concretely this means that the class that represents capital will employ a myriad of strategies regarding wages and the organisation of work—which will be contested by workers, individually or collectively, to varying degrees.

Second, in a broader sense the conditions of production are shaped by the struggle between competing factions of both capital and labour (Herod, 2006; Rainnie, Herod, & McGrath-Champ, 2011). First-order determinations, driven by the inner workings of capitalism, give rise to second-order determinations manifest as institutional forms such as international and national regulatory regimes, sectoral specificities, and structural power (Selwyn, 2007) and the shifting power between organised workers and capital. Within this conceptual framework the objective and potential role of labour is therefore at the apex of the analysis. The subjective nature of labour and realisation of labour power in contesting capital at the point of production is the outcome of complex and contingent factors, such as, for example, competition in the sector for the product, the demands of the customers, and power relations in value chains. Social relations of production, class conflict, and resistance vary by sector and location, both reflecting and producing new unevenness.

The next section turns to looking at how new forms of unevenness have been generated by China's increasing integration with the global economy and response to the 2008 crisis.

China's Integration with the Global Economy: Exacerbated Tensions Since 2008

Tensions in China's economy have been well elaborated from a Marxist perspective by Li (2008) and since 2008 by Hung (2009, 2015). The aim of this section is to elaborate the way in which tensions generated since 2008 as a result of integration with the global economy have been exacerbated and generated new forms of unevenness. The following three sections discuss the way in which China's mode of accumulation has resulted in internal imbalances between consumption and investment, which are fundamentally interlinked with and dependent on other parts of the global economy, and the US and Europe in particular.

An 'Unbalanced' Economy: Towards a Crisis of Over-accumulation

A key factor in China's rapid growth has been unparalleled capital accumulation. The proportion of national output going into investment is significantly higher than in other developing economies and over twice the average for the core capitalist G7 countries. This colossal rate of investment was enabled by the exploitation of low-paid workers and by the high levels of savings of workers and peasants, characteristic of all the rapidly industrialising Asian economies after 1945. These savings are recycled by state-run banks to provide loans to industry (Ma & Yi, 2010).

From 2000 to 2013 the annual growth of investment averaged 12.2%, compared with the growth of private consumption of 7.3% (World Bank Statistics, 2014). As a consequence over the same period the share of private consumption in GDP decreased from 62% to 48%, while the share of fixed investment rose from 34% to 47% (World Bank, 2014a, 2014b). Further, wages as a proportion of national income fell for 22 consecutive years, from 56.5% in 1983 to 36.7% in 2005 (Hou, 2010). Externally this accumulation has been fuelled by foreign capital—both from overseas Chinese and the core capitalist economies—attracted by the low wages of Chinese workers and with longer term expectations of the growth of the potentially gargantuan Chinese consumer market. Internally accumulation has been driven by central government and exacerbated by competition between local governments—what Huang (2003) describes as 'one country, thirty two economies'. Rather than producing a more specialised economy this reinforced China's 'duplicative industrial structure by allowing every production branch at both central and local levels continued expanded reproduction in the extensive mode' (Hart-Landsberg and Burkett, 2006, p. 62 quoting Lau, 1999, p. 4). This competition between local governments has accentuated what Marx identified as the anarchic nature of accumulation and resulted in the uncoordinated construction of redundant production capacity.

There are other problems of over-accumulation. From the early 1990s the uneven and breakneck speed of development created shortages and inflationary pressures, which were intensified by the government's fiscal injection prompted by the sharp fall in exports to EU and US after the 2008 crisis. The 2008 mega-stimulus package's headline figure of $570 billion substantially under-stated the real stimulus as, in addition, the state directed banks to increase their loans to firms and local government (Huang, 2003). This in turn reinforced the tendency towards over-accumulation. As Hung (2008) points out, only 20% of the rescue package was directed towards social spending, the bulk of it going to fixed asset investment in sectors already plagued by over capacity—such as steel and concrete—and the construction of the world's fastest high-speed rail system (Soh & Wang, 2011). The infrastructure boom and massive expansion of credit insulated the Chinese economy from the collapse of exports in the wake of the crisis, but laid the basis for other problems.

By autumn 2011, other sources of systemic risk were appearing. There was an increasing reliance on credit for investment; with the latter increasing from 130% of GDP in 2008 to 200% by 2013 (Nabar & N'Diaye, 2013). The huge debts amassed by local governments and the rapid expansion of informal markets to supply credit threatened to boomerang back on the real economy. In response to government exhortations to borrow and stimulate regional economies after the 2008 crisis, local governments accumulated unprecedented debts; new credit is being taken to service existing debt (Jiang & Wu, 2014). The liabilities of local governments increased by 67% from 10.7 trillion yuan in 2010 to 17.9 trillion yuan in 2013, representing 27% and 33% of national GDP, respectively (Jiang & Xu, 2014). This problem appears even more acute as some local governments are now being sued for late payments (Mitchell & Wildau, 2015).

By 2011 the government was trying to dampen the overheating property market and halt the speculative boom by instructing banks to cut back on credit. This led to the growth of an informal finance sector or 'shadow banking', as underground lenders and trust companies extended credit to individuals and firms who might not have otherwise qualified (Hung, 2008; Nabar & N'Diaye, 2013). These loans were then 'sliced and diced' into investment packages that resemble the 'toxic' collateralised debt that triggered the first phase of the current global crisis. Burgeoning informal lending has been described as a 'time bomb' that poses a bigger risk to the Chinese economy than even the amassing of debts by local government (Soh & Wang, 2011). These cheap loans to firms and local government have amplified over-investment into a generalised risk to the economy and produced parallels with the sub-prime crisis that engulfed the US and European economies from 2007.

The Problems of Balancing and Rebalancing

China's ruling class are concerned about their ability to control the tempo of competitive accumulation and the over-dependence of China's growth on exports to the world's major markets. Although the share of exports in GDP has fallen from a high of 39% in 2006 to 26% in 2013, China's growth model remains highly dependent on exports to the US and Europe (World Bank Statistics). In 2007 Premier Wen Jiabao told the People's Congress that the economy was 'unstable, unbalanced, uncoordinated and ultimately unsustainable' (Wolf, 2011). Reflecting the fears of China's ruling class that the scale of accumulation is not sustainable, the 12th Five Year Plan (2011–2015) called for a sharp change in the pace and structure of economic growth, which included slower growth and a rebalancing from investment to consumption (see Jiabao, 2011). However, while recent years have seen some increase in wages, partly as a result of workers' struggles, a more substantial increase in domestic consumption driven by rising wages presents immense difficulties for the ruling class.

A further problem with attempting to raise incomes to increase demand for domestic production lies in the fact that China's high personal savings are difficult to translate into consumption. For most workers these are needed to compensate for the lack of welfare and to pay for medical expenses, children's education, and retirement (Ma & Yi, 2010). Additionally, it is estimated that more than 80% of total housing saving deposits are owned by less than 20% of the population (Hung, 2009).

Rebalancing the economy towards domestic consumption that entails the contradictory impetus to increase wages and simultaneously keep costs sufficiently low to maintain competitiveness poses a significant dilemma for the ruling class. Further, the unevenness of different regions, sectors, and firms means that measures that serve the interests of China's capitalism as a whole may have differential impacts spatially and sectorally, and therefore the interests of different sections of the ruling class are fractured.

From 2005 the government tried to fuel domestic consumption to rebalance the economy by boosting the disposable income of peasants and urban workers. Measures included the abolition of agricultural taxes and a rise in government procurement prices for agricultural products.

Although these measures to raise rural living standards were a small step, their effect was instantaneous. Slightly improved conditions in the rural-agricultural sector slowed the flow of migration to the cities and produced a sudden shortage of labour and a hike in wages in the coastal export-processing zones (Hung, 2009). No sooner had the government taken its first step towards domestic consumption-driven growth, than some sections of the ruling class in the coastal export sector complained about the impact on their profitability. They demanded compensating policies to safeguard their competitiveness, and attempted to sabotage further initiatives to raise workers' living standards (Hung, 2009). Nevertheless, such is the pressure on China's rulers that measures to stave off social unrest have included the raising of the minimum wage and threshold for tax along with plans to build 36 million units of low-cost housing (Hung, 2009). The next section discusses how this tension in interrelated with the co-dependence of China and the US.

China–US: A Major Fault Line in the Global Economy

China's major export markets are the US and EU, accounting, respectively, for 17.2% and 16.3% of its exports in 2013 (World Trade Organisation, 2014). The expansion of the US market, highly dependent on both private and public borrowing, has sucked in colossal volumes of imports from China and produced a huge Chinese trade surplus. In this way China has become the world's largest holder of foreign exchange reserves. China's official holdings of US Treasury securities have been growing exponentially to reach $1.3 trillion as of December 2013. Financing 22% of US debt, China is the largest foreign holder of US Treasury securities (it overtook Japan as the largest holder in 2008) (Salidjanova, 2014). At first glance, these figures may suggest a simple rebalancing of global economic power in China's favour. However, more importantly, they are part of a set of deepening interdependencies between China and the core capitalist economies.

China's trade surplus finds its way back to the US, chiefly via buying government debt, in order to enable further purchases of Chinese exports. Such are the dependencies involved that, despite China's rulers' desire to reorient the economy, when they faced a one-fifth fall in exports between late 2008 and early 2009 they intensified export promotion by, for example, granting VAT rebates on exports, rather than rebalancing towards domestic consumption.

The analogy of Marx's 'hostile brothers' comes to mind when assessing the dollar-renminbi exchange rate skirmishes between the ruling classes of the US and China as they strive for competitive advantage. In July 2005, the Chinese government announced that the *renminbi* would be allowed limited appreciation against the dollar. In the wake of the crisis, between 2008 and 2010, the exchange rate was frozen, but appreciation has again been allowed from early 2010 (see Morrison & Labonte, 2011). Since 2005 the *renminbi* has appreciated by 28% (and by 40% when China's higher inflation is taken into account), seriously eroding Chinese competitiveness. Despite talk of China's capacity to destroy the dollar's reserve status and construct a new financial order, China has little choice in the short term than to continue US dominance by extending more credit and perpetuating their interdependence. A collapse in the dollar would deal a severe blow to China's export machine and its financial power through the drastic devaluation of its dollar investments.

Therefore China's regime of accumulation with a huge imbalance between consumption and investment leaves it heavily dependent on exports to the US and Europe, a vulnerability that was exposed after the 2008 crisis. The contradictory drives to both increase consumption and therefore wages in order to reduce dependence on the US and Europe, and at the same time to keep wages competitive and increasing productivity, are shaping responses to labour.

China's Capital in the Global Division of Labour

This section explores China's place in emerging divisions of labour with regard to unevenness, spatiality, and labour. In particular, it discusses China's place in production hierarchies and how far it is making technological leaps to catch up with competitors in advanced capitalist economies. Further, the discussion focuses on the problem of China as a 'temporary fix' for TNCs and the extent to which its comparative advantage of low labour costs is being challenged.

Moving Up the Value Chain?

There are debates about whether China is moving up the value chain to pose a serious challenge to the advanced capitalist economies. Information and communications technology (ICT) industries illustrate the problem China faces. China is a major exporter of ICT products, such as personal computers and laptops, and consumer electronics more generally. These sectors, however, are dominated by foreign-owned TNCs employing Chinese workers to assemble high value-added goods, such as micro-processors and memory chips, produced elsewhere (Nanto & Chanlett-Avery, 2006). China has subsequently made little advance in raising the local value-added content of exports. Koopman, Wang, and Wei (2013) estimate that the share of domestic content in its manufactured exports was about 50% before WTO membership and has risen to nearly 60% since then. However, for processed exports dominated by foreign TNCs the figure is much higher. There are also variations across sectors and those that are labelled as relatively sophisticated, such as electronic devices, have a low domestic content of 30% or less (Koopman, Wang, & Wei, 2013).

Nevertheless, to suggest that in the global division of labour China is either trapped in low-skilled production or at the other end of the spectrum moving towards advanced manufacturing is to misunderstand the unevenness of China's capital and technological capacity in the context of dynamic changes and shifts in the global economy. The technological capacity of China combines primitive and low-technology production with medium-technology and pockets of advanced and even very advanced technology. Giant companies have developed in areas that play to their domestic comparative advantage (white and electrical goods, trucks and cars, for example). Furthermore, China's banks, construction and oil firms have emerged as global giants with 8 firms now in the *Financial Timestop* 100 firms in 2011 (Dullforce, 2011). A number of other firms have the potential to develop into major competitors in sectors such as Aerospace (AVIC1), telecommunications (China Mobile and Huawei), and computers (Lenovo).

However, a huge technological gap between China and the advanced capitalist countries remains, as it is heavily dependent on imported technologies. Foreign companies control virtually all intellectual property in China and accounted for 85% of exports in 2010 (Salidjanova, 2011). Sustained efforts are being made to 'move up the value chain'. In aerospace, for example, huge investment is planned to challenge the global giants Airbus and Boeing. In 2010 this was identified as one of seven industries in the category of 'high end equipment manufacturing' whose share of the economy the ruling class wants to increase from 2% in 2011 to 20% by 2020 (MacCarthy & Waldmeir, 2011; Rabinovitch & Anderlini, 2011). To have any chance of meeting such a goal China's rulers are compelled to intensify their role in what the Communist Manifesto called the 'chase across the globe' for new markets, technology, and raw materials. In the domestic economy the role of Chinese firms in the global value chains of TNCs producing income- and price-sensitive goods locks workers into intense competitive pressures in the global economy and increases the objective necessity for their exploitation.

The Temporary 'Spatial Fix' of Relocation

China's competitive advantage of low labour costs in terms of offering a 'spatial fix' for global TNCs and more generally to resolve the contradictions of capital is taken for granted (Harvey, 2006; Li, 2008). However, moving to new locations, re-jigging contractual arrangements with other capital and/or adopting new technology are only temporary fixes for individual capitals and the system as a whole. Competition drives other capitalists in the same sector to follow a similar strategy—in other words, if one capitalist expands output and relocates production, then other capitalists are compelled to follow a similar strategy to defend their competitive position. This is the concrete manifestation of the tension between differentiation and equalisation referred to by Smith (2008) and discussed earlier.

By relocating across national boundaries firms may be able to employ workers for a lower wage or compel them to work longer and harder. This is one of the countervailing influences on the falling rate of profit identified by Marx. However, the higher the rate of profit achieved in a particular sector, the more rapidly that exceptional rate of profit will be eroded by the entry of new capital into that sector (assuming that there are no barriers to entry). Competition on the labour market and the attendant rise in confidence of workers collectively or individually will push up wages and erode the differential. However, the fact that labour has less freedom to move across national boundaries than capital means that differences in the rate of exploitation may be sustained for long periods of time—depending on the strength and combativity of workers.

There is a complex interplay between the rate of exploitation and the level of investment per worker which means that the impact on profits cannot be simply read off from the strategies of firms and sectors. However, the dynamics of foreign investment into China on the basis of low costs reflects the contradictions of this model of social relations.

China's Eroding Low Wage Advantage

According to the CEO of Collective Brands, a US footwear company shifting some of its production from China to Indonesia, '[t]he utopia for one stop sourcing for quality and low price has been China . . . but utopias never last' (Brown, 2011). The advantages that can be gained from a particular locality can only be temporary, and the opportunities for excess profits (economic rents) from location are eliminated by the mobility of capital. The advantages and excess profits to be extracted from China's regime of low-wage, labour-intensive production are being eroded. The meteoric rise of China's economy and average growth rates of 10% for the last 30 years were based on an endless supply of cheap migrant workers from inland China to the Special Economic Zones in the coastal regions. Labour markets have tightened with the availability of migrant workers slowing down from 2005. This has meant expectations of better working conditions, the possibility of trading jobs, a higher turnover of workers, and upward pressure on wages. All of these reduce the level of profit that firms can make in a particular locality. Buttolo (2015) demonstrated empirically how these forces have played out in the garment and LED lighting sectors in Guangdong as a regime of accumulation based on low wages became unsustainable.

What emerges are complex patterns of capital mobility with firms moving from urban to suburban locations, from large to small cities, from the coastal regions to inland China and out of China completely (Yang, 2014). Citing numerous examples of companies moving their production back to the US, Sirkin, Zinser, and Hohner (2011) argued that the differential is closing between the opportunities offered in China and in the southern states of the US. They concluded that China's overwhelming cost advantage over the US is shrinking and that higher US productivity, a weaker dollar, and other factors will close the cost gap between the US and China. Further, differentials are eroded by the appreciation of the *renmimbi* against the dollar, and the 'costs and headaches' (Sirkin, Zinser, & Hohner, 2011, p. 11) of extended supply chains, as well as inventory expenses, quality control, unanticipated travel needs, and the threat of disruption due to port closures and natural disasters.

In addition to the threat of relocation some sections of capital that are reaching the limits of operating in low-cost locations may look to another strategy for staving off, limiting, or temporarily resolving the aggregate crisis of accumulation by adopting more or newer technology. In China, Foxconn has diversified its strategies by planning to relocate some of its production to Brazil, Mexico, and Eastern Europe. Further, although Foxconn continues to build new plants and hire thousands of extra workers to make smart phones, it also plans to install a million robots inside of three years to supplement its workforce in China (Markillie, 2012).

Therefore the calculus on how to extract maximum surplus value from China can change, and an alternative strategy is to return some or all production to the higher labour cost home country and invest in new technology. It is not suggested that all foreign firms will switch their production from China or that workers will be replaced by robots. Automating assembly lines would require the restructuring of entire manufacturing processes. Smaller firms have more limited capital to invest in robotics. The technological capacity of capitalism changes incessantly and with it the incentives for capital including its mobility. There will be developments in technology that will change how things are produced in incremental or revolutionary ways and which will alter the potential for profits. How far and how quickly new technologies will be adopted is not predictable, and it will be uneven between firms. However, there will be a pressure on them to adopt these new technologies in order to keep pace with their rivals.

Strategies for Extracting Absolute and Relative Surplus Value

As Chinese capital has become ever more integrated with global circuits of capital accumulation, the question of competitiveness looms increasingly large for China's rulers. Not only is this much lower than in the advanced capitalist countries, and other East Asian economies, but it is falling. Total factor productivity (TFP) fell during the global crisis and only marginally increased in 2010. Estimates of TFP between 2001 and 2007 range between 4.7% to 4.1% per annum (Wu, 2014); between 2008 and 2012, however, TFP slowed down to between 2.8% per annum and 0.8% (Wu, 2014). The implications of these figures are that repressing wages or increased exploitation is needed to compensate for poor relative increases in productivity.

Conclusion

The rise of China's economy offers further evidence of the abiding significance of Trotsky's concept of uneven and combined development. By its very nature, competitive accumulation is anarchic and does not proceed on a smooth upward path. Unevenness is reinforced, as we are now witnessing, by the aftermath of the 2008 economic crisis differentiated by sector and region. If China is subject to the dynamic of uneven development between and within states, it is also locked into the pattern, albeit less dramatically, of the booms and slumps of mature capitalism. In the early years of its transformation it was able to draw on its vast labour surplus to generate spectacular growth and accumulation and, as it did so, was remorselessly incorporated into the global system and so subject to the same crisis tendencies as the rest of the world.

From a macro perspective this article concurs with Hung's (2015) compelling argument that any restructuring of capitalist development in China will involve an increase in the share of domestic consumption in GDP. In turn this would require a profound redistribution of wealth and income. Without such a change of direction the question is raised as to the ability of the Chinese state and existing political institutions to contain the labour unrest and proliferation of disputes that have occurred since the late 1990s.

This is the context in which labour relations need to be understood. Therefore at a broad level of analysis, China's integration with the global economy locks workers into the competitive dynamics of world capitalism. The 'law of value' provides an impetus for individual employers to intensify work, hold down wages and/or increase efficiency. Uneven and combined development enables an understanding of the specificities of how the law of value unfolds spatially and sectorally and within different workplaces and therefore the context within which labour struggles are played out.

In particular, presented in Marxist terms this raises the question as to how far it is the case that China has exhausted the possibility of primitive accumulation (the capacity to convert an agrarian into an industrial workforce) and reached the limits of extracting absolute surplus value by extending the number of hours worked to which there are physical and political limits. The key question is how far they can increase relative surplus value by reducing the necessary labour time to produce a given good or service through using new managerial methods and organisation, training and education. Whichever direction is taken all present a challenge for the relationship between the state, managers, and workers.

Disclosure Statement

No potential conflict of interest was reported by the author.

References

Anievas, A. (Ed.). (2010). *Marxism and world politics: Contesting global capitalism.* Oxford: Routledge.

Ashman, S. (2006). From world market to world economy. In B. Dunn & H. Radice (Eds.), *100 years of permanent revolution: Results and prospects* (pp. 88–104). London: Pluto Press.

Ashman, S. (2010). Capitalism, uneven and combined development and the transhistoric. In A. Anievas (Eds.), *Marxism and world politics: Contesting global capitalism* (pp. 183–197). Oxford: Routledge.

Barker, C. (2006). Beyond Trotsky: Extending combined and uneven development. In B. Dunn & H. Radice (Eds.), *100 years of permanent revolution: Results and prospects* (pp. 78–87). London: Pluto Press.

Brown, K. (2011, February 15). Rising Chinese wages pose relocation risk. *Financial Times.*

Butollo, F. (2015). *The end of cheap labour? Industrial transformation and social upgrading in China.* Frankfurt-on-Main: Campus Verlag.

Coe, N., Dicken, P., & Hess, M. (2008). Global production networks: Realizing the potential. *Journal of Economic Geography, 8*(3), 271–295.

Dullforce, A. B. (2011, June 25). FT Global 500 2011. *Financial Times Weekend.*

Dunn, B. & Radice, H. (Eds.). (2006). *100 years of permanent revolution: Results and prospects.* London: Pluto.

Harvey, D. (2006). *Limits to capital.* London: Verso.

Herod, A. (2006). Trotsky's omission: Labour's role in combined and uneven development. In B. Dunn & H. Radice (Eds.), *100 years of permanent revolution: Results and prospects* (pp. 152–179). London: Pluto Press.

Hou, L. (2010, May 12). Official: Wage share decreases 22 years in a row. *China Daily*. Retrieved from www.chinadaily.com.cn/china/2010-05/12/content_9841109.htm

Huang, Y. (2003). *Selling China: Foreign direct investment during the reform Era*. Cambridge: Cambridge University Press.

Hung, H. F. (2008). Rise of China and the global overaccumulation crisis. *Review of International Political Economy, 15*(2), 143–179.

Hung, H. F. (2009). America's head servant? The PRC's dilemma in the global crisis. *New Left Review, 60*, 5–25.

Hung, H. F. (2015). *The China boom: Why China will not rule the world*. New York, NY: Columbia University Press.

Jiabao, W. (2011, June 24). How China plans to reinforce the global recovery. *Financial Times*.

Jiang, L., & Wu, Y. (2014). Will China's local debt crisis break out? Evidence from local government financing practice. *International Journal of Business and Commerce, 3*(10), 32–42.

Koopman, R., Wang, Z., & Wei, S. J. (2012). Estimating the domestic content in exports when processing trade is pervasive. *Journal of Development Economics, 99*(1), 178–189.

Lau, W. K. (1999). The fifteenth congress of the Chinese communist party: Milestone in China's privatization. *Capital and Class, 23*(2), 51–87.

Li, M. (2008). *The rise of China and the demise of the capitalist world economy*. London: Pluto Press.

van der Linden, M. (2007). The 'Law' of uneven and combined development: Some underdeveloped thoughts. *Historical Materialism, 15*(1), 145–165.

Ma, G., & Yi, W. (2010). *China's high saving rate: Myth and reality*. Bank for International Settlements Working Paper, number 312, Bank for International Settlements.

MacCarthy, C., & Waldemeir, P. (2011, May 17). China drive to rescue Saab. *Financial Times*.

Markillie, P. (2012, April 21). The third industrial revolution. *The Economist*.

Marx, K. (1976). *Capital volume 1*. Penguin Books.

McGrath-Champ, S., Herod, A., & Rainnie, A. (2010). *Handbook of employment and society: Working space*. Cheltenham: Edward Elgar.

Meckstroth, D. J. (2014). *China has a dominant share of world manufacturing*. MAPI (Manufacturing Alliance for Productivity and Innovation). Retrieved from https://www.mapi.net/china-has-dominant-share-world-manufacturing

Mitchell, T., & Wildau, G. (2015, January 26). Chinese tycoon sues local governments for late payment. *Financial Times*.

Morrison, W. M., & Labonte, M. (2011, August 3). *China's currency: An analysis of the economic issues*. Congressional Research Service.

Nabar, M., & N'Diaye, P. (2013). *Enhancing China's medium-term growth prospects the path to a high-income economy*. International Monetary Fund Working Paper. WP/13/204.

Nanto, D. K., & Chanlett-Avery, E. (2006). *The rise of China and its effect on Taiwan, Japan, and South Korea: U.S. policy choices*. Washington, DC: Congressional Research Service, Library of Congress.

Novack, G. (1972). *Understanding history: Marxist essays*. New York, NY: Pathfinder Press.

Rabinovitch, S., & Anderlini, J. (2011, June 28). Audit lays bare extent of local debts in China. *Financial Times*.

Rainnie, A., Herod, A., & McGrath-Champ, S. (2011). Global production networks and labour. *Competition & Change, 15*(2), 155–169.

Rainnie, A., Herod, A., & McGrath-Champ, S. (2013). Global production networks, labour and small firms. *Capital & Class, 37*(3), 177–195.

Salidjanova, N. (2011, March 30). *Going out: An overview of China's foreign direct investment*. USCC Staff Research Report, US-China Economic and Security Review Commission.

Salidjanova, N. (2014). *China's foreign exchange reserves and holdings of U.S. Securities*. USCC Economic Issue Brief, Washington.

Selwyn, B. (2007). Labour process and workers bargaining power in export grape production, north east Brazil. *Journal of Agrarian Change, 7*(4), 526–553.

Sirkin, H. L., Zinser, M., & Hohner, D. (2011). *Made in America, again: Why manufacturing will return to the U.S.* The Boston Consulting Group.

Smith, N. (2006). The geography of uneven development. In B. Dunn & H. Radici (Eds.), *100 years of permanent revolution: Results and prospects* (pp. 180–195). London: Pluto Press.

Smith, N. (2008). *Uneven development: Nature, capital and the production of space*. Georgia: University of Georgia Press.

Soh, K., & Wang, A. (2011, October 10). China's debts pileup raises risk of hard landing. *Reuters*. Retrieved from http://old.news.yahoo.com/s/nm/20111010/bs_nm/us_china_debt

Starosta, G. (2010). Global commodity chains and the Marxian law of value. *Antipode, 42*(2), 433–465.

Trotsky, L. ([1932–1933] 2008). *History of the Russian revolution.* (Max Eastman, Trans.). Chicago, IL: Haymarket Books.

United Nations Conference on Trade and Development. (2014). Retrieved from http://unctad.org/en/PublicationsLibrary/wir2014_en.pdf.

Wolf, M. (2011, June 15). How China could yet fail like Japan. *Financial Times.*

World Bank Database. (2014a). Retrieved from http://data.worldbank.org/indicator/NE.GDI.TOTL.ZS.

World Bank Database. (2014b). Retrieved from http://data.worldbank.org/indicator/NY.GDP.MKTP.CD.

World Bank Statistics. (2014). Retrieved from http://data.worldbank.org/.

World Trade Organisation Country Database. (2014). Retrieved from http://stat.wto.org/CountryProfile/WSDBCountryPFView.aspx?Language=E&Country=CN.

Wu, H. X. (2014). *China's growth and productivity performance revisited: Accounting for China's sources of growth with a new data set.* Economics Program Working Paper Series, New York, 14–01. Retrieved from https://www.conferenceboard.org/pdf_free/workingpapers/EPWP1401.pdf.

Yang, C. (2014). Market rebalancing of global production networks in the Post-Washington consensus globalizing era: Transformation of export-oriented development in China. *Review of International Political Economy*, *21*(1), 130–156.

Exploitation and Resistance: A Comparative Analysis of the Chinese Cheap Labour Electronics and High-Value Added IT Sectors

ANDREAS BIELER & CHUN-YI LEE

University of Nottingham, Nottingham, UK

ABSTRACT *This article compares the electronics sector in the area of Shenzhen, based on cheap labour assembling goods for export, with the IT sector in the area of Shanghai, relying on a more skilled workforce manufacturing high value-added goods. It is asked in what way these rather different locations within the global political economy condition the form and contents of resistance in these two sectors. The article concludes that industrial relations are more confrontational in the electronics sector with informal labour NGOs supporting workers in getting their individual and collective rights. The IT sector, in contrast, is characterised by consensual relationships. Informal labour NGOs concentrate on organising cultural activities for workers' free time, performing a mediating role between employers and employees, supported by the government.*

Introduction

China is frequently considered to be an example of successful developmental catch-up. And yet, the country's impressive growth rates are to a large extent based on the super-exploitation of its workforce expressed in long working hours, low wages, and a general lack of basic welfare benefits such as medical insurance and work-injury insurance (Chan & Selden, 2014, p. 606). Wages are often so low that a normal working day is not enough for the reproduction of labour power. Hence, workers are pushed towards performing 'excessive amounts of overtime work' to make ends meet (Li & Hao, 2014, p. 483). In recent years, Chinese workers have started to resist these exploitative conditions and a new movement is emerging spear-headed by migrant workers (Pringle, 2013). The purpose of this article is to analyse these dynamics of resistance within the wider structuring conditions of the global political economy.

Empirically, this paper will provide a comparative analysis of the electronics sector based around Shenzhen with the IT sector in the area of Shanghai. While the former is predominantly based on cheap labour, assembling electronic goods for export—see, for example, Foxconn and the assembling of Apple products—the latter relies on a more skilled workforce manufacturing higher value-added goods. In what way do these rather different locations within the global political economy condition the form and contents of resistance in these two sectors?

Conceptually, this paper will be based on a neo-Gramscian, historical materialist perspective, which starts through an analysis of the social relations of production and the different ways of how these two sectors are integrated into the global political economy (Bieler & Morton, 2004). Unlike liberal or neo-realist approaches, a historical materialist theory allows us to comprehend the historical specificity of capitalism. State and market only appear as separate in capitalism, because of the way production is organised around wage labour and the private ownership of the means of production. In this arrangement, the accumulation of surplus value is not politically enforced, but workers are indirectly, economically compelled to sell their labour power to ensure their subsistence. In turn, this will then allow us to identify key social class forces and provide the structural background within which these forces struggle against exploitation (Bieler, 2014).

The terrain of class struggle is, of course, the factory floor, but also the wider social relations of production, which regulate the work process. Production is, thus, understood broadly in that it also includes the wider institutional and normative settings around the production process including government involvement and broader research environment. In the next section, we will, therefore, first analyse the position of Chinese production in the global economy and the kind of social class forces this generates. In line with a neo-Gramscian, historical materialist perspective, these struggles take also place at the form of state level. Hence, the second section will assess the particular Chinese form of state and the way especially informal labour NGOs interact with Chinese state institutions in the two industrial sectors under investigation. These two sections, in turn, will provide the background for our comparative analysis in the third section. The Conclusion will draw out the main implications of our findings.

Methodologically, the empirical argument is partly based on a set of 21 semi-structured elite interviews with representatives of informal labour NGOs, employers, local government and researchers between 2009 and 2014. All interviewees were guaranteed anonymity and are not mentioned by name. The validity of information was cross-checked through the information from other interviews as well as the consultation of further primary and secondary printed sources.

Chinese Production in the Global Economy

China's GDP growth figures are impressive indeed. Although they are currently no longer in the double digits, they have remained high since 2012 with about 7.5 five per cent (http://www.tradingeconomics.com/china/gdp-growth-annual, accessed 26/06/2014). No other country in the world seems to make such good use of the opportunities presented by globalisation, observers assert. Hence the discussions of China's rise as potential new hegemon in the global economy and be it only as an economic super-power for the moment. And yet, a closer analysis of the Chinese production structure reveals a rather more fragile picture of Chinese economic growth. First, 'it is largely in low-value, labour-intensive sectors that China has played a major role in out-competing other developing countries' (Kiely, 2010, p. 226). As discussed in the introduction to this volume, China has become the major regional assembly platform in Asia. A large part of regional trade is the trade in parts and components especially in ICT products and electrical goods in the direction of China, where they are assembled on the basis of cheap labour (Hart-Landsberg, 2013, p. 34). In turn, these products are mainly destined for markets in North America and Europe integrating East Asia tightly with the global economy, but also making it dependent on continuing demand in the Global North. Equally important, Chinese exports are dominated by foreign transnational corporations (TNCs), which control about 85% of China's high technology exports (Hart-Landsberg, 2015, p. 5). Expressed differently, 'China's growth has become increasingly dependent on exports produced by transnational corporations' (Hart-Landsberg, 2013, p. 43). In short, China's production is mainly based on cheap labour, low value-added activities, dominated by foreign TNCs and highly dependent on access to markets elsewhere.

The focus on cheap labour and dependence on foreign TNCs, however, has significant implications for the Chinese social relations of production. Most importantly, there needs to be a continuing supply of workers, who are prepared to work for low wages. In the process of privatising state-owned companies during the 1990s 60 million workers were made redundant and turned into a source of cheap labour. They are joined by the ever growing group of migrant workers from the countryside, making up 269 million in 2013 (Chan & Selden, 2014, pp. 600–601). As a result of this large pool of cheap labour, Chinese workers have not benefitted from the economic boom. Labour's share of GDP 'fell from approximately 53% of GDP in 1992 to below 40% in 2006. Private consumption as a percent of GDP also declined, falling from approximately 47% to 36% over the same period' (Hart-Landsberg, 2013, p. 50; see also Qi, 2014). The Chinese government has started to stimulate domestic consumption since the 2008 financial crisis in the expectation that increasing domestic purchasing capacity will boost consumption. Nevertheless, 'China's level of consumption, at 36 percent of GDP, is much lower than the world average, which measures in at 60 percent of GDP' (Hsu, 2015). In a situation of unsatisfactory pensions, health care and public services, people are reluctant to invest more in luxury goods. Although China has introduced a minimum wage in 2008, this minimum wage is still far below a level, which would allow more extensive consumption patterns.

Our first case study the electronics goods sector in the Pearl River Delta (PRD) characterised by companies such as Foxconn is precisely part of this cheap labour, export-oriented strategy. The PRD is the earliest developing area after the 1979 open door policy. As a result of generous tax breaks for foreign companies, the PRD benefited from waves of foreign direct investment (FDI) from the mid-1980s onwards (Yeung, 2001, p. 44). While higher value-added functions of production remained in Hong Kong or Taiwan, manufacturing production in the PRD is mostly confined to assembling and finishing at the low value-added segment of the international production chain organised by and through Hong Kong or Taiwan investors, who have reaped profits from cheap land and labour (Airriess, 2008, p. 140). Because both raw material and half-finished and finished components of computer products have to come from and go through Hong Kong, the PRD has been stuck in the low value-added part of production (Mao, Liu, & Hu, 2004).

Another characteristic of PRD's industrial development is the lack of long-term planning by local government. Though the PRD was one of the earliest regions to open up for FDI, local governments in the region did not prepare well for attracting sustainable foreign investment. As Shen indicates, there was minimal transportation, communication and electricity supply during the mid-1980s when the PRD just opened for foreign investors (Shen, 2002, p. 135).

After 2000 with increasing labour costs and capital shifting production to the hinterland in the search for cheaper labour, there were some attempts at upgrading to attract higher value-added investment. For example, with the help of national government, nine industrial technology parks have been established in the PRD; three of them were located in Dongguan (Airriess, 2008, p. 141). However, whether those technology industrial parks really triggered industrial upgrading is rather doubtful. As Tuan and Ng indicate, the PRD is limited in technology upgrading due to the deepening cross-border processing trading, characterised by declining wages and labour expertise (Tuan & Ng, 2004, p. 1618). And if there is industrial upgrading as, for example, in the textile industry, ensuring China's continuing competitiveness in global textile, this has not gone hand in hand with social upgrading. Rather, while a small proportion of workers have become highly skilled to operate new machinery, the larger part of the workforce has become deskilled (Butollo, 2014).

Unsurprisingly, as a result of an emphasis on cheap labour and control by foreign TNCs, the social relations of production are characterised by super-exploitation. The source of the pressure results from international competition and here the key role of TNCs in the organisation of transnational production networks. As Ngai Pun et al. make clear in their analysis of a series of suicides by Foxconn workers, the pressure comes directly from Apple, which is Foxconn's main customer. 'Our studies show that compressed delivery time of new products has repeatedly taken precedence over protecting workers' health, safety and rights, at times with tragic consequences' (Pun et al., 2014, p. 9). In a situation of clear power asymmetries between Apple and its suppliers, it is Apple's drive to reduce costs and maximise profits, which 'is the source of the pressure placed on Chinese workers employed by Foxconn, many of them producing signature Apple products' (Chan, Pun, & Selden, 2013, p. 106). The US retail giant Wal-Mart is another example. 'Seventy per cent of all products sold by Wal-Mart in 2005 were made in China and 80 per cent of the 6000 factories that supply it were Chinese' (Sum, 2009, pp. 162–163). This has given Wal-Mart enormous leverage vis-à-vis these suppliers. 'This firm grip over suppliers-manufacturers and the unrelenting push for cost and price-value competitiveness means that manufacturers, in turn, must pass on their costs and production insecurity (e.g. stopping orders) to their workers' (Sum, 2009, p. 163).

Nevertheless, as Jane Hardy (2016) points out in her contribution to this volume, China's technological capacity is also characterised by unevenness. Cheap labour and low technology production are combined in some areas with medium and small pockets of advanced technology. Our second case study of the IT industry in the area around Shanghai, the Yangtze River Delta (YRD), is an example of higher value-added production. It rose as the second regional driver of massive FDI into and export out of central costal China during the 1990s and into the twenty-first century (Chen, 2007, p. 171). As Chen indicates, the YRD is less export-oriented than the PRD, and has a consistently lower export-to-foreign investment ratio. Unlike the larger percentage of foreign investment especially from Taiwan and Hong Kong in the PRD, the YRD regions is characterised by more domestic private and state-owned enterprises. In comparison to the PRD, from the early 1980s to the early 1990s, the government-led development of the YRD economy type focused on township and collective enterprises, that is, social relations of production which were comprised by human capital, business networks, technical expertise, and technology transfer provided by urban youth and urban young adults from Shanghai to Suzhou (Ngo, 2011, p. 4; see also Chen, 2007, p. 185). Airriess argues that this model is different from the PRD's production relationship with Hong Kong (Airriess, 2008, p. 144). While the latter focuses primarily on short-term investment benefits, vast land and cheap labour, this model heavily relies on careful planning and aggressive action by the municipal government

Table 1. Different characteristics of the social relations of production in PRD and YRD

	Ownership types	Production types	Government role	Incubating environment
Electronics industry in PRD	FDI by large foreign TNCs especially from Hong Kong and Taiwan	Low value-added production, assembling and processing trade based on cheap labour	Little long-term planning by local government	Only one top university
IT industry in YRD	More domestic investment or joint venture with local government	Higher value-added production, with more R&D input	Government-led development	Several top universities

to create an attractive environment. In many respects, this resembles closely earlier strategies by Newly Industrialised Countries in the region such as South Korea and Taiwan, which had heavily relied on state involvement (see Gray, 2015). The most prominent and successful planned projects are the Suzhou Industrial Park (SIP) as well as the Suzhou New District (SND). The SIP is a joint project between both national and local governments (Airriess, 2008, p. 144). The SIP and SND have mainly attracted electronics and telecommunications companies in higher value-added production lines, including firms such as Panasonics, Philips, Nokia, and Alcatel.

The SIP and SND are research and development (R&D) friendly zones, necessary for higher value-added industries. Apart from governmental planning to retain the capacity of R&D, the incubating environment is also rather different from the PRD. In the PRD, there is only one top university, that is, the Sun Yat-Sen University in Guangzhou. In the YRD, by contrast, there are several top universities including Fu-Dan University in Shanghai, Jiao-tong University in Shanghai and also Shanghai University of Finance and Economics. To nourish human capital is crucial for pushing R&D and higher value-added industries. For a comparative overview of the social relations of production in the electronics industry and the IT sector, see the Table 1.

As a result of these different locations within the global political economy and diverging social relations of production, the social class forces of labour are rather different in both industrial sectors. In the electronics sector in the PRD, workers are generally less skilled and the turnover of the workforce is high with cheap labour being easily replaced (see also the contribution by Butollo & Lüthje, 2016). By contrast, employment relations in the IT sector in the YRD are more stable and the workforce more highly skilled. In the YRD, China's economic development has adjusted from 'fast and good' to 'good and fast' (Wang, Appelbaum, Degiuli, & Lichtenstein, 2009, p. 489). Skill and quality have become the main focus. In the next section, we will first assess the Chinese form of state and the different kinds of labour organisations, before we then compare the labour struggles taking place in the electronics with those in the IT sector.

Informal Labour NGOs within the Chinese Form of State

When analysing class struggle within forms of state, Gramsci's notion of the 'integral state' is important. The integral state consists of 'political society', that is, the coercive apparatus of the state more narrowly understood including ministries, the police and other state institutions, and 'civil society', made up of political parties, unions, employers' associations, churches, etc. (Gramsci, 1971, pp. 257–263, p. 271). For Gramsci, civil society is the sphere of hegemonic struggle over the purpose of a particular state form. 'Civil society is simultaneously the terrain of hegemony and of opposition to hegemony' (Buttigieg, 2005, p. 38). Linked back to the social relations of production, it is clear that different social class forces operate within and through a particular form of state to establish their particular interests as part of the national interest. The methodological task is then to identify which institutions in civil and political society are the formal expression of the interests of which particular social class forces. We need to identify the relevant institutions representing workers' interests in the electronics sector based around Shenzhen, compare them with the institutions representing workers in the IT sector in the area of Shanghai as well as analyse the nature of their interaction with state institutions.

Analysing capitalist restructuring in China, Kevin Gray highlights the important role of the state in a strategy of passive revolution. As there is no dominant class fraction or class alliance in support of restructuring, state officials are crucial in sustaining the conditions of restructuring, simultaneously drawing on international expertise as well as negotiating domestic restructuring within the wider global economy. Gramsci's framework, Gray asserts, 'can help to address the issue of the role of the state in facilitating the restoration of capitalism, and how this "revolution from above" has been embedded within broader processes of transnational accumulation and inter-state rivalry' (Gray, 2010, p. 455). The Chinese state, therefore, plays a crucial role in mediating the tensions between foreign TNCs focused on super-profits and Chinese workers labouring under conditions of severe economic hardship.

Unsurprisingly, the state is heavily involved in organising civil society in China:

> Instead of lifting restrictions on freedom of association in China, the CCP has established a system of state-corporatist industrial relations, and the All-China Federation of Trade Unions (ACFTU) has been given a new role in the representation of workers' interests, and has itself played a greater role in the design of reform policies. (Gray, 2010, p. 459)

Independent trade unions, however, are not permitted. There is no right to free association and 'the right to strike was removed entirely from the 1982 constitution and has not been reinstated' (Gray, 2015, p. 149). In parallel to these official efforts of structuring civil society, a whole range of more informal labour NGOs have emerged in recent years as a form of support and organisation of Chinese workers. The Chinese state is also heavily involved in the control of these labour NGOs. There are three basic strategies for labour NGOs to survive in China (Chan, 2013, pp. 5–6; Pun, 2008, pp. 154–170). The first one is to collaborate with organisations with a clear legal status, for instance local official trade unions, the Communist Youth League, or academic institutions. By doing so labour NGOs can operate their projects under their host's names, but still retain some autonomy in actual work. The second strategy is that the NGO will register as a self-employed person, an independent enterprise or a limited company. One of our interviewees actually registered his organisation as a commercial company. As he said: *I am using my company's resource to support my organisation ... ; therefore during the week days I focus on my 'company' but I will organise activities for workers during the weekend* (Interview data, S1).The third strategy is to choose not to register at all. Labour NGOs of this type go underground and keep a low profile. Unsurprisingly, the latter type of labour NGO is the most important target for the government and finds it more difficult to survive under official surveillance.

The funding of labour NGOs is coming either from government institutions, making them into so-called Gongos (Government organised NGOs), or foreign foundations. Gongos are controversial in terms of their identity. Some argue that although they receive government funds, they still can serve society to a limited extent, as long as they do not cross the government's official lines (Ma, 2006, p. 10). However some scholars argue that although coming under the government's protection will ensure NGOs' legitimacy and most importantly, financial status, these NGOs will either intentionally or inadvertently sacrifice workers' solidarity or the collective capacity of self-protection (Lee & Shen, 2011, p. 177). The struggle of whether to accept governmental funds has gone on for quite some time. Nevertheless, as a leader of a labour NGO in Guangzhou stated in an interview after the crack-down on Shenzhen labour NGOs from June to October 2012 (see below), *it's a difficult choice for us to consider whether to accept government help. For us, the important thing is to survive first. Some organisations stubbornly refuse to take government help. Therefore, they have to move out from their offices or have their electricity and water cut off* (Interview data, G2). The government version is: *If these organisations don't promote illegal activities, and if it is so difficult to maintain an organisation, why don't they accept government funding* (Interview data, G4)*?* This clearly demonstrates the close involvement of Chinese political society, the government, in civil society in line with a strategy of passive revolution.

Foreign foundations are an alternative source of funding. However, due to the unstable financial situation, labour NGOs are in danger of becoming commercialised. They become part of a market competing for funding from institutions such as the European Union, foreign governmental bodies, the International Labour Organization (ILO), the United Nations or even large, branded corporations (Lee & Shen, 2011, p. 179). Compared to Gongos, it could be easily assumed that these 'independent' labour NGOs, which are funded by foreign foundations, would have more courage to challenge state regulations and control, to initiate some activities which inspire workers' consciousness. This assumption, however, is not always correct. In fact, many foreign foundations deliberately avoid sponsoring projects that may be considered politically incorrect or violating governmental policies (Interview data, S5). More importantly, NGOs which receive foreign funding are the main target of the government (Chan, 2013, p. 6, Interview data, G5). It is easy for the Chinese government to close down NGOs, while it is difficult for labour NGOs to obtain legal status. It is precisely because of this that some labour NGOs did not register with the government at all, whereas others did register but as commercial companies. Overall, it can be concluded that:

> the CCP has attempted to restructure civil society so that social organisations such as trade unions serve to mediate social tensions, and their revival as part of a wider legalization of industrial relations can be seen as a key element of the CCP's passive revolution. (Gray, 2015, p. 142)

In the next section, we will analyse what kind of NGOs operate within the PRD and YRD, the kind of government response they receive and how this is related to the different positions within which the two industrial sectors are located in the global economy.

Comparing Labour NGO Activities in the PRD with Labour NGO Activities in the YRD

The Electronics Sector in PRD

As outlined above, this sector is characterised by cheap labour and a large migrant work force, working often in highly exploitative and hazardous working conditions. In general, the cheap labour-based industrial sector in PRD has experienced a large amount of labour protests. In the absence of official data, scholars have estimated the amount of industrial conflicts. Wedeman (2009) investigates a sample of 947 'mass incidents', reported in domestic and foreign news articles from 1990 to 2008, to find that 345 incidents or 36.7% of the total number of incidents in his sample involved workers and employment issues. According to a research report (China Labour Bulletin, 2014, p. 17), from the beginning of June 2011 to the end of December 2013, 470 strikes and protests by factory workers across the country were recorded. The bulk of China's factory protests occurred in the manufacturing heartland of Guangdong, and especially in the PRD. There were 267 incidents in Guangdong alone, some 57% of the total. In short, the cheap labour electronics sector is characterised by high levels of industrial dispute.

Labour NGOs in the PRD mainly rely on funding from foreign foundations including the World Bank, Ford Foundation, Oxfam, etc. Funding is channelled through Hong Kong as a transit passage (He & Huang, 2008, p. 66). Certainly, the government has been very sensitive and defensive towards these foreign-funded foundations. A former ACFTU chairman in Guangzhou, expressed this as follows: *It is not that the government doesn't support labour NGOs. The taboo for the government is to see these labour NGOs accepting foreign foundations' funding. The government cannot be sure whether these foreign foundations will not control mainland labour NGOs through funding them* (Interview data, G3). As we discussed above, labour NGOs have struggled over the issue of whether to accept government funding. Importantly, this struggle is much more severe in the PRD than in the YRD. Though government's persuasion is strong and even coercive in funding labour NGOs, organisations in the PRD emphasise much more the importance of being financially independent from government funding. From 2010 to 2014, periodically we visited eight grass-root labour organisations in the PRD. One is commissioned by companies to conduct factory audits, while the others have distanced themselves from government funding. It has to be noted that under the current President Xi Jing-Ping's governance, the regulation in terms of monitoring NGOs to receive foreign funds has been tightened, putting pressure on labour NGOs, who accepted foreign funding (People's Republic of China, 2015).

Apart from receiving funding from foreign foundations, labour NGOs in the south are trying to survive by providing Corporate Social Responsibility (CSR) training inside enterprises. For instance, the organiser of the Institute of Contemporary Observation (ICO) in Shenzhen remarked that *the ICO is working with the enterprises to build the concept of responsible CSR. We send out advisers to the companies to train their managers and also accept big brands' (for instance Disney and Adidas) requests to inspect their contracted factories from time to time, just to check whether their contracted factories are up to standard regulations* (Interview data, S10).

A similar line of independence vis-à-vis government is visible in the choice of labour NGOs of whether to register or not with government. A majority of labour NGOs in the PRD decides for option three, that is, not to register officially at all. Unsurprisingly, the unwillingness to accept government money and to register officially, has resulted in rather conflictual relations with local government. Between June 2012 and October 2012, the Chinese government came down hard on labour NGOs in the area of Shenzen, part of PRD (Zhang, 2012), triggering a group of scholars (more than 140) from the outside world to sign an open letter to Guangdong Municipal to express their grave concern at the Guangdong government's repression of grass-roots labour NGOs (Sacom, 2012). The same happened again on 3 December 2015, when authorities detained 20 labour activists in Guangdong Province. 'All of these activists are associated with four grass-roots labor NGOs in the Pearl River Delta' (see http://www.ipetitions.com/petition/scholars-opposing-the-abuse-of-state-power; accessed 16 December 2015).

In the PRD, many labour organisations focus on providing workers with legal consultancy (see Chan and Hui, 2016, in this volume). Hence, the priority is on helping individual workers to get their rights, including, for example, back pay owed to them by their companies. The practice of the Laowei labour law firm in Shenzhen is a good example. Established in 2007, Laowei has focused on helping workers in their disputes with their employer and also on spreading the concept of 'collective bargaining' to workers. According to a partner of the law firm, the *workers' movement should be initiated and led by workers, and only through collective bargaining, workers will have equal rights vis-à-vis the employers* (Interview data, S3). To date, Laowei has handled more than two hundred cases of collective bargaining (Interview data, S8). With the reputation spread through workers' mouths, Laowei has become an important source of advice and support for workers in the PRD. When workers encounter unjustified dismissal cases, they have also gone to Laowei for help. Furthermore, there are clear indications that labour NGOs have been actively involved in strike activities. The Yue Yuen strike in mid-April 2014 was a good example in this respect (Interview data, S8). Yue Yuen is a shoe factory in Dongguan, a city in the south of China built with Taiwanese investment. On 16 April 2014, 40,000 workers from this factory went on strike over unpaid social insurance payments by the employer (see also Schmalz, Sommer, & Xu, 2016). It is not only the sheer number of striking workers, which triggered international attention. More importantly, it was the fact that the grass-roots labour organisation *Spring Breeze* was helping workers to negotiate with the factory owner, thereby introducing them to the concept of collective bargaining, which was noted widely at the international level (Interview data, SH6).

Moreover, because the staff at labour NGOs and lawyers of labour law firms cannot represent workers, *workers are the protagonists to negotiate with employers* (Interview data, S3). Hence, Laowei and some anonymous community labour NGOs have been engaged in training interested workers to be 'workers' representatives' since 2012. This includes labour contract law, strategies of collective bargaining and the concept of 'decent work environment'.

The IT Sector in YRD

The IT sector in YRD is characterised by more highly-qualified workers. In contrast to the electronics sector, it is noticeable that there are significantly fewer labour NGOs in the YRD than the PRD. Second, they generally tend to be officially registered with the government. Third, these labour NGOs have not really got problems with accepting government funding. They are even bidding for funding from the government. According to one of the labour NGO organisers in Shanghai, the funding of labour NGOs in the YRD is *most likely from the government, but also organisations such as the Red Cross. Sometimes, even enterprises will offer funding for NGOs. However, the most common situation is that the government has a project and looks for some NGOs to implement it.* This labour NGO leader expressed his definition of a 'good labour organisation' as follows: *First, it has to aim for being awarded the 'five-star'. Local government has a set of criteria to access the performance of NGOs, the best of which can be rewarded as a 'five-star' NGO. Second, the NGO has to set up its own mission and endeavour to achieve its own objectives* (Interview data, SH1). Another NGO in Shanghai also stated that they mainly receive project funding from the *Shanghai Civil Affair Bureau* (Interview data, SH2). From these two quotes, it can be concluded that labour NGOs in the YRD apply more strategy one and two in relation to registration. Equally, it is obvious that the relations between labour NGOs and government institutions are characterised by co-operation and less conflict.

The collective organisation of workers to enable them to obtain their rights is not a major concern for labour NGOs in the YRD. During the time of the Yue Yuen strike in PRD (see above), the second author of this paper was in Shanghai for fieldwork. This was a good opportunity to ask labour NGOs in Shanghai, what their reflections on these issues were. Most of the interviewees argued that it was almost impossible that such a big strike would take place in the YRD and there was little understanding for the striking workers' objectives. At times, these workers were presented as being confused about what their real objectives are (e.g. Interview data, SH2). The main focus of labour NGOs in the YRD, by contrast, is to organise cultural activities and provide social space for workers to meet up in their free time. *We want to enrich workers' after-work time. We also hold a migrant workers' salon, so workers can come over to discuss with each other various issues. For instance, workers can come together to discuss their future career, girls, the latest fashion, etc. We try to transform a person from the inside to the outside.* (Interview data, SH2). The organiser of another workers' community centre describes the objectives of his NGO as follows (Interview data, SH1): *We aim to create an 'open space' for workers, either a theatre or a play, performance is just a form, it aims to mix people from different ages, professions, rich or poor, pretty or ugly. It is a total un-organised space. However, I have to say, people who come to my play or theatre, are not really poor workers, they are not from the bottom of society.* From these two quotes of labour organisations in the YRD, we can see the differences between labour organisations' styles in the YRD and PRD. In the PRD, labour NGOs mainly focus on collective bargaining, getting payment and social insurance for workers, providing legal consultancy in labour disputes, and training workers' representatives. In the YRD, by contrast, the activities of labour NGOs are more culturally oriented. Clearly, unlike informal labour NGOs in the PRD, these NGOs in the YRD understand their role mainly as a service provider rather than an organiser of exploited workers. Interestingly, a Human Resource manager in the YRD in an interview directly referred to the higher value-added production carried out in his company, when reflecting on the lower level of industrial disputes: *Here (in the SIP) workers are much more obedient, compared to the south, workers here don't cause so much troubles. One reason is that the government has a tighter control here in the YRD; another reason is, we are doing a bit more of high-value added production than the PRD* (Interview data, SUH1).

Conclusion

The social relations of production in the electronics sector differ drastically from the ones in the IT sector. While the former is characterised by cheap labour and the dominance of foreign TNCs, the latter has more domestic investment and involvement. Moreover, while the governance style in the PRD is more laissez-faire without a long-term plan, municipal governments in the YRD have not been transformed into free and independent administrations. The YRD, in contrast to the PRD, is much more characterised by an entrenched planning system and sustained regional governance with the task to direct and foster the local economy as well as to exercise strong control over social groups. The IT sector is also characterised by a stronger R&T environment. While the electronics sector in the PRD is characterised by cheap labour, long working hours and conditions of super-exploitation, the YRD is an example of regulated working hours and jobs with better benefits attached for the workers themselves as well as their families. Production based on cheap labour in PRD, predominantly organised by foreign TNCs, is in constant and extremely heavy competition with other cheap labour locations in the Global South. The resulting relentless downward pressure on wages and working conditions makes any other system of industrial relations almost impossible. Thanks to a larger reserve army of labour, dissatisfied workers can be replaced easily. Production in IT in YRD, by contrast, is integrated in more high value-added areas of global production. In order to be successful, a skilled, satisfied, and stable workforce is necessary and this requires as a precondition more stable industrial relations, higher salaries, and better working conditions.

These rather different social relations of production and their different locations in the global political economy, we argue, have a strong influence on the type of informal labour NGOs in the two sectors as well as the nature of labour NGO—government relations. With work in the electronics industry being based on cheap labour and super-exploitation, industrial conflict is more likely. Labour NGOs, often not officially registered and not accepting government money, assist workers in getting their individual, but also collective rights vis-à-vis employers. By contrast, the higher value-added production in the IT sector requires more stable employment relations and, therefore, better working conditions to ensure a more satisfied workforce. The state is much more involved and informal labour NGOs, which willingly accept government funding and register officially, concentrate on organising interesting cultural activities for workers' free time. They almost perform a mediating role between employers and employees, supported by the government, in order to ensure a smooth functioning of the more high value-added production process.

As a result of improved rural conditions in China, the younger generation of migrant workers is no longer willing to accept the conditions of super-exploitation in the electronics industry (Gray, 2010, p. 463). Related cheap labour shortages especially in the PRD have put further pressure on employers and strengthened workers' bargaining power. As a result of class struggle, export industries have been forced to accept significant wage increases in recent years. 'Between 2008 and 2012, nominal statutory minimum wages increased annually by 12.6 percent on average' (Chan & Selden, 2014, p. 605). As Chan and Hui (2016), when the Chinese economy recovered after the global financial crisis and workers became stronger and more militant again, the Chinese state felt compelled to take their demands seriously and intervene with more pro-labour policies. Hence, the fact that global competitive dynamics put downward pressure on cheap labour sectors does not imply that resistance by workers could not result in an improvement of their working conditions. Nor do higher salaries necessarily imply that capital would simply leave. As Butollo and Lüthje (2016), despite the tendency of capitalists to relocate production sites globally in the search for cheaper labour, the PRD has continued to be a large, increasingly diverse and more mature production site in electronic appliances production. Nevertheless, the state and employers have not only given in to workers' increasing unrest. On the one hand, yes, the state passed some pro-labour policies including increases in the official minimum wage. On the other, it has clamped down on informal labour NGOs especially in the PRD, considered to be involved in recent unrest (Pringle, 2015). Equally, while employers have upgraded some of their production facilities, these struggles continue to be embedded within the wider global capitalist dynamics. 'Global manufacturers may also respond [to increasing wages] by shifting production to lower-cost economies, and there are already signs that this is happening' (Gray, 2010, p. 463). Hence, the success of struggles in China will ultimately also depend on the outcome of struggles in other countries.

Acknowledgements

We are grateful for the comments by two anonymous referees and Barry Gills on previous drafts of this article.

Funding

We thankfully acknowledge the grant of £275k by the Economic and Social Research Council (ESRC) for the project on 'Globalisation, national transformation and workers' rights: an analysis of Chinese labour within the global economy' [grant number RES-062-23-2777]. This article is part of our outputs from this research project.

Disclosure statement

No potential conflict of interest was reported by the authors.

Interview data

D1, August 22, 2009, Dongguan, Taiwanese investor.
G1, January 4, 2012, Guangzhou, Lecturer at School of Law, Sun Yat-sen University.
G2 January 10, 2012, Guangzhou, Leader of Labour NGO1.
G3, June 7, 2012, Guangzhou, Leader of Labour NGO 2.
G4, December 14 2012, Guangzhou, former chairman of Guangzhou ACFTU.
G5, January 13 2012, Guangzhou, Visiting scholar at Labour Study Centre of Yun Yet-Sen University.
S1, June 5, 2012, Shenzhen, Organiser of Labour NGO 1.
S2, January 22, 2013, Shenzhen, Labour NGO 2, lawyer 1.
S3, January 21, 2013, Shenzhen, Labour NGO 2, lawyer 2.
S4 August 18, 2011, Shenzhen, Formal Leader of Labour NGO 3.
S5 May 23, 2012, Shenzhen, Organiser of Labour NGO 4.
S6, January 20, 2013, Shenzhen, Leader of Labour NGO 5.
S7, December 9, 2012, Shenzhen, representative of workers' centre at Tsinghua library.
S8, April 24, 2014, Shenzhen, phone interview with labour organiser.
S9, July 24, 2014, Shenzhen, labour lawyer at Laowei labour law firm.
S10 , December 10, 2012, Shenzhen, leading organiser of ICO.
SH4, April 22, 2014, Shanghai, Organizer of worker's community centre 1.
SH5, April 26, 2014, Shanghai, Organizer of worker's community centre 2.
SH6, April 27, 2014, Shanghai, phone interview with organiser of Spring breeze after the Yue Yuan Strike.
SUH1, January 15, 2012, Suzhou, Human Resource Manager of Siemens.
SUH2, January 16, 2012, Suzhou, Human Resource Manager of Canmax.

References

Airriess, C. (2008). The geographies of secondary city growth in a globalised China—comparing Dongguan and Suzhou. *Journal of Urban History*, *35*(1), 134–149.

Bieler, A. (2014). Transnational labour solidarity in (the) crisis. *Global Labour Journal*, *5*(2), 114–133.

Bieler, A., & Morton, A. D. (2004). A critical theory route to hegemony, world order and historical change: Neo-Gramscian perspectives in international relations. *Capital & Class*, *82*, 85–113.

Butollo, F. (2014). *The end of cheap labour? Industrial transformation and 'social upgrading' in China*. Frankfurt: Campus.

Butollo, F., & Lüthje, B. (2016). Why the Foxconn model does not die: Global production and labour relations in the IT industry in South China. *Globalizations*. doi:10.1080/14747731.2016.1203132

Buttigieg, J. A. (2005). The contemporary discourse on civil society: A Gramscian critique. *Boundary 2*, *32*(1), 33–52.

Chan, C. (2013). Community-based organisations for migrant workers' rights: The emergence of labour NGOs in China. *Community Development Journal*, *48*(1), 1–17.

Chan, K. C. C., & Hui, E. S. (2016). Bringing class struggles back: A Marxian analysis of the state and class relations in China. *Globalizations*. doi:10.1080/14747731.2016.1207935

Chan, J., Pun, N., & Selden, M. (2013). The politics of global production: Apple, Foxconn and China's new working class. *New Technology, Work and Employment*, *28*(2), 100–115.

Chan, J., & Selden, M. (2014). China's rural migrant workers, the state, and labor politics. *Critical Asian Studies*, *46*(4), 599–620.

Chen, X. (2007). A tale of two regions in China: Rapid economic development and slow industrial upgrading in the Pearl River Delta and the Yangtze River Deltas. *International Journal of Comparative Sociology*, *48*(2), 167–201.

China Labour Bulletin. (2014, February). *Searching for the union, the workers movement in China 2011-13*. Retrieved July 6, 2014, from http://www.clb.org.hk/en/sites/default/files/File/research_reports/searching%20for%20the%20union%201.pdf

Gramsci, A. (1971). *Selections from the prison notebooks*. (Q. Hoare & G. Nowell Smith, Ed. and Trans.). London: Lawrence and Wishart.

Gray, K. (2010). Labour and the state in China's passive revolution. *Capital & Class*, *34*(3), 449–467.

Gray, K. (2015). *Labour and development in East Asia: Social forces and passive revolution*. London: Routledge.

Hardy, J. (2016). China's place in global divisions of labour: An uneven and combined development perspective. *Globalizations*. doi:10.1080/14747731.2016.1200264

Hart-Landsberg, M. (2013). *Capitalist globalization: Consequences, resistance, and alternatives*. New York, NY: Monthly Review Press.

Hart-Landsberg, M. (2015). From the claw to the lion: A critical look at capitalist globalization. *Critical Asian Studies*. doi:10.1080/14672715.2015.997024

He, J., & Huang, H. (2008). NGOs defending migrant labour rights in the Pearl River Delta region. *Hong Kong Journal of Social Science*, *35*, 41–71. [In Chinese].

Hsu, S. (2015, May 3). China's efforts to boost consumption: Are they enough? *The Diplomat*. Retrieved December 4, 2015, from http://thediplomat.com/2015/05/chinas-efforts-to-boost-consumption-are-they-enough

Kiely, R. (2010). *Rethinking imperialism*. London: Palgrave.

Lee, C. K. & Shen, Y. (2011). The anti-solidarity machine? Labour nongovernmental organisations in China. In S. Kuruvilla, C. K. Lee, & M. Gallagher (Eds.), *From iron rice bowl to informalisation* (pp. 173–188). New York, NY: Cornell University.

Li, Z., & Hao, Q. (2014). Labor process and the social structure of accumulation in China. *Review of Radical Political Economics*, *46*(4), 481–488.

Ma, Q. (2006). *Non-governmental organisations in contemporary China*. London: Routledge.

Mao, Y., Liu, W., & Hu, J. (2004). Dynamics of SEMs clusters and networks: An analysis of the export network economy of it industries in Dongguan. *Web Journal of China Management Review*, *7*(1), 49–65.

Ngo. (2011). *Globalising Suzhou: Exogenous growth and chinese urban development*. Retrieved August 25, 2014, from http://blogs.ubc.ca/victorngo/files/2012/07/GEOG352_Suzhou.pdf

People's Republic of China. (2015). *Foreign non-governmental organisations management law (draft) (second reviewed draft)*. Retrieved November 10, 2015, from http://chinalawtranslate.com/foreign-ngo-draft-2/?lang=en

Pringle, T. (2013). Reflections on labor in China: From a moment to a movement. *The South Atlantic Quarterly*, *112*(1), 191–202.

Pringle, T. (2015). Labour under threat: The rise and (possible) fall of 'collective bargaining' in South China. *Union Rights*, *22*(4), 3–5.

Pun, N. (2008). The making of a global dormitory labour regime: Labour NGOs and workers empowerment in South China. In R. Murphy (Ed.), *Labour migration and social development in contemporary China* (pp. 154–171). New York, NY: Routledge.

Pun, N., Yuan, S., Yuhua, G., Huilin, L., Chan, J., & Seldon, M. (2014). Worker-intellectual unity: Trans-border sociological intervention in Foxconn. *Current Sociology*. doi:10.1177/0011392113514892

Qi, H. (2014). The labor share question in China. *Monthly Review*, 65/8. Retrieved June 23, 2014, from http://monthlyreview.org/2014/01/01/labor-share-question-china

Sacom. (2012). *Open letter to Guangdong government*. Retrieved July 7, 2014, from http://sacom.hk/archives/953

Schmalz, S., Sommer, B., & Xu, H. (2016). The Yue Yuen Strike: Industrial transformation and labour unrest in the Pearl River Delta. *Globalizations*. doi:10.1080/14747731.2016.1203188

Shen, J. (2002). Urban and regional development in post-reform China: The case of Zhujian delta. *Progress in Planning*, *57*, 91–140.

Sum, N.-L. (2009). Struggles against Wal-Martisation and neoliberal competitiveness in (southern) China—towards postneoliberalism as an alternative? *Development Dialogue*, *51*, 157–168. Retrieved July 9, 2014, from http://www.dhf.uu.se/pdffiler/DD2009_51_postneoliberalism/Development_Dialogue_51-art13.pdf

Tuan, C., & Ng, L.-Y. (2004). FDI and industrial restructuring in post-WTO Greater PRD: Implications on regional growth in China. *The World Economy*, *27*(10), 1609–1630.

Wang, H., Appelbaum, R. P., Degiuli, F., & Lichtenstein, N. (2009). China's new labour contract law: Is China moving towards increased power for workers? *Third World Quarterly*, *30*(3), 485–501.

Wedeman, A. (2009, September 3–6). *Enemies of the state: Mass incidents and subversion in China*. Paper presented at the annual meeting of the American Political Science Association, Toronto, Canada.

Yeung, G. (2001). *Foreign investment and socio-economic development in China: The case of Dongguan*. New York, NY: Palgrave.

Zhang, Z. (2012). *Guangdong NGOs face grand-scale regulation: The government is using a two-handed policy, suppression and incorporation (in Chinese)*. Retrieved July 6, 2014, from http://www.szwlg.org/news/lgnew/2012/0608/911.html

Why the Foxconn Model Does Not Die: Production Networks and Labour Relations in the IT Industry in South China

BOY LÜTHJE* & FLORIAN BUTOLLO**

*Sun Yat-sen University, Guangzhou, People's Republic of China
**Friedrich-Schiller-University of Jena, Jena, Germany

ABSTRACT *This contribution tracks the recent geographical and structural changes in the electronics contract manufacturing (ECM) industry in China's Pearl River Delta (PRD) and the corresponding modifications in labour relations. We find that a diversified ECM industry in the PRD has been expanding in spite of rising production costs and that investments in other regions in China should therefore be seen as a complement, rather than a substitute, for production capacities in the PRD. Our investigation of working conditions at three major production sites in the PRD in May 2013 based on 167 worker interviews shows that substantial changes in employment regimes are absent and that wage rises remain modest. The industry continues to operate on the flexible employment of low-skilled and poorly paid migrant workers. We conclude that improvements of working conditions must rely on the associational power of workers and global efforts to regulate the highly competitive ECM industry.*

Since China's export-oriented industrialisation took off in the 1990s, the Pearl River Delta (PRD) has emerged as the country's primary hub of large-scale sub-contracted manufacturing for overseas markets. Propelled by annual growth rates of 20% and more in the early 2000s, the PRD became the largest agglomeration of manufacturing industries in the world. Most of its roughly 25 million industrial workers are employed in labour-intensive industries, such as clothing, shoes, or household appliances. But the PRD also hosts vast networks of globalised high-tech production with capital-intensive mega factories, such as the Foxconn industrial park in Shenzhen Longhua. It is the largest location for the manufacturing of advanced information technologies in the world, particularly in mobile communications.

As widely analysed in the recent literature, the labour-intensive, export-driven production model in the PRD and similar regions in China has increasingly come under pressure due to the combined influences of rising costs and diminishing markets (Yang, 2012). Especially after the world financial crisis of 2008/2009 no-name mass manufacturing for global brands was deemed to be unsustainable by Chinese political leaders and commentators. Although advanced electronics manufacturing is regarded as a crucial base for China's quest for world-power status in high-tech industries, the industry has been subjected to public criticism. On the one hand, mass production for foreign brands, as epitomised in the symbiosis of Apple and its key supplier Foxconn, is seen as detrimental to indigenous innovation in China (e.g. Qiu, 2011). On the other hand, the notoriously poor labour practices, symbolised by the tragic series of suicides among young migrant workers at Foxconn's industrial park in Shenzhen in 2010 (Chan, Pun, & Selden, 2013, pp. 104–108) are considered a continuing threat to social stability. At the same time the electronics contract manufacturing (ECM) industry continues to suffer from low profit margins, rising costs for production inputs (including labour), and structural overcapacity in global information technology (IT) production (Lüthje, Hürtgen, Schumm, & Sproll, 2013; Lüthje, Luo, & Zhang, 2013).

In this contribution, we track the recent changes in the ECM industry of the PRD and ask whether they entail a transformation towards more sustainable patterns of industrial development and labour regulation. In contrast to the often heard prediction that the industry was about to leave the PRD (Yang, 2014, p. 148), we find that a more differentiated geography of production has emerged in China, in which the PRD continues to play a leading role. However, despite efforts to diversify and upgrade production models and commitments to improve working conditions, the fundamental characteristics of the regime of flexible mass production (Lüthje, Luo et al., 2013) remain unchanged. This is the prime reason for the persistence of labour conflicts, which also have spread to the new production sites in central and western China.

The article is organised as follows: in the subsequent section, we give a brief overview of the structure and main characteristics of the global ECM industry. We then present the results of our investigation about the diversification and expansion of the industry in the PRD based on the evaluation of secondary sources. This is complemented by the results of a survey of labour conditions at three major production sites of ECM companies in the PRD based on 169 workers interviews, which demonstrate a persistence of exploitative labour regimes despite the upgrading and diversification of the industry. In the final section, we summarise our results and discuss policy implications. Our main conclusion is that substantial reform of labour policies, supported by social organisation among rank and file workers and democratically elected workplace-trade unions, is needed to achieve sustainable forms of economic and social development.

China's Electronics Manufacturing Industry in the Global Context

During the recent three decades the electronics industry has undergone massive changes of global dimensions. Today the production of IT systems and devices takes place in complex networks of technology development firms, component suppliers, and assembly service companies. These networks have replaced the traditional type of large, integrated multinational corporations (like IBM, Siemens, or Fujitsu) that controlled the electronics industry in earlier periods of capitalist development. Since the 1990s, the IT industry became dominated by specialised companies with global leadership in some key technologies, such as Apple, Microsoft, or Cisco. The downside of this model was the massive outsourcing of manufacturing from lead companies to large-scale contract manufacturers, which in fact became global corporations themselves and the backbone of electronics manufacturing (Borrus & Zysman, 1997; Lüthje, Hürtgen et al., 2013; Lüthje, Schumm, & Sproll, 2002).

The shift of large-scale production resources and important elements of product development to China and other emerging economies was part of this restructuring. Hence the shape of China's IT manufacturing mirrors contemporary industry structures at the global level and shows relatively little heritage from the planned economy. The industry is heavily dominated by foreign transnational corporations (TNCs) and their production models which are grounded on the specialisation of component suppliers in modular production systems (cf. Borrus, Ernst, & Haggard, 2000; Lüthje, Hürtgen et al., 2013; Sturgeon & Kawakami, 2011 for comprehensive analyses).

Table 1 presents the sectoral structure of IT manufacturing in China and its development from 2007 to 2010. In 2010, the entire production volume reached 5.69 trillion RMB (approximately 630 billion Euro at 2010 exchange rates), probably the largest volume of its kind in the world. A stunning 72.5% of revenues are held by foreign-invested or overseas Chinese companies, whereas state-owned enterprises account for less than 10%.

China's IT sector is deeply integrated into the capitalist world market. In 2010, the export volume of IT products stood at 534.8 bn US$, about 80% of the total production volume. IT products accounted for 34.1% of China's total exports. At the same time, there was a very high volume of imports of IT components which reflects China's role as a global assembly hub for the industry. Imports amounted to 377 bn US$ or 30% of the country's total imports in 2009 (Ministry of Industry and Information Technology (MIIT) of the People's Republic of China, 2010).

These figures reflect the rapid expansion of the industry since the late 1990s, particularly between 2001 and 2007, when a massive crisis in the IT industry pushed enormous amounts of foreign investment into IT production in China. The average annual growth rate of the

Table 1. China IT industry revenues by subsectors (2010)

		Revenues in billion RMB	Revenue growth (%)	Percentage of total (%)
Entire industry		5688.03	28.5	100
Components	Telecommunications equipment	847.74	14.9	14.9
	Radar and radio equipment	172.81	46.1	3.0
	Broadcasting and TV equipment	433.89	32.5	8.0
	Electronic computers	1739.56	25.2	30.6
	Video and audio home equipment	402.74	21.5	7.1
	Components for electronic devices	853.72	44	15.0
	Electronic components (chips)	1044.61	33.4	18.4
	Electronic measuring instrument	82.68	35.7	1.5
	Special-purpose electronic equipment	198.73	36.4	3.5
	Electric machinery for electronic information systems	166.08	33.5	2.9
	Others	291.50	35.6	5.1
By ownership	Foreign-invested enterprises	4120.29	26.9	72.4
	State-owned enterprises	455.85	28.1	8.0

Source: Ministry of Industry and Information Technology.

information electronics industry reached 28.8% between 2000 and 2005, which was significantly higher than the average growth for all manufacturing industries (10.9%). This fast pace of growth resumed after the global crisis in 2008–2009, which led to severe employment reductions during winter 2008 and 2009. After a contraction of industry-wide revenues by 2.7% in 2009, revenue again increased by around 30% in 2010 (ibid.).

The integration of China's information electronics industry into global production networks has produced a highly complex scenario of company organisation and production models. Four main types can be distinguished among multinational and national companies (cf. Lüthje, Hürtgen et al., 2013):

(1) *Brand-name companies that have kept substantial amounts of in-house production.* This group once was led by traditional multinational electronics companies such as Siemens, Philips, or Motorola. It is now mainly represented by multinationals from Japan and Korea, such as Sony or Samsung. Some major electronics manufacturers from China, namely TCL and Konka have adapted this model.

(2) *Systems and component manufacturers with no factories of their own.* Such companies focus on the design of hardware, semiconductors, and other components, but do not operate production facilities under their own name. These companies cooperate extensively with ECM. This group is represented by major vendors of personal computer (PC) and data networking equipment, such as Dell or Cisco. Also, a number of leading Chinese IT companies, such as Huawei and ZTE adhere to this model. There are many 'factoryless' design houses for high-end chips and software.

Table 2. Top electronics control manufacturers (2007/2011)

Rank 2007	Company	Country of origin	Revenues 2007[a]	Revenues 2011[a]	Dominant production model
1	Foxconn (Hon Hai)	Taiwan	40,527	93,100	EMS[b]
2	Flextronics	Singapore/US	17,708	27,450	EMS
3	Asustek	Taiwan	17,196	14,730	ODM[c]/OBM[d]
4	Quanta Computer	Taiwan	16,503	33,487	ODM/OBM
5	Solectron	US	11,200	Acquired by Flextronics	EMS
6	Sanmina-SCI	US	10,955	6040	EMS
7	Jabil	US	10,300	16,760	EMS
8	Clestica	Canada	8800	7210	EMS
9	Inventec	Taiwan	7890	12,562	ODM/OBM
10	TPV Technology	Hong Kong	7176	n.a.	NN
11	Wistron	Taiwan	6800	n.a.	EMS
12	BenQ	Taiwan	6094	n.a.	ODM/OBM
13	Elcoteq	Finland	5677	Out of business	EMS
14	Benchmark Electronics	US	2907	2300	EMS
15	Cal-Comp Electronics	Thailand	2050	4469	EMS

[a]In million USD.

[b]Electronic manufacturing services (EMS): companies providing test, manufacture, distribute and repair services on behalf of brandname companies.

[c]Original design manufacturing (ODM): like the former but with additional product design services.

[d]Original brand manufacturing (OBM): manufacturing companies that sell products to consumer markets under their own brand name.

Source: Electronic Business, www.edn.com, Bloomberg.

(3) *Large electronic contract manufacturers* of electronics systems with no brand name of their own. ECM form the largest segment of IT production in China by revenues, production facilities, and employment. This group is led by Foxconn, Flextronics, and the Taiwanese companies Compal, Asustek, and Quanta (cf. table 2). These companies integrate large-scale resources of high-end mass manufacturing of electronic products, extensive networks of supply-chain management and logistics, and substantial capacities of engineering and technology development. They provide comprehensive manufacturing services for brand-name firms at global scale, including process engineering, product testing and design of components, and sometimes entire products.

(4) *Suppliers of electronic and non-electronic components* without extensive ECM capabilities. Large-scale component manufacturers can mostly be found in production of computer motherboards, assembly of specialised printed circuit boards (PCBs), or manufacturing of such components as computer displays or graphic cards. Small and medium-sized companies dominate the manufacturing of non-electronic components, such as connectors, cable assemblies, metal, and plastic parts. This sector is very large and dominated by family- and privately owned companies. They form the backbone of labour-intensive assembly in electronics. The largest concentration of such companies can be found in the PRD, where about 2700 companies were located around 2005 (Lüthje, Hürtgen et al., 2013).

In spite of the massive growth of electronics contract and component manufacturing this industry structure clearly contains drawbacks for China's industrial and social development. As Sturgeon and Kawakami explain, the market power of large electronics contract manufacturers has remained low, since the industry was 'characterized by intense competition, low profitability, and dramatic consolidation, even as it has experienced rapid growth' (2011, p. 127). Therefore, 'the world's major contract manufacturers have been trapped in low value-added segments of the electronics GVC: manufacturing and iterative, detailed design' (ibid., p. 137). As the No.1 location for ECM in the world, the electronics industry in China and in the PRD in particular is exposed to the rapid ups and downs of the global IT industry. In fact, it acts as a safety valve for global markets cycles. As we will explain in detail below, extreme employment flexibility and huge fluctuations of the workforce are essentially an outcome of China's present position in global networks of mass production.

ECM in the PRD: Persistent, Growing, and Increasingly Differentiated

IT manufacturing in China is highly regionalised. The main industry clusters have emerged from large-scale investment of foreign and overseas Chinese companies. South China's PRD is the largest and historically oldest location for export-oriented IT manufacturing with a strong presence of Hong Kong- and Taiwan-owned companies. The region is primarily specialised on the assembly of consumer electronics products, such as PCs or cellphones, and a hot spot of the ECM industry. As Table 3 shows, Guangdong province earns by far the highest revenues in IT manufacturing in China, followed by Jiangsu, Shandong, Fujian, and Shanghai.

The decision by Foxconn in 2009 to build another giant factory for the production of Apple's iPad in Chengdu in Sichuan province symbolised an important change in the geography of IT production in China. Until then, the industry had been concentrated mainly in the large industrial areas of the Pearl River Delta (PRD) and the Yangtze River Delta (YRD). In fact, Foxconn's investment was only one step in a larger regional diversification of electronics manufacturing. After years of geographic diversification, there exist Foxconn factories in over 20 Chinese cities, many of them in inland provinces (Pun, Lu, Guo, & Shen, 2012). Likewise, other electronics contract manufacturers, such as Flextronics, Quanta, Pegatron, Compal, Wistron, and

Table 3. Regional distribution of IT manufacturing revenues (2010)

		Revenues in bn RMB	Annual growth (%)	Percentage of total (%)
By province (top 10)	Total	5688.03		
	Guangdong	1797.66	29.3	31.6
	Jiangsu	1347.36	27.4	23.7
	Shanghai	582.60	23.1	10.2
	Shandong	434.18	21	7.6
	Zhejiang	277.14	35.3	4.9
	Beijing	245.72	13.6	4.3
	Fujian	222.26	33.3	3.9
	Tianjin	165.01	23.8	2.9
	Sichuan	119.52	47.4	2.1
	Liaoning	97.41	44.4	1.7

Source: MIIT.

Inventec, have established subsidiaries in western provinces. The cities of Chengdu and Chongqing emerged as new hubs for volume manufacturing.

The trend of regional expansion has been well observed in recent studies and media coverage. However, the consequences for established industrial centres like the PRD have been grossly exaggerated by the media and some industry experts (cf. Jung & Wagner, 2008). For instance, many expected a rapid downsizing of Foxconńs operations in Shenzhen. But these factories still employed a combined workforce of at least 500,000 in 2011, two years after the inauguration of Foxconn's Chengdu branch. Although some contracts indeed were shifted to other provinces in the meantime, more recent figures show that Foxconn's Shenzhen operations still function as a giant complex for mass production with a combined workforce of at least 440,000 in the second quarter of 2013, according to media sources (NanfangDushibao, 2013).

Our investigation based on an evaluation of company websites, recent literature (Pun et al., 2012; Yang, 2014) and English as well as Chinese online resources reveals a surprisingly dense network of ECM factories in the PRD, which involve a number of highly diversified production sites of the largest enterprises (cf. Figure 1). Additionally, there are new investments of global ECM companies that had not been present in the PRD before. Some very large factories, particularly Foxconn's giant industrial park in Shenzhen Longhua, while still employing around 200,000 workers in autumn 2015 (Interview data), will prospectively be downsized due to the relocation of certain tasks. Yet other factories in the region were significantly expanded, for example the operations of Flextronics in Zhuhai, of Jabil in Guangzhou, and of Wistron in Zhongshan.

A closer look at the largest ECM companies, Foxconn and Flextronics, demonstrates the ongoing importance of the PRD. Both companies have established complex networks of factories beyond their main production sites.

Foxconn by now operates ten factories in the PRD. Its best known and largest branches are in Shenzhen Longhua and Guanlan. These industrial parks focus on the production of various products of the '3C' category (= computers, consumer electronics, and communication). But the Foxconn group maintains several other factories in the area, some of which focus on certain product groups which require specialised manufacturing equipment and skills, for instance three factories in the city of Foshan that produce digital cameras (over 20,000 employees), TFT-LCD monitors (17,000 employees), and LED lighting products (12,000 employees).

Other specialised factories include one in the city of Zhongshan (power amplifiers and Wi-Fi equipment, 2000 employees) and one in Huizhou, producing electric components, mobile phones, and white goods (25,000 employees).

Not all of these facilities are new investments. Some were acquired by Foxconn, such as the digital camera maker Pulihua in 2006. Although this factory is currently experiencing a relocation of a part of its operations to the city of Yantai in Shandong province, most other enterprises are set to stay. Foxconn's latest investment in the region, a factory in Dongguan, has been started in 2011 (Pun et al., 2012). The factory in Huizhou is supposed to be expanded soon from current 25,000 to about 30,000 employees (Boluo government, 2012). In other words, Foxconn has significantly expanded a number of investments in the PRD well after the financial and economic crisis of 2008–2009. This contradicts the assumption of a comprehensive relocation of operations.

Similarly, *Flextronics* has expanded its portfolio to currently seven factories in the area. By far the largest is the industrial park in Zhuhai's Doumen district. The complex covers more than 1.5 square kilometres with at least seven production units and a total number of about 60,000 employees—more than a quarter of Flextronics' global workforce. The number of employees at this location was reduced from 50,000 to slightly over 30,000 in the course of the crisis of 2008/2009, but since then almost doubled again. Other operations of Flextronics include a number of smaller factories of 3000–5000 employees located in Shenzhen that focus on the assembly of PCBs. A larger operation with currently 11,000 employees with a more diversified production portfolio, including tooling, plastic injection parts manufacturing and PCB assembly, is located in the town of Dalingshan in Dongguan. Again, the complex and diversified production network of Flextronics illustrates the ongoing importance of the PRD as a production site. However, it remains to be seen whether the planned opening of a factory of 100,000 in Chengdu, a size which exceeds the current combined number of employees in the PRD, will lead to a reconfiguration of the company's internal division of labour.

Other ECM companies do not possess production networks of similar size and scope, but most have expanded their operations in the region. Jabil's Guangzhou branch has experienced rapid growth over the past five years and doubled the number of its employees to about 13,000. Apart from this factory which mainly assembles PCBs and the related final products, the company also operates a plant in Shenzhen with around 4000 employees that makes special components, such as moulded plastic parts for communication, motor vehicle structures, optical lenses, and back light modules.

The PRD also experienced additional investment of Taiwanese original design manufacturing (ODM) companies in recent years. This is remarkable since companies that operated under this more sophisticated production model were previously almost exclusively located in the YRD. *Wistron*, the fourth largest company of this category, operates a factory with a workforce of 18,000 in the city of Zhongshan—almost one-third of its 60,000 employees globally. The worlds second largest company ODM contract manufacturer, *Pegatron*, runs three factories in the PRD. Its largest facility with 10,500 employees produces digital cameras in Dongguan. Another significant development is the rise of Chinese ECM companies like *3CEMS* and *Nam Tai Electronics*. These companies have entered the global top 50 of the ECM industry after the economic crisis and are expanding their businesses by supplying to large Chinese consumer electronics companies like Huawei or ZTE, among others.

The large production volumes in the PRD demonstrate the ongoing vitality of the regional ECM industry. However, it should be noted that contract manufacturers do not only do more of the same, but have increasingly diversified their production. This has counteracted the

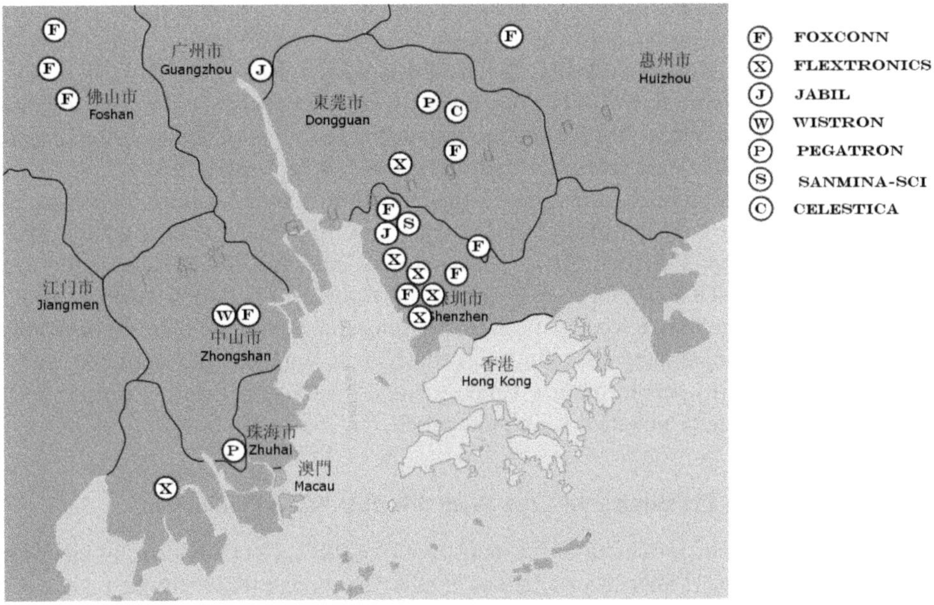

Figure 1. Location of major production sites of contract manufacturers in the PRD.

predicted emerging division of labour between the YRD as a location for more complex and specialised manufacturing and the PRD as site for high-volume assemblies of lower complexity. In this sense there has been a substantial upgrading of the ECM industry in the PRD, as shown by the examples of the Zhuhai industrial park of Flextronics, the specialised factories of Foxconn that produce digital cameras, large TFT-LCD displays, and LED lighting products, and the new investments of ODM contract manufacturers.

What is more, there has been rapid growth of Chinese telecommunications equipment makers headquartered in the PRD, such as Huawei and ZTE. This, in turn, fostered a new generation of smaller Chinese contract manufacturers. For smartphones the PRD has emerged as the most important location of production and design in China and worldwide, with complete supply chains, including software, displays, PCB design and production, and chip development. Finally, the rapid growth of the automotive sector, of the electric car industry, and of the LED industry in the region partially relies on ECM companies as suppliers and bears considerable potential for future product diversification.

The restructuring and diversification of production in the PRD, however, is occurring under the auspices of ongoing low profit margins and cut-throat competition in ECM. Rising production costs in China now amplify the squeeze in profitability, for which ECM is notorious. However, the industry has not embarked on the path of simply moving to the next cheaper production site. There are simultaneous endeavours to raise the share of value added through industrial upgrading which either implies to offer more specialised and complex products ('high mix, low volume') or to move into new areas that complement the core business of volume manufacturing. The recent actions of Foxconn illustrate this tendency as the company aimed to diversify its range of functions by starting divisions in the field of robotics, automotive parts, and retailing. The company also launched its own brand in the field of LED lighting and entered a joint venture with the Japanese TNC Sharp.

Such strategies to escape pressures in the low-margin business of volume manufacturing have not been thoroughly successful, however. Foxconn diversification efforts have remained precarious in many aspects. Most remarkably, the flamboyant announcement of 2011 that Foxconn would introduce one million 'Foxbots'—Foxconn's own robot brand—did not materialise. In autumn of 2015, only about 30,000 Foxbots are installed in Foxconn's China divisions according to an expert active in this field (personal communication, 24 September 2015).

Seen from this perspective, the struggle to escape from low-margin business remains an uphill battle. The option to become consumer brands in their own right and thus reap a larger share of value added, as had been practised by the Taiwanese brands ASUS, ACER, and more recently HTC, has not been copied by the large EMC firms. This would be a high-risk strategy, since contract manufacturers would enter competition in consumer markets with their main customers. Thus, large contract manufacturers only indirectly benefit from China's booming consumer markets which are rather served by new Chinese brands, such as Xiaomi, Coolpad, or Oppo, which in turn heavily rely on outsourcing production.

The Labour Regime: Persistence of Low-Wage Flexible Mass Production

How does the recent transformation of the industry of the PRD affect the forms of labour regulation at ECM companies? Shop-floor relations in ECM are representative for the regime of production in the capital-intensive and technologically advanced sectors of sub-contracted mass production in China that we have called 'flexible mass production' (cf. Lüthje, Luo et al., 2013). It is based on neo-Taylorist work organisation, characterised by the combination of technologically sophisticated automated equipment, and large workforces of rural migrant workers at low wages. Work is highly segmented and systematically de-skilled in order to facilitate flexible employment of large numbers of workers. The wage and employment system is designed to extract extensive overtime work. The base wage, usually near the local legal minimum wage, is low and provides not more than 50% of workers' regular incomes. Workers achieve the larger part of their wages through extensive overtime work and bonuses for personal performance and disciplined behaviour. Workers are housed in factory dormitories and eat in canteens, usually at very low cost or free. The dormitory regime (cf. Pun, 2005) has become the hallmark of this system; it plays a central role in maintaining social control and stability in the factories. Nevertheless, the turnover in ECM factories is notoriously high, working hours regularly surpass the legal maximum, and labour conflicts are frequent (Lüthje, Hürtgen et al., 2013).

The social costs of this production regime became obvious after the series of suicides at the Foxconn plant in Shenzhen in the summer of 2010. This increased public awareness about labour rights violations at ECM companies, along with some massive labour conflicts in the newly established ECM factories in central and western China (Chan et al., 2013). As a reaction to public pressure from Chinese officials and international media, companies such as Apple have pledged to exert a tighter control over labour conditions at their suppliers. The Fair Labour Association (FLA) conducted investigations at Foxconn subsidiaries on behalf of Apple. The FLA (2013a) published an action plan for the correction of the observed labour rights violations and concluded in May 2013 that '[o]ver the past nine months, steady progress has been made at the three facilities employing an estimated 178,000 workers' (p. 5). This contributed to the overall impression that Apple was about to fix the problems in its supply chain.

Our investigation was conducted in May 2013, immediately after the second verification report on Foxconn was published by the FLA. Its aim was to find out whether management reforms combined with changes in production models would result in substantial changes of the regimes of flexible mass production, in particular with regard to workforce recruitment, turnover, working hours, and wage systems.

Our survey consisting of 167 workers' questionnaires[1]was conducted at three major subsidiaries in the PRD which belong to globally operating electronics contract manufacturers owned by foreign investors. All of them manufacture finished products or components of the '3C' category, that is, computer, communication, and consumer electronics. The size of the workforces was between 10,000 and 50,000 employees, of which between 75% and 80% were migrant workers.

In terms of the employment regimes, the results from our survey reflect the persistence of highly flexible employment of a very young migrant workforce. This is obvious when factories A and B are concerned. In these cases, the average age of the interviewed workers was between 23 and 24 years and the average employment period was between one and two years (cf. Table 4). When asked about how long the interviewees worked in the company, 49% of workers at factory A and 60% at factory B gave periods of below one year. This confirms that there have been no changes in the stability of employment in the period of the investigation. The implementation of the Labour Contract Law, which was supposed to counteract such employment practices, has changed little in this respect. Neither did the management encourage long-term employment as a response to the widespread labour shortage in this region.

Factory C seems to be the exception to this rule since workers at this factory had stayed there for a longer period of time. Apparently this company relies on a layer of long-term migrant employees. However, the data most likely reflect the imminent relocation of the factory. The management has basically stopped to recruit workers about one year before our investigation and consequently there has been no expansion of the workforce.

Since employment remains highly flexible, the surveyed companies relied mainly on low-skilled work which is reflected in very short training periods for line workers that lasted between five and nine days. About half of all manufacturing workers only received an introductory training of up to three days only. Conversely, the share of manufacturing workers that were trained for one month or more was lower than 7% in all companies of the sample.

Since workers do not possess comprehensive skills, work is very monotonous. Between a third and half of all workers perform only one task in their current position and only a minority of manufacturing workers deals with more than three tasks at the same time. Likewise, the bulk of the workers stated that they switch their positions very rarely and mostly go on performing the same tasks over and over again.

The average total wage for manufacturing workers ranges between RMB 2578 and RMB 2887. These figures clearly reflect the trend towards higher basic incomes which has been

Table 4. Age and turnover of the workforce

	Average age	Average employment period	Highest value employment period	Employed since 3 years or less (%)	Employed since1 year or less (%)	Employed since spring festival or less (%)
Factory A	23.34	1 year, 11 months	7 years	21.6	49.0	25.5
Factory B	24.09	1 year, 2 months	10 years	8.6	60.3	43.1
Factory C	26.91	4 year, 4 months	16 years	63.6	9.1	2.3

Table 5. Workers' wages

	Last income Base wage	Total wage	Flexible wage share[a] %	Average income Total wage	Lowest income Total wage	Highest income Total wage
Factory A	1490	2636	43.5	2578	1891	3819
Factory B	1566	2879	45.6	2887	2370	3336
Factory C	1852	3192	42.0	2726	1734	3790

[a]Total wage (last income)—base wage (last income) / total wage (last income), that is, calculated from average incomes.

prevalent in this region and led to frequent government-induced rises of the minimum wage. However, the wage systems still rely on a very high amount of flexible, performance-based bonuses and overtime payments while base wages remain well below the figure of RMB 2200 which was proclaimed by Foxconn in 2012 as a benchmark for workers in another plant in the region. Base wages rather correspond roughly to the local minimum wages which ranged between RMB 1310 and RMB 1600 in the respective localities at the time of investigation (Table 5).

The high proportion of flexible pay led to significant variations in income. Asked for their minimum monthly incomes since they started working at the company, workers gave amounts between RMB 1734 and RMB 2370. The highest monthly incomes, however, ranged between RMB 3336 and RMB 3819.

The data on working hours show that all companies rely on excessive amounts of overtime, which exceed the stipulations by the Chinese labour law (cf. Table 6). The regular working hours are close to the maximum of 60 hours to which the industry subscribed in voluntary initiatives such as the Electronic Industry Citizenship Coalition Code of Conduct. Contract manufacturers thus continue with the illegal practice of aligning to self-proclaimed codes of conduct instead of the local labour law and obviously are given a free hand of doing so by local governments.

The excesses in terms of illegal overtime work are not obvious when only average figures are considered. But a significant number of workers stated that they had already worked for more than 70 hours per week since hired by the company. At factory B, where 43% of the interviewed workers were hired less than 3 months before the investigation, more than 57% of the sample said that they already had worked more than 70 hours per week. Excessive working hours continue to be a hallmark of the ECM industry and there are little signs of change. Consequently, the FLA had to address this issue as one of the 'remaining deficiencies' which had not been corrected after Foxconn had committed to an action plan in 2012 (FLA, 2013b, p. 3).

Table 6. Working hours

	Regular working hours	Regular OT per week	Max. working hours	Max of > 70h (share)
Factory A	59.80	17.63	62.72	20.00
Factory B	n.s.	17.79	69.78	57.41
Factory C	58.63	16.28	65.77	51.22

Trade Unions and Labour Conflicts

At all three companies in our sample there exists an enterprise trade union which was set up following the governments' initiatives to establish trade unions in private companies. However, our data suggest that in all of the three cases the unions fail to represent workers.

At factories A and B, a trade union does exist, but it seems to be virtually invisible. Almost one-third of the interviewed workers at factory A either did not know whether there was a trade union at the company or thought it would not exist. At factory B, most workers did not have contact with the trade union and had no opinion about it. At both factories, there is no indication that the trade union would play any role in wage negotiations.

In the aftermath of a strike at factory C shortly before the investigation, workers' awareness of the enterprise trade union was higher, but there was a significant number of workers who were dissatisfied with it (13% said that they were 'very dissatisfied' and another 13% said that they were 'fairly dissatisfied'). This reflects a failure of the trade union to represent workers during the strike. Significantly, the practice of this union was largely limited to a (traditional) role of organising leisure activities.

The trigger for this strike was the relocation of parts of the production to a city in the Northern Bohai region between March and July 2013. Most workers were not prepared to continue working for the company in that distant region and therefore were leaving the company. However, the compensation pay offered to the workers was much lower than the amount that had been promised before. This added to the discontent about dissatisfying wages and working conditions which had been deteriorating since the factory was taken over by the current owners in 2006. There was additional tension, because the management tried to prevent workers from leaving, in order to maintain production for their ongoing customer orders.

There was considerable insecurity among workers about the motivation and the extent of the relocation since it was announced that not all capacity in the PRD would be shut down. According to workers' information, the economic situation of the company had been deteriorating because of economic pressures in the highly competitive segment of digital cameras and due to 'management problems'. Additionally, rent contracts and tax benefits were about to expire, which made it less attractive to maintain production in the PRD.

Overall, the strike seems to have been fairly successful since the management finally agreed to pay compensation at the rate that was initially promised and granted wage increases. Yet, there was neither an agreement allowing the workers to leave the factory at their own decision nor on the question of the housing fund. The interviewed workers tended to see the strike as a success, although some remained sceptical whether the announced measures would actually be implemented.

The case of the relocation and strike at factory C is another expression of the instability of production regimes in the contract manufacturing industry. Of the companies in our sample, factory C had the most experienced and a relatively skilled workforce. Yet, there seem to be no schemes to offer long-standing employees jobs in other company branches in the region, Even workers with a long history at this company were dismissed. It seems more appropriate for the management to count on a re-launch of the factory in another location with new workers than to build on the skills and experience of the existing workforce.

In this sense, this strike has become representative for the growing number of labour conflicts in the PRD electronics industry over relocations, plant closures, and compensation in recent years. Since 2013 there has been a number of collective work stoppages at major electronic firms, some of them well publicised. Most prominently, workers in a computer factory of

IBM waged a strike in early 2014, when the plant was sold to Chinese computer giant Lenovo. Similarly, a factory in Dongguan, formerly owned by Nokia, was hit by a week-long strike of several thousand workers, as its new owner, Microsoft, closed the plant in the wake of taking over Nokia's mobile phone business in 2013. In fall 2015, a number of plant downsizing announcements by Taiwanese contract manufacturers, such as Pegatron, provoked short-term work stoppages in Dongguan and Shenzhen (interview data 2015).

Conclusion: Industrial Upgrading Without Social Upgrading

In this article we addressed the question of how ECM companies react to the present challenges to their business models due to rising production costs in China. We asked how this would affect company strategies and the spatial structure of the industry and whether industrial upgrading would have positive effects on workers in the PRD. Our findings show substantial changes on the technological and organisational side, but only a few on the social side. The PRD has continued to be a large, increasingly differentiated production site in ECM, and continues to attract major investments. Rather than leaving the region in search of cheaper labour, large contract manufacturers are set to stay. Relocation is not primarily driven by rising labour costs, but by strategic decisions to restructure capital-intensive production networks across various locations in China and abroad. A relatively capital- and knowledge-intensive industry as advanced electronics manufacturing cannot and will not leave the region overnight.

The accelerated restructuring of global production networks in the wake of the global financial and economic crisis 2008–2009 has rendered new strategic importance to the traditional locational advantages of the PRD region such as large-scale vertical integration, extensive clustering of assembly, and component manufacturing, and increasingly strong potentials in product development and design. While some products and tasks were relocated, all major contract manufacturers maintain their core operations and often their flagship operations in the PRD and many of them expanded investment since the economic crisis. The huge new manufacturing sites in the Chinese interior provinces therefore should rather be seen as complementary to operations in the traditional core regions.

In terms of working conditions, our study reveals that there are no substantial changes in the regimes of production of ECM companies in the PRD. Certainly, there have been moderate, but constant wage increases in recent years. But these have been mostly driven by the rises of government-controlled minimum wages. However, this does not go along with qualitative changes in employment patterns, wage systems, and task assignments. Rather, the surveyed companies maintain their established production regimes even under the condition of rising wages and labour shortages. The highly flexible employment schemes based on a high share of short-term migrant workers are upheld despite the mounting evidence that such practices are unsustainable. Especially, the existing wage system with low base wages that force workers to work extensive overtime hours has not been changed.

The central and the provincial governments have time and again emphasised the necessity of overcoming a growth model which predominately rests on exports and cheap labour. Additionally, Guangdong has seen some important steps to reform industrial relations in the aftermath of particularly intense labour conflicts in recent years (Butollo & ten Brink,2012; China Labour Bulletin, 2012). However, the linkages between industrial upgrading on the one hand and upgrading of work and labour relations on the other are weak (Butollo, 2014; Lüthje, Luo et al., 2013, pp. 315–342). The provincial government and trade unions so far have failed to address this connection in rhetoric and practice. Clearly, a reform of labour relations needs to go beyond occasional public criticism of working conditions in the IT industry by government agencies and trade unions. Rather, it must rely on democratic workplace representation, the establishment of collective bargaining at factory and industry levels, and the inclusion of labour standards into the general regulatory framework of the IT industry in China and internationally.

The escalation of labour conflicts since the middle of the last decade has put the reform of labour relations high on the political agenda. After years of discussion and against political lobbying by corporate interests, especially from Hong Kong and Taiwan, the Guangdong government has implemented guidelines on collective negotiations in January 2015. Although their language is much weaker than many trade unionists and worker activists would have hoped for, the guidelines establish independence of trade unions from management, democratic elections of workplace-trade union representatives, and collective negotiations between employers and trade unions at workplace, regional and industry levels basic principles of labour relations in Guangdong province (Brown, 2015). Although such initiatives will not solve the problem of notoriously weak trade unions and insufficient regulation of labour relations especially in the electronics industry, they may further improve the conditions for workers action on the shop floor that can curb labour right violations in the ECM industry.

Although slow and tepid, labour reforms of this kind are changing the conditions for workers' demands for higher wages, better workplace representation, and an end of discrimination against migrant workers. Common wage standards across the industry and its various locations in the region and a break-up of the repressive wage system based on local minimum wages are the key to the agenda for future change. Job security has become an important issue in the face of ongoing restructuring of production networks. Companies must be obliged to issue long-term labour contracts in order to support the development of a skilled workforce and to end the current hire-and-fire practices. Comprehensive training and task diversification at the shop floor must become a key element of industrial upgrading strategies, as outlined in the national government's report 'Made in China 2025' and the draft documents for the 13th Five-Year-Plan 2016–2020. There can be no 'rebalancing' of China's economy without substantial social innovations at the workplace.

Acknowledgements

Our research assistants Qin Yu, Xu Hui and HuanZhihang and our students Yang Hong, Fu Zheng, Zhu Yingzhi, Wen Xin, He Yunbing, Ma Sai, Mo Jiangli, Lu Peiyi, Yang Zhiqiang, Lu Xilang, Wu Di, Liu Chuncheng and Qin Liu provided excellent assistance during our field research.

Disclosure Statement

No potential conflict of interest was reported by the authors.

Funding

This research was supported by Rosa-Luxemburg-Foundation in Beijing.

Note

1 During our field study, workers were approached in the vicinity of the factory buildings. Since the selection of interviewees involves a degree of chance, the sample is not representative for the workforce at each of the

companies. Still, the responses give a valid impression of the general conditions which will be discussed subsequently. The data were evaluated by quantitative and qualitative means. The quantitative analysis covered the core information concerning the social characteristics of the respondents, wages, working hours, work-related injuries, and housing. This information was evaluated statistically. Additionally, the questionnaires at each company were scanned for peculiarities and qualitative information. This qualitative analysis resulted in a description of working conditions, relocation plans, and the strike at one factory of the sample in April 2013.

References

Boluo government. (2012). *Fushikangboluo long xi xiangmuyuanqu* [FoxconnBoluoLongxi industrial parkproject]. Retrieved from http://lx.boluo.gov.cn: http://lx.boluo.gov.cn/show.asp?id=532

Borrus, M., Ernst, D., & Haggard, S. (Ed.). (2000). *International production networks in Asia: Rivalry or riches?* Abingdon: Routledge.

Borrus, M., & Zysman, J. (1997). *Wintelism and the changing terms of global competition. Prototype of the future?* (BRIE Working Paper 96B). Berkeley, CA: Berkeley Roundtable on the International Economy.

Brown, R. C. (2015). Collective bargaining in China: Guangdong regulation as a harbinger of a national model? *The China-EU Law Journal*, *4*(2), 135–154.

Butollo, F. (2014). *The end of cheap labour? Industrial transformation and 'social upgrading' in China.* Frankfurt: Campus.

Butollo, F., & ten Brink, T. (2012). Challenging the atomization of discontent. Patterns of migrant workers' protest in China during the series of strikes in 2010. *Critical Asian Studies*, *44*(3), 419–440. doi:10.1080/14672715.2012.711978

Chan, J., Pun, N., & Selden, M. (2013). The politics of global production: Apple, Foxconn and China's new working class. *New Technology, Work and Employment*, *28*, 100–115. doi:10.1111/ntwe.12008

China Labour Bulletin. (2012). *A decade of change. The workers' movement in China 2000-2010.* Hong Kong: Author.

Fair Labor Association. (2013a). *Second Foxconn verification status report.* Author. Retrieved from http://www.fairlabor.org: http://www.fairlabor.org/sites/default/files/documents/reports/second_foxconn_verification_status_report_0.pdf

Fair Labor Association. (2013b). *Final Foxconn verification status report.* Author. Retrieved from http://www.fairlabor.org/sites/default/files/documents/reports/final_foxconn_verification_report_0.pdf

Jung, A., & Wagner, W. (2008). *Vietnam is the New China: Globalization's victors hunt for the next low-wage country.* Retrieved from http://www.spiegel.de: http://www.spiegel.de/international/business/vietnam-is-the-new-china-globalization-s-victors-hunt-for-the-next-low-wage-country-a-553301.html

Lüthje, B., Hürtgen, S., Schumm, W., & Sproll, M. (2013). *From Silicon Valley to Shenzhen: Global production and work in the IT industry.* Boulder, CO: Rowman & Littlefield.

Lüthje, B., Luo, S., & Zhang, H. (2013). *Beyond the iron rice bowl. Regimes of production and industrial relations in China.* Frankfurt: Campus.

Lüthje, B., Schumm, W., & Sproll, M. (2002). *Contract manufacturing: Transnationale produktion und industriearbeit in der IT-branche.* Frankfurt: Campus.

Ministry of Industry and Information Technology (MIIT) of the People's Republic of China. (2010). *China national information electronics industry economic development indicators, January-November 2010.* Beijing: MIIT.

Nanfangdushibao. (2013). *Fu shikang: Shen zhen'zijoncheng'* [Foxconn: Shenzhen, 'forbitten city']. Retrieved from http://www.c114.net: http://www.c114.net/news/84/a511321.html

Pun, N. (2005). *Made in China. Women factory workers in a global workplace.* Durham, NC: Duke University Press.

Pun, N., Lu, H., Guo, Y., & Shen, Y. (2012). *Islaves. Ausbeutung und Widerstand in Chinas Foxconn-Fabriken.* Vienna: Mandelbaum.

Qiu, H. (2011, December 6). *Industrial upgrading and social development in the Pearl-River Delta.* Speech given at the conference 'Global production, economic development, and labor relations in the information technology industry', Guangzhou.

Sturgeon, T., & Kawakami, M. (2011). Global value chains in the electronics industry: Characteristics, crisis, and upgrading opportunities for firms from developing countries. *International Journal of Technological Learning, Innovation and Development*, *4*, 120–147.

Yang, C. (2012). Restructuring the export-oriented industrialization in the Pearl River Delta, China: Institutional evolution and emerging tension. *Applied Geography*, *32*, 143–157. doi:10.1016/j.apgeog.2010.10.013

Yang, C. (2014). Market rebalancing of global production networks in the post-Washington consensus globalizing era: Transformation of export-oriented development in China. *Review of International Political Economy*, *21*, 130–156. Retrieved from doi:10.1080/09692290.2013.776616

Bringing Class Struggles Back: A Marxian Analysis of the State and Class Relations in China

CHRIS KING-CHI CHAN* & ELAINE SIO-IENG HUI**

**City University of Hong Kong, Kowloon, Hong Kong*
***The Pennsylvania State University, University Park, PA, USA*

ABSTRACT *This article finds both the 'weakening-state' hypothesis of neo-liberalism and the 'state as autonomous actor' approach adopted by many current China studies dissatisfying towards an understanding of the Chinese state. The authors have therefore conducted a Marxian investigation of the Chinese state. We argue that the state is socially embedded; it is the field and condensation of class struggle. The gulf separating global capital and internal migrant workers on interests such as wage standards, pensions, and other labour regulations in China is a major form of class struggle, which continues to shape the state's policies and behaviours. The attack on Chinese workers by global capital after the global economic crisis in 2008 precipitated a new wave of migrant worker protests and contributed to their articulation of worker demands on the Chinese state. To substantiate these arguments, we examine the (global) capital and (migrant) labour relations during and after the global economic crisis in 2008, with detailed analysis of the Honda strike and Yue Yuen strike, which took place in 2010 and 2014, respectively. The central theme is that the Chinese state's development and labour policies can be fully comprehended only by bringing class struggle back into the analysis.*

Introduction: A Marxian Approach to the Chinese State[1]

Due to the growing dominance of neo-liberalism and global capitalism, the role of the state in Western countries has been regarded as dwindling by many political scientists and economists (see Mann, 1997). First, neo-liberal reforms pushed forwarded by Margaret Thatcher in the UK and Ronald Reagan in the USA led to large-scale privatisation of public services and reduction of social welfare. The role of the state is now considered to be less significant compared to the post-war period. Second, some advocates believe that the promotion of free trade, the rise of transnational corporations, and the emergence of numerous international organisations (e.g. World Trade Organisation (WTO) and IMF) have weakened the regulatory power of states over capital. However, contrary to the belief that the role of the state has been declining in the era of global capitalism, the authors argue that it is presumptive to completely dismiss the role of the state. We will illustrate our argument by drawing upon the case of China.

Many scholars have noted the role of the Chinese state in restructuring and boosting the domestic economy. They attribute the 'success' of China to a strong state that plays a critical role in planning and coordinating the economy (Blecher, 1991; Oi, 1995). The global financial crisis in 2008 brought the world economy into a new era. While the advanced capitalist countries have suffered seriously and waves of protests against welfare cuts and government austerity have been triggered, China stands out as one of the few countries that could resist economic recession and sustain a high rate of growth.[2] The development in China thus has somehow served as a counter-argument to the weakening state hypothesis in the era of globalisation.

However, many advocates of the strong Chinese state thesis have revealed a tendency towards statism and treat the Chinese state as an all-powerful, free, and independent actor. For instance, Baek demonstrates that China follows the same developmental state model pursued by Taiwan, Japan, and South Korea. The Chinese state has strict control over the financial sector, provides tremendous support to state-owned enterprises, and plays a vital role in promoting the export-oriented economy (Baek, 2001).[3] We, however, do not agree with this statist perspective and argue that a critical Marxian approach is needed to examine the Chinese state. In the past century, there have been significant attempts to theorise the capitalist state within the Marxian paradigm. For example, discontenting with economic reductionism, Gramsci (1971) has broadened the definition of the state with the concept of integral state by considering both the political and civil society parts of the state; Poulantzas' idea of the relatively autonomous state has pointed to the partial independence of the state from the capitalist class, which is to promote the latter's long-term dominance (1973, 2000). Miliband's notable debate with Poulantzas on the state has aroused reflections on structuralism and class agency (Miliband, 1969, 1977). Jessop's strategic relational approach seeks to solve the dichotomy between the abstract structural determination and concrete class struggles (1990, 2008). Despite the different emphases developed by these theorists, there are some points concerning the capitalist state that they do agree. First, although the state helps promote capital accumulation, it is never the direct instrument of capitalists. The state cannot be simply reduced to the economic (Barrow, 1993; Jessop, 1990; Poulantzas, 1973). Second, the state is not a free-standing and autonomous actor; instead it is a field and condensation of class struggles between capital and labour. It is embedded in the social relations of production and therefore can be fully understood only if the capital–labour relations and class struggles are seriously examined (Clarke, 1991; Jessop, 2008; Poulantzas, 2000). Poulantzas has summarised this as follows:

> ... the state crystallizes the relations of production and class relations. The modern political state does not translate the 'interest' of the dominant classes at the political level, but the relationship between those interests and the interests of the dominated classes—which means that it precisely constitutes the 'political' expression of the interests of the dominant classes. (2008, p. 80)

Following the Marxian approach, we see the Chinese state neither as an independent and mighty actor nor as a tool for class rule. It is true that it possesses strong capacity to facilitate the reproduction of capital class' domination, but at the same time its formation has been constantly shaped by the social relations of production in society. And the Chinese state's social policies and development strategies often reflect its response to emerging class struggles within the limit set up by the capitalist social relations of production. In this article, we seek to bring the role of workers' struggles to the discussion of China's economic development and state policies. As China today has been highly integrated into global capitalism and foreign investment could be seen in almost every part of China, the structural antagonism between global capital and internal migrant workers has been intensified around the issue of wage levels, social insurance, and labour regulations. We argue that in China the ongoing class struggles between global capital and internal migrant workers have exerted a remarkable impact on the state's policies and behaviour. The Chinese state cannot be adequately understood if class struggle is not incorporated into the analysis.[4] We present the thesis that an increase in workers' organisational and structural power subjects the state to greater pressure to respond to worker demands and thus reduces its previous pro-capital orientation in policy- and law-making. Rather than viewing Chinese migrant workers only with sympathy for their exploitation, we hold that their struggles in influencing history and politics should be fully considered. To provide evidence for our arguments, this paper examines (global) capital and (migrant) labour relations during and after the global economic crisis in 2008, with detailed analysis of the Honda strike and the Yue Yuen strike that took place in 2010 and 2014, respectively.[5]

The data in this article were primarily collected from the authors' intensive fieldwork starting from 2005 in China, through participation observation in labour-NGO-run workers' service centres, documentary research, and interviews with workers during their strikes. For the Honda strike and Yue Yuen strike, the authors paid visits to the strikers during the course of the strikes and interviewed 60 workers altogether. This article is organised as follows: the second section outlines the state–capital–labour relations in China during the global economic crisis, highlighting how the state's policies had been shaped by the capitalist class while the working class was in a structurally weak position. The third section explicates the class relations during economic recovery, showing how the state's policies have been a field of class struggles with the illustration of the Honda strike and Yue Yuen strike. The fourth section summarises the key findings of this article.

State, Capital, and Labour during the Global Economic Crisis[6]

As a consequence of the global economic crisis, China's total exports in 2009 dropped by 16% to US$1,201,610 million, from US$1,430,690 million in 2008 (Chinese National Statistics Bureau, 2010). To rise to the financial challenges, various strategies were deployed by global capital in China. First, it tried to lower labour costs by slimming down the workforce. Twenty million migrant workers are reckoned to have been laid off in the wake of the economic crisis (Hong Kong Liaison Office at the International Trade Union Movement [IHLO], 2009b). The official urban unemployment rate, which does not factor internal migrant workers, reached 4.3% by January 2009—though the real level as estimated by the Chinese Academy of Social Sciences was 9.4% (China Labour Bulletin [CLB], 2009).The second strategy deployed by capital was to evade its legal responsibility. After the global economic meltdown, many factories in China shut down or scaled down without paying due compensation to workers. One such example was a *Dongguan* factory called Kai Da, which owed its workers severance payment. This triggered labour protests in November 2008 (CLB, 2009). Third, many factory owners pressured the government for assistance. For example, the Taiwanese business association strongly requested the governments in the Pearl River Delta (PRD) via Taiwanese politicians to waive employers' contribution for workers' social insurance, and reduce taxes and land charges, as well as put off the implementation of the Labour Contract Law (Window of Guangdong and Taiwan, 2009).

The Chinese government responded promptly to capital's pressure by temporarily and selectively retreating from labour regulations. A testimony to this is the central government's advice to the provincial governments in February 2009 to take provisional measures, including the reduction of social insurance rates and freeze of the minimum wage rate to lower firms' labour costs (IHLO, 2009b). As a result, the *Guangdong* provincial government froze the minimum wage rate, put off wage consultations in enterprises and reduced enterprises' contributions to social insurance. The *Shenzhen* government removed the punitive clauses on wage arrears in the Regulations of the *Shenzhen* Municipality on the Wage Payment to Employees (*Yuangong gong zizhifutiao li*) in October 2009 and altered the definition of wages and overtime work in ways that help reduce enterprises' labour costs.

The Chinese state's pro-capital initiative has induced massive labour resistance which appeared in two major forms. First, many workers sought help from the legal system. The Supreme People's Court reported that the total number of labour disputes in the country went up drastically by 30% in the first half of 2009; and a 41.63%, 50.32%, and 159.61% increase was recorded in the *Guangdong*, *Jiangsu*, and *Zhejing* province, respectively (IHLO, 2009b). Second, workers have resorted to collective protests, especially when litigation is time-consuming and complicated for them. The state-run *Liaowang* magazine observed that labour protests in the first 10 months of 2008 increased 93.52% when compared with the same period of the previous year. Even more dramatically, a 300% increase in workers protests was recorded in Beijing (IHLO, 2009c).

To avoid social and political instability, the Chinese state responded swiftly to the waves of workers' protests during the economic crisis. For instance, the *Shenzhen* government gave 500 yuan to each employees of a factory whose owner suddenly disappeared in December 2008; the *Guangzhou* government offered 300 yuan to each of the 900 workers of a Taiwanese factory that was shut down (IHLO, 2009a). This government practice is in tune with what Louis Rocca has observed in China: 'in many cities social stability is "bought" by localities through money given to protesters' (Lee, 2008, p. 244). This shows that the Chinese state does not simply reflect the capitalist class's interests. It is a field of class struggles and its policies are simultaneously shaped by capital and labour (Clarke, 1991).

Class Relations during Economic Recovery

Context for Post-crisis Labour Unrest

China has managed to stay more or less immune from the world economic crisis. It set a target of 8% growth for the year 2009 while the actual growth surpassed expectation and reached 8.7% (Xinhua Net, 2010). In 2010, the growth rate returned to double digits and jumped to 10.3% (*Global Times*, 2011). Concomitant with the economic revival was the re-emergence of labour shortage. Newspaper reports that a total number of two million workers were needed in the PRD in early 2010 and some production lines were suspended due to labour shortages (*Chengdu Commercial Daily*, 2010). The phenomenon of labour shortage was reported by the media in China since 2004. A number of factors can account for the changes in the labour market. First, the flooding of FDI into China after its entry to the WTO in 2001 increased job opportunities (Chan, 2010). Second, the one-child policy implemented since 1979 reduced the supply of workers in the new millennium (Lee, 2007). Third, the development of the rural economy, driven by the campaign of then President Hu Jintao to build the 'socialist new rural villages' since 2003, as well as the relocation of production to the inland, western and northern provinces, have encouraged some migrant workers to stay and look for jobs in their homeland (Chan, 2014). Fourth, living costs and inflation in cities has increased tremendously. It is cheaper for workers to live in inland areas than in the coastal cities. Labour shortage became less serious during the economic crisis in 2008 and 2009 as many factories in the coastal areas were closed down and many workers lost their jobs. In response to the wave of factory closures in the coastal areas, the central government attempted to direct the surplus migrant workers from urban to rural areas during the economic crisis.[7] However, the GDP growth returned to double digits (10.06%) in 2010 after a slow-down in 2008 and 2009 and labour shortage was again widely reported by the media in early 2010.

Labour shortage means that 'marketplace bargaining power'[8] of Chinese workers has been enhanced (Chan, 2010), which has great implications for the balance of power between capital and labour in the post-crisis period. First, endeavouring to cope with the labour shortage, capitalists took initiatives to improve workers' wages and working conditions so as to stabilise the labour supply. Many factories raised workers' wages, extended the age limit from 25 to 40, employed more male workers and lowered the educational qualification requirement (*Chengdu Commercial Daily*, 2010). Second, many local governments started to adjust the legal minimum wage rate, which helped wring greater economic concessions from capital to labour. In April 2010, the *Guangdong Province* government announced an upward adjustment, with a maximum of 21% increase in some cities. This again illustrates that although the Chinese state has been supporting class reproduction, its policies are somehow shaped by class struggles and reflect the balance of power between capital and labour.

Enhanced marketplace bargaining power has heightened migrant workers' confidence and thus their 'workplace bargaining power' to resist capitalist exploitation (Chan, 2010). Many workers we interviewed before the crisis indicated that the appalling working conditions in their factories made them frustrated and that they would move to other factories if circumstances permitted. Knowing that it is not difficult to get a job in a time of labour shortage, now more workers demonstrate their discontent by quitting their jobs. In other words, labour shortage is not simply a result of the change in labour market, the state, and economic policies as explicated above. It is at the same time a manifestation of workers' anger towards the aggravating alienation and exploitation, which had intensified during the global economic recession when labour was under serious assault.

Stronger marketplace bargaining power has also emboldened migrant workers to take offensive actions at the workplace level to advance their interests (see e.g. Franzosi, 1995); this explains why waves of protests took place in different industries and in many parts of the country in the few years after the crisis to demand higher wages and benefits, as demonstrated by the Honda and the Yue Yuen strikes.

The Honda Strike

The Honda strike in 2010, with workers, among other things, demanding 800 yuan wage increase and a democratic reform of the enterprise trade union, attracted nation-wide as well as international attention. This strike lasted for 17 days and involved around 1000 workers. Despite the failure of the enterprise trade union to protect their interests, the Honda workers' strong organisation and persistence was able to compel the state and its official trade unions to intervene strongly into the strike securing workers a 32.4% wage increase to 2044 yuan. Moreover, it had also exercised a knock-on effect at the industrial level (within the car industry)[9] and national level (across different regions of the country).[10] Moreover, it has also been influencing the state's broader labour regulations.

Shortly after the Honda strike, *Wangyang*, the then Chinese Communist Party (CCP) secretary of *Guangdong* province, emphasised that when handling collective labour grievances, workplace trade unions should position themselves as workers' representatives and help safeguard workers' rights according to legal regulations (*Yangchengwanbao*, 2010). Additionally, the then vice president of the *Guangdong* Provincial Federation of Trade Unions (GDFTU), *Kong Xiang Hong*, confirmed that the democratisation of Chinese trade unions would be sped up so that members could elect their own president in the near future. He also announced that a pilot scheme of democratic election of workplace trade unions would be carried out in 10 factories, including the Honda factory in Foshan (Chan & Hui, 2014).

Moreover, shortly before the Honda strike ended, *Xinhua* agency, the official press, highlighted that it was of great urgency to push forward collective wage consultation in enterprises, so as to further safeguard workers' legal rights and promote harmonious labour relations (Chan & Hui, 2014). Afterwards, the central and local governments have sought to introduce a legal framework for workplace collective consultation. The *Guangdong* provincial government debated the second draft of the Regulations on the Democratic Management of Enterprises in August 2010 after a suspension of almost two years, while the *Shenzhen* Collective Consultation Ordinance (amended draft), which had also been suspended since the world economic crisis, was under public consultation at around the same period. Alongside this, 13 provinces have issued documents in the name of the CCP branch committee or the local governments to promote collective wage consultation (Hui & Chan, 2015).

Although the introduction of collective workplace consultation has seemingly come to the top of the government's agenda, in reality it is undetermined and attempts to build up a collective interest-based legal framework has been hampered by the pressure of capital. Many overseas business chambers were strongly against the legislation on collective negotiation. In Hong Kong, over 40 business associations published their petition in newspapers while some of their representatives paid an official visit to the *Guangdong* and central governments to voice their concern. The American Chamber of Commerce in South China and the Japanese External Trade Organization were also against the two proposed legislations. As a consequence, the Regulations on the Democratic Management of Enterprises and the *Shenzhen* Collective Consultation Ordinance have been put off (Hui & Chan, 2014).

Due to the legacy of state socialism in China, various bureaucracies and elite politicians were said to have strong influence on labour legislation (Johnston, 2002). In recent years, however, global capital and its agencies, including the commercial chambers, have become more active in lobbying Chinese legislators, as evidenced in the case of the Labour Contract Law legislation in 2008 (Santoro, 2009). After the strike wave in 2010, when the Chinese government took workplace collective bargaining in the global factories more seriously than at any other time since the reform in 1978, global capital (which has a structural conflict of interest with the migrant workers) opposed the initiative vigorously. The ebb and flow of the legislations related to collective bargaining in Shenzhen and Guangdong over the years reflects the balance of power between the working and the capitalist class in this particular historical moment.

The Yue Yuen Strike

Subsequent to the Honda strike, there were a number of significant strikes that caught the attention of the general public, including the Yue Yuen strike in a shoes factory in the district of Gao Po in the city of Dongguan (thereafter called Dongguan Yue Yuen) in April 2014. Under the Taiwanese Pou Chen Group, this factory has operated since 1988. It produces shoes for global brands such as Addidas, Puma, Reebok, and Nike. The Yue Yuen strike involved over 60,000 workers whose pension insurance had been underpaid by the factory over a long period of time. Before 2008, Yue Yuen only paid social insurance for workers above the position of group leaders (*Banzhang*). Even though it had extended the social insurance coverage to all the workers after 2008, its contribution for the rank and file workers was based only on the monthly minimum wage of Dongguan (an unlawful practice), rather than the workers' actual monthly salaries. Since July 2013, the basis of its contribution was lifted to 1810 yuan, which was still much less than the workers' actual monthly wages, around 3000 yuan. Moreover, many workers were listed incorrectly as temporary workers in documents submitted by the factory to the Social Security Department in Dongguan, allowing the employer to make lower contributions. In addition, although the 2011 Social Insurance Law stipulates that both employers and their workers should contribute to the pension insurance at a designated rate decided at the local level, Yue Yuen only deducted workers' wages and put them into the pension fund, and did not contribute its own share. Furthermore, the factory did not pay for the housing fund for workers as required by law.

As a result of the illegal practices of Yue Yuen, many workers received much lower pensions than their legal entitlement. For example, one of the workers only got a pension of around 400 yuan upon her retirement. Another worker, whose monthly wage was around 4400 yuan, was supposed to have around 350 yuan monthly pension contribution from the factory, but in reality the company only paid 144.8 yuan.

Having discovered the illegal conduct of Yue Yuen, the workers stopped working and went to block the road on 5 April 2014. They demanded that the factory pay their social insurance. The workers' action was triggered when a soon-retiring worker went to the Social Security Department to enquire about his pension. He realised that Yue Yuen had never insured him as required by law. This news soon spread among the workers, who became highly agitated and worried about their own situation and thus joined the road blockage. On 14 April, the workers' unrest grew into a large-scale strike, with participation of over 30,000 workers from 4 factory sites. Starting from 15 April, the number of strikers increased to over 50,000. Workers of the same corporation in Huangjiang city, Zhongshan City, and other factory areas also joined the strike.

Despite the intimidating strategies of the factory (such as threatening to fire strikers, who stopped working for more than three days, without paying them any compensation), the strike did not resolve. This strike of an unprecedented scale drew tremendous attention from the general public in China and overseas. Activists from Hong Kong, Taiwan, the UK, the USA, Canada, and Turkey took solidarity actions to support the Yue Yuen workers. Students from the Sun Yat-sen University in Guangzhou formed a concern group undertaking public actions to protest against Yue Yuen's exploitation. Some labour NGOs in China initiated petitions to back the strikers. In response to the immense pressure by the strikers and wider society, on 21 April 2014 Dongguan Yue Yuen issued two notices highlighting its corrective measures, to take effect on 1 May. These measures included (i) paying, according to the law, in full for the workers' pension insurance and housing fund (but did not specify if the workers' actual salaries were the basis of the contribution), (ii) the factory would back pay the pension insurance and housing fund contributions should the workers request so, and (iii) the factory will give the workers a monthly living allowance of 230 yuan.

The workers found the factory's proposal unsatisfactory, especially concerning point (2) stated above. On the surface, the factory was willing to back pay the pension insurance and housing fund contributions it owed workers, but it was only on the condition that the workers themselves also pay their share, which could be as in the tens of thousands of yuan. It was impossible for the workers to pay this huge amount of money out of their own pocket at one time, which basically meant that the factory did not have to compensate workers for its illegal misconduct. The workers were furious because it was due to the complete fault of the factory that they could not enjoy the pension insurance and housing fund as legally stipulated. They argued that the factory should, therefore, assume full responsibilities for the problem and fix it at its own costs. The workers continued to strike after the factory's announcement of its corrective measures, but Yue Yuen did not make further offers. Later, the strike withered.

Although the Yue Yuen workers could not achieve all of their demands, their struggle had a significant impact on the social insurance policies of Dongguan city. For a long time, many employers in Donguan (and other parts of China), like Yue Yuen, have not paid for their employees' pension insurance as legally required, but the Dongguan government just turned a blind eye to employer's violation of laws. A labour activist assisting the Yue Yuen strikers pointed out as long as employers take a basis not lower than the legal minimum wages for their social insurance contribution, the government would give its tacit assent even though this breaches the laws. Some managers suggested that underpaying the social insurance contribution is a highly common practice in Dongguan. One manager revealed that the Dongguan government only requested enterprises to contribute to pension fund for 55% of their employees. When employers paid pension insurance at a lower rate than legally required, the government did not take any legal action (*Financial Times*, 2014). In other words, the legal implementation concerning pension in Dongguan (and probably many other cities in the country) was highly biased towards capital. However, the Yue Yuen strike has changed the balance of class forces as reflected and condensed in the legal enforcement of the Social Insurance Law. Subjected to the immense pressure of the Yue Yuen workers and broader society, the Dongguan government and the national government have reoriented themselves regarding their pension policies. After the unfolding of the Yue Yuen workers' actions, the Dongguan government stated publicly that Yue Yuen should contribute to workers' pension insurance on the basis of their actual salaries including overtime premium, rather than a lower rate (the basic wages). The Social Security Department of Dongguan issued Yue Yuen a 'Letter of Order on Redressing Practices related to Social Insurance within Designated Period of Time' (ShehuiBaoxianXianqiGaizhengZhiling Shu), ordering it to correct its unlawful practices by 25 April 2014. In addition, not only the Dongguan government, but also the Guangdong provincial government has taken investigative actions and given instructions to its subordinate to redress the issue (Ifeng Finance, 2014). Furthermore, the spokesperson of the Ministry of Human Resources and Social Security of PRC highlighted in a media conference, held during the course of the Yue Yuen strike, that it would strengthen its instructions over local subordinates to seriously enforce the Social Insurance Law and to strictly monitor if enterprises have contributed their right share of social insurance.

In the past few decades, pension insurance was never a top agenda for workers. Workers did not care so much if their employers contributed the pension insurance for them. Many of them even preferred their employers not to deduct their salaries for paying the pension insurance (as required by the law), because this would reduce their already very-low income. In this circumstance, many employers who had good connections with the government did not act according to the law and their misconduct was tolerated and covered up by the government. The government's tacit assent to the loose compliance with the Social Insurance Law was somehow a crystallisation of class forces between labour and capital at that particular historical period. Labour was not active in striving for their rights in association to pension and capital and the state were not eager to enforce the laws strictly.

However, the Yue Yuen strike and other subsequent strike cases that demanded lawful social insurance contribution from employers demonstrated that labour has become more conscious of their social rights and is willing to strive for their legally entitled pensions with strikes. Rising labour unrest in relation to pension has inflicted substantial pressure on the Dongguan and Guangdong governments and tipped the balance of power between class forces. The governments' old inclination towards the capitalists has now given way to an increasing concern for labour. Prior to the meeting of the National People's Congress and People's Political Consultative Conferences in March 2015, in response to the opinion that the five types of social insurance (pension, medical, work accident, unemployed, and maternity insurance) and the housing fund have created a huge burden for enterprises, the head of the Guangdong Social Security Bureau, Lin Yingwu, emphasised: 'the Social Insurance Law of our country never states that policies related to social insurance should be responsible for solving enterprises' operational difficulties', implying that the government should not take into consideration enterprises' financial situations when making social insurance-related policies. He added that it is the legal obligations of enterprises to pay for workers' social insurance in accordance to law. If they have financial difficulties, they should solve their problems through credit-borrowing, rather than sacrificing the legal rights of the popular masses (Sina news, 2014). This strike case illustrates that although the Chinese state has a tendency to defend the capitalist class's interests, labour still has the potential to influence the state's position and capital's attitude when their struggles escalate.

Conclusion: Class Struggle and Labour Politics in China

The central argument of this article is that contrary to the neo-liberal belief that the role of the state has been undermined in the age of global capitalism, it still plays a predominant role in facilitating capital accumulation and in mediating class relations. We contend that a Marxian analysis of the state is still useful and we have illustrated our argument with the case of China.[12] We found both the 'weakening-state' and 'state as autonomous actor' approaches inadequate to shed light on the Chinese state and its policy-making processes. Rather we conceive the Chinese state as socially embedded and to be a field and reflection of class struggles. This article has brought the role of class struggles into the picture in order to better comprehend how class struggles between capital and labour have been shaping the Chinese state's policies. As Clarke contends, the development of the state and the capitalist social relations have to be seen as the object and effect brought about by class struggle, and the theory of the state has to be located in the context of the development of class struggle (Clarke, 1991).

This article demonstrates how global businesses in China have pressured the government's policies towards the protection of capital interests after the global economic downturn. However, capital's attack on Chinese workers has sown the seeds of workers' discontent and indignation towards the worsening of labour rights. Therefore, once China's economy showed signs of recovery and labour shortages re-emerged, migrant workers' struggles have gone from being on the defensive onto the offensive, as attested by the Honda strike and the Yue Yuen strike. A new wave of strikes has swept through many parts of the country demanding higher wages, better working conditions, pensions, and in some cases democratic election of trade unions. According to the CLB

(2016), the number of labour strikes and protests in 2015 in China reaches 2774, more than a double of the number for 2014. Workers' militancy has compelled the Chinese state to respond seriously to their demands and to implement more pro-labour policies. Poulantzas' concept of relative autonomy of the state is useful for understanding the Chinese state (1978, 2000). He explains that direct political coercion of the state is unnecessary for the conversion of surplus labour into surplus value in capitalist societies. Instead, the state's intervention takes an indirect and legal-political form by creating the formal and abstract equality among exchangers of labour power in the market. It is because of this relative autonomy of the state that at times it can act independently from the capitalist class to enact policies and laws that seem to harm their interests.[11]

Subsequent to the Honda strike and the waves of strikes it triggered, due to the strong pressure imposed by workers, the Shenzhen and Guangdong governments have attempted to build up a legal framework for collective bargaining and democratic management of enterprises. However, their attempt was easily halted by capital, which does not want to be subjected to so many legal constraints. The legislation of collective bargaining in Shenzhen and Guangdong over the years was shaped by the dynamics of class struggles in the country.

Another example to illustrate that the Chinese state's labour policies are shaped by class struggles is the Yue Yuen strike. Many local governments used to tolerate employers' unlawful practices in relation to social insurance, because they have close relations with enterprises and workers did not struggle around this issue. However, as workers' consciousness of their social rights grows, they have staged more actions to demand pension and social insurance which has in turns shaped the governments' policies, pressuring it to take the issue more seriously. In other words, the governments' rising concern for workers' social insurance and its commitment to stricter enforcement of the Social Insurance Law reflects and condenses the balance of class forces between labour and capital; and the social insurance policy indeed is a field of class struggles.

The development strategy of the Chinese state is not separated from class struggle. The main form of class struggle in China today is between internal migrant workers and global capital around the issues of wage standards, pensions, and other labour regulations. The implication drawn from our analysis is that the struggles of migrant workers should be given due attention when examining the Chinese state's development strategy and its policies. The political bedrock of China's labour-intensive and export-led development model is the unorganised working class. For this reason, when workers start to better organise themselves and pursue their demands by means of collective action, the Chinese government seeks to find ways to address them and make concessions. However, these concessions are very often met with opposition from global capital. State policies are never made independently of social forces. They are both the field and condensation of class struggles in the country.

Funding

The authors would like to thank the Research Grants Council (RGC) of Hong Kong (project no. CityU 140313) and the City University of Hong Kong for the financial support to their research. This paper was partly influenced by Elaine Hui's PhD research at the University of Kassel, Germany. She thanks Prof. Christoph Scherrer for his advice and the Heinrich Böll Stiftung for offering her full scholarship.

Disclosure Statement

No potential conflict of interest was reported by the authors.

Notes

1 This part is partially drawn from Elaine Hui's PhD research. For more information about the Marxian debate on the state, see Hui (in press).

2 Its gross domestic product (GDP) growth rate in 2010 was 10.4%, in 2011 9.3%, in 2012 7.7%, and in 2013 7.7% (see http://data.worldbank.org/indicator/NY.GDP.MKTP.KD.ZG).

3 Some studies manifest a more sophisticated analysis of the Chinese state and the state–society relations (see Lee, 2007; Lee & Yonghong, 2013; Pun, Chan, & Chan, 2010), but they have not explicitly highlighted what kind of analytical approach they have adopted to examine the Chinese state. This article differs from these studies in two aspects. First, it has applied the Marxian perspective to investigate the Chinese State. Second, instead of focusing only specifically on China, this article has engaged with a debate of wider conceptual/analytical significance, that is, the role of state in global capitalism. China is a case used to illustrate our argument.

4 This paper highlights the class antagonism between global capital and migrant workers, due to the fact that most of the labour-intensive and export-oriented industries are owned by overseas investors. However, the authors do not intend to dismiss the exploitative role of local Chinese capital.

5 One of the reasons that this article focuses on the period during and after the 2008 global economic crisis is that labour strikes prior to this period have been widely studied (such as Chan 2010; Lee, 2007; Pun et al., 2010) while an overview of class relations during this particular period is not available.

6 See Chan (2010) for the analysis of changing state, labour, and capital relations before the economic crisis in 2008; Hui and Chan (2012) and Chan (2014) for an analysis after the crisis till 2011.

7 Many NGO and government reports have elaborated this strategy. See, for example, IHLO (2009b), CLB (2009).

8 Eric Wright has categorised workers' powers as marketplace bargaining power, workplace bargaining power, and association power (2000). Wright's concepts have been used by Silver to analyse the pattern of strikes and globalisation (Silver, 2003).

9 It was reported that workers from a Hyundai supplier factory in Beijing had launched a strike to demand higher wages after or around the time of the Honda strike. Adding to this, workers from two Toyota factories in Tianjin, Atsumitec Co (a supplier to Honda) and Ormon (a supplier to Honda, Ford and BWM), followed the example of their counterparts and went on strike in June.

10 The strike waves since May 2010 took place all over the country, including Beijing, Tianjin, Jiangsu, Henan, Yunan, and Chongqing. See *Asian Weekly* 23, Volume 2010, *Economist* 31 July–6 August 2010.

11 However, Poulantzas also reminds us that the relative autonomy of the state is to reproduce the capitalist class's long-term dominance through offering short-term benefits to the exploited class so that they will not revolt against the capitalist system.

12 Similar approaches of bringing the role of class struggle in analysing Chinese state and labour relations can also be seen in Chan (2012) and Hui and Chan (2012).

References

Baek, S-W. (2001). Does China follow 'the east Asian development model?' *Journal of Contemporary Asia, 35*(4), 485–498.

Barrow, C. W. (1993). *Critical theories of the state: Marxist, neo-Marxist, post-Marxist.* Madison: University of Wisconsin Press.

Blecher, M. (1991). Development state, entrepreneurial state: The political economy of socialist reform in Xinji municipality and Guanghan county. In G. White (Ed.), *The Chinese state in the era of economic reform: The road to crisis* (pp. 263–294). Basingstoke: Macmillan.

Chan, C. K. C. (2012). Class or citizenship? Debating workplace conflict in China. *Journal of Contemporary Asia, 42*(2), 308–327.

Chan, K-C. C. (2010). *The challenge of labour in China: Strikes and the changing labour regime in global factories.* New York, NY: Routledge.

Chan, K-C. C. (2014). Constrained labour agency and the changing regulatory regime in China. *Development and Change, 45*(4), 685–709.

Chan, K-C. C., & Hui, S-I. E. (2014). The development of collective bargaining in China: From 'collective bargaining by Riot' to 'party state-led wage bargaining'. *China Quarterly, 217*, 221–242.

Chengdu Commercial Daily. (2010, February 22). Labour shortage in the Pearl River Delta is getting worse, 2 million workers are needed (chusanjiaomingongfanjiaju, quekouchao 200 wan). Retrieved from http://e.chengdu.cn/html/2010-02/22/content_119019.htm

China Labour Bulletin. (2009). *The observer: China fears riots will spread as boom goes sour*. Retrieved from http://www.china-labour.org.hk/en/node/100376

China Labour Bulletin. (2016). *Strikes and protests by China's workers soar to record heights in 2015*. Retrieved from http://www.clb.org.hk/en/content/strikes-and-protests-china%E2%80%99s-workers-soar-record-heights-2015

Chinese National Statistics Bureau. (2010). *Total value of imports and exports*. Retrieved from http://www.stats.gov.cn/tjsj/ndsj/2010/html/R0603e.htm

Clarke, S. (1991). *The state debate*. London: Macmillan.

Financial Times Chinese. (2014). Issues related to back payment of pension insurance caused concern in China [Zhongguo Yanglaojin Qianjiao Wenti Yinfa Guanzhu]. Retrieved from http://www.ftchinese.com/story/001056117?full=y

Franzosi, R. (1995). *The puzzle of strikes: Class and state strategies in postwar Italy*. Cambridge: Cambridge University Press.

Global Times. (2011, January 20). Some workers at Honda's China parts plant still on strike. Retrieved from http://business.globaltimes.cn/data/2011-04/614673.html

Gramsci, A. (1971). *Selections from the prison notebooks* (Q. Hoare & G. N. Smith, Trans. and Eds.). New York, NY: International Publishers.

Hui, S-I. E. (in press). *Hegemonic transformation: The state, laws and labour relations in post-socialist China*. New York, NY: Palgrave Macmillan.

Hui, S-I. E., & Chan, K-C. C. (2012). The 'harmonious society' as a hegemonic project: Labour conflicts and changing labour policies in China. *Labour, Capital and Society*, *44*(2), 154–183.

Hui, S-I. E., & Chan, K-C. C. (2014). The politics of labour legislation in southern China: How foreign chambers of commerce and government agencies influence collective bargaining laws. *International Labour Review*, *153*(4), 587–607.

Hui, S-I. E., & Chan, K-C. C. (2015). Going beyond the union-centred approach: A critical evaluation of recent trade union elections in China. *British Journal of Industrial Relations*, *53*(3), 601–627.

Hong Kong Liaison Office of the International Trade Union Movement. (2009a).*The observer: China fears riots will spread as boom goes sour*. Retrieved from http://www.china-labour.org.hk/en/node/100376

Hong Kong Liaison Office at the International Trade Union Movement. (2009b). *ACFTU in a time of crisis: Back to the old ways?* Retrieved from http://www.ihlo.org/LRC/ACFTU/070509

Hong Kong Liaison Office at the International Trade Union Movement. (2009c). *As labour disputes rise 30 percent in the first half of 2009, courts emphasize stability*. Retrieved from http://www.china-labour.org.hk/en/node/100518

Ifeng Finance. (2014). The Ministry of Human Resources and Social Security: Yue Yuen indeed has not honestly reported it pension insurance fees [Renshebu: Dongguan Yue Yuen Xiechang jueshi cunzai weirushi shenbu shebao jiaofei wenti]. Retrieved from http://finance.ifeng.com/a/20140425/12206756_0.shtml

Jessop, B. (1990). *State theory: Putting the capitalist state in its place*. Cambridge: Polity Press.

Jessop, B. (2008). *State power: A strategic-relational approach*. Cambridge: Polity Press.

Johnston, M. F. (2002). Elites and agencies: Forging labour policy at China's central level. *Modern China*, *28*(2), 147–176.

Lee, C. K. (2007). *Against the law: Labor protests in China's rustbelt and sunbelt*. Berkeley: University of California Press.

Lee, C. K. (2008). Is labour a political force in China? In E J. Perry & M. Goldman (Eds.), *Grassroots political reform in contemporary China* (pp. 227–252). Cambridge, MA: Harvard University Press.

Lee, C. K., & Yonghong, Z. (2013). The power of instability: Unraveling the microfoundations of bargained authoritarianism in China. *American Journal of Sociology*, *118*(6), 1475–1508.

Mann, M. (1997). Has globalization ended the rise and rise of the nation-state? *Review of International Political Economy*, *4*(3), 472–496.

Miliband, R. (1969). *The state in capitalist society*. New York, NY: Basic Books.

Miliband, R. (1977). *Marxism and politics (Marxist introductions)*. Oxford: Oxford University Press.

Oi, J. (1995). The role of the local state in China's transitional economy. *China Quarterly*, *144*, 1132–1149.

Poulantzas, N. (1973). *Political power and social classes*. London: New Left Review and Sheed and Ward.

Poulantzas, N. (1978). *Classes in contemporary capitalism*. London: Verso.

Poulantzas, N. (2000). *State, power, socialism*. New York, NY: Verso.

Pun, N., Chan, K-C. C., & Chan, J. (2010). The role of the state, labour policy and migrant workers' struggles in globalized China. *Global Labour Journal*, *1*(1), 132–151.

Santoro, M. A. (2009). *China 2020: How western businesses can-and should-influence social and political change in the coming decade.* Ithaca, NY: Cornell University Press.

Silver, B. (2003). *Forces of labour: Workers' movements and globalization since 1870.* Cambridge: Cambridge University Press.

Sina news. (2014). Minister of the Guangdong Ministry of Human Resources and Social Security: Guangdong will not be a pilot in unifying the pension system [Guangdong rensheting tingzhang: yanglaojin binggui Guangdong buhui xian-xinxianshi]. Retrieved from http://news.sina.com.cn/c/2015-02-11/061931507031.shtml

Window of Guangdong and Taiwan (yuetaizhichuang) (A Guangdong province run website). (2009). Association for relations across the Taiwan straits and straits exchange foundation jointly organized a forum in Guangzhou for Taiwanese businesses in Guangdong [Haixiehui yu haijihui zai Guangzhou lianhe juban Guangdong Taishang zuotan-hui]. Retrieved from http://www.huaxia.com/gdtb/sthd/2009/01/1285133.html

Wright, E. O. (2000). Working-class power, capitalist-interests, and class compromise. *American Journal of Sociology, 105*(4), 957–1002.

Xinhua Net. (2010). National Statistic Bureau adjusted the GDP growth for 2009 upward to 9.1% [Guojia tongjiju Qiang 2009 nian GDP zengsu xiangshang xiuding wei 9.1%]. Retrieved from http://news.xinhuanet.com/fortune/2010-07/02/c_12291379.htm

Yangchengwanbao. (2010, June 13). *Adopt a human-oriented approach to create a good employment environment (chongfentixianyirenweiben, yingzuolianhaoyonggonghuijing).* Retrieved from http://www.ycwb.com/ePaper/ycwb/html/2010-06/13/content_851916.htm

A Class Against Capital: Class and Collective Bargaining in Guangdong

TIM PRINGLE

School of Oriental and African Studies, London, UK

ABSTRACT *This paper argues that a class against capital emerged in Guangdong province between 2007 and 2014. I base my arguments on data drawn from significant strikes in the province and the processes of collective bargaining that partially resolved them. I observe that the formation of a working class against capital in Guangdong, made up primarily of migrant workers, has at least partially overcome fragmentary pressures it continues to face. I argue that it is the self-activity of workers themselves that is chiefly responsible for the significant improvement in wages and, to a lesser extent, working conditions that unfolded during this period. While collective bargaining remains mostly—but not exclusively—outside institutional norms, workers' agency pushed the practical application of forms of collective bargaining on to both the political and labour relations agenda in Guangdong and beyond. Continued pressure from below will keep it there.*

Introduction

The cautious emergence of collective bargaining has been the most intriguing aspect of China's evolving labour relations framework. While class struggle has been the impetus for this experiment, there is little doubt that the Communist Party of China (CPC) still controls the rules of the game as recent detentions of activists in Guangdong province have demonstrated all too clearly. The Party's attempts to ameliorate labour unrest arising from the antagonistic interests of capital and labour has been especially marked in Guangdong where mainstream notions of collective consultation (*jitixieshang*) have been challenged by recognisable processes of collective bargaining (*jititanpan*). This paper will examine the appearance of nascent forms of collective bargaining, which, it should not be forgotten, are unfurling in the context of Party-led trade unionism and authoritarian rule. I base the paper on the Marxist conceptualisation of class formation, namely a class against capital. I argue that the growth of interest-based strikes in the period 2007 to 2014 in Guangdong suggests that the class fragmentation that characterised China's period of high economic growth has been undermined by the emergence of a class against capital.

First, however, I will clarify my preference for the formulation of class against capital over the more traditional 'class in itself' that is frequently juxtaposed against a more class conscious and confrontational 'class for itself'. In this I am guided by the work in particular of Andrew and his analysis of 'Karl Marx and his Classifiers' (Andrew, 1983, p. 577). Andrew argues, with wonderful clarity, that Marx 'never referred to classes in themselves or distinguished a class in itself from a class for itself' (Andrew, 1983, p. 577). In doing so Andrew draws directly on Thompson's famous representation of class as a form of conflictive behaviour generated by shared experiences in the production processes. This relational approach is contrasted to Cohen's structural class in itself—class for itself dichotomy. For Cohen, a person's class 'is established by nothing but his objective place in the network of ownership relations' (Cohen, 1980; p. 76 cited in Andrew, 1983, p. 578). Thus the concept of a class in itself separates class from class conflict—an approach analogous with the administrative categorisation of migrant workers in China as peasant workers (*nongmingong*). This descriptor hardly captures the dynamic class struggles that have both forced state and capital to collective bargaining tables in Guangdong province. Following Andrew's citation from Marx's *Poverty of Philosophy*, my approach focuses on the combination of economic conditions and class struggles.

> Economic conditions at first transformed the mass of the people of the country into workers. The combination of capital has created for this mass a common situation, common interests. This mass is thus already a class against capital, but not yet for itself. In the struggle ... this mass becomes united, and constitutes a class for itself. (Marx and Engels, 1976, p. 211 cited in Andrew, 1983, p. 280)

Three decades of economic reform have provided a 'combination of capital' distinguished in Guangdong by massive inflows of foreign investment and the plurality—or 'network' to use Marx's word—of property relations. In the Chinese-language literature this is often described as the 'complication' (*fuzahua*) of enterprise ownership. As the translations of Chan (1998), China Labour Bulletin (CLB) (2001) and others have demonstrated, the millions of young women and men who left the land to work in Guangdong's export boom were never not against capital and the concomitant injustices of rapid industrialisation that has been the hallmark of East Asian development (see e.g., Koo's [2001] account of working class formation in Korea). But it was not until the early years of the present century that the material conditions emerged—at least in Guangdong—for the largely individualised grievances of migrant workers 'under assault' (Chan, 1998) from globalisation to cohere into a class against capital. Whether the forces of labour will overcome renewed onslaughts of fragmentation and repression from capital and state to constitute a class for itself that can be the driving force pushing further progress towards centralised collective bargaining remains a moot point. However, my focus is on the substitution of the formulation 'class in itself' with 'class against capital'.

Although this paper engages with the issue of class consciousness by implication, it is not explicit. I consider the relationship between individual consciousness and collective action as highly complex, especially in a post-socialist authoritarian state where 'the phrasing of demands is more likely a tactical judgement than a spontaneous expression of "consciousness"'

(Clarke, 2014, p. 760). As such, by pinning the recent progress in collective bargaining to levels of consciousness, there is a danger of idealising what is essentially an instrument of class compromise into a transformative—even revolutionary—device that will attain its full potential once the class consciousness of workers has matured beyond a narrow focus on the pay packet. This in turn generates room for misinterpretations: on the one hand, under-acknowledging the significant gains made by strikes; and on the other hand, attaching too much *political* significance to the institutional response of such gains namely—for the purposes of this paper—evolving forms of collective bargaining.

Rather, I use primary research on sanitation workers in Guangzhou alongside an analysis of three major class struggles across Guangdong to demonstrate the emergence of a class against capital drawn primarily from the ranks of migrant workers. One result of this process has been a concomitant struggle for participatory collective bargaining—a classic instrument of class compromise that I employ as an approximate bell-weather to evaluate the forces of labour in the province. By participatory collective bargaining, I mean scenarios in which workers are engaged—directly or indirectly—in negotiations with capitalists, state officials and sometimes both. By indirectly I mean at the very least aware of such negotiations; and by directly I mean as strikers, workers representatives or both. In either case, these negotiations are in stark contrast to the tradition of collective consultation that is characterised by the disengagement of workers as a social class from the entire process.

The remainder of this paper is organised as follows: the next section will review the key literature on class formation in China in the context of my adoption of the class against capital approach. The following section will discuss key strikes in relation to the literature covered in the previous section and provides a context for my case study of strikes by sanitation workers in Guangzhou. I conclude with a summary discussion that will make some cautious observations on the future development of collective bargaining in Guangdong.

My paper draws on interviews conducted during fieldwork in Guangdong and Hong Kong in June–July 2013 spread over two 12-day research trips; Hong Kong in July–August and October 2014 spread over two 10-day trips; and Beijing in December 2014. This fieldwork included interviews with 20 sanitation workers—most of these with the supervised assistance of a labour NGO with over a decade of experience in conducting such interviews—two auto parts factory workers, 12 labour NGO staff as well as numerous conversations with labour relations academics, union officials and activists in Shenzhen, Panyu, Guangzhou, Hong Kong and Beijing. The primary data on the Yantian port strike in 2007 are drawn from the author's participation as a co-investigator on an ESRC project entitled Post-Socialist Trade Unions, Low Pay and Decent Work: Russia, China and Vietnam (Grant Reference RES-155-25-0071). Interviewees' names are not stated in accordance with the conditions under which most of the interviews were agreed. My primary research is supported by secondary sources drawn from relevant academic journals, books and newspaper articles in Chinese and English as well as material elicited from labour NGO websites and reports. The fieldwork in Guangdong was funded by faculty research grants from SOAS, University of London where the author is employed as a Senior Lecturer in Labour, Social Movements and Development.

Class Formation

At the national level, the potential for working-class solidarity against the forces of capital is fragmented from above via categorisations defined by the state or capital: peasant worker (*nongmin gong*), urban worker (*zhigong*), part-time worker (*linshi gong*), dispatch worker (*paiqian gong*) student worker (*xuesheng gong*) as well as temporarily (in theory) laid-off state-enterprise workers (*xiaganggongren*) (Pringle, 2011, pp. 11–55). These administrative and contract-based categories are fractured further by gendered state-constructed ideal type narratives of economic migration via such labels as *dagongzhe* (migrant worker) and *dagongmei* (Fu, 2009, p. 527). Fragmentation from below in the form of home-town associations rarely organised around class interests can also serve the interests of capital and weaken the potential for solidarity. On the other hand, Chan has shown vividly how such organisations can quickly transform into conduits for class solidarity in the course of struggles (Chan, 2009, p. 60). Indeed, it is precisely in this conflictive behaviour that lines of fragmentation—be they imposed from above or formed from below—are reconfigured and joined up along class lines as migrant workers 'find common interest against other men whose interests are different from (and opposed to) theirs' (Thompson, 1963, p. 9). Indeed, I see this phenomenon as an illustration in support of Andrew's critique of structuralist interpretations of Marx's ideas on class formation in which there is a tendency to reduce class to a sociological category.

Nevertheless, Pun and Lu track a process of 'unfinished proletarianisation' to capture the second generation of migrant workers and the constraints on organising. They argue that because the restrictions of the *hukou* regime effectively tie one's right to permanent residence to place of birth, workers are prevented from establishing their own 'working class community' (Pun & Lu, 2010, p. 498). Consequent incomplete class formation is further compounded by the other side of the *hukou* regime that retains peasant workers' access to land. Pun and Lu argue that this differentiates the current period of industrialisation in Guangdong from the English industrial revolution: '[U]nlike the English working class, the Chinese working class faced no coercion effectively forcing on them a process of industrialisation' (Pun & Lu, 2010, p. 505). Drawing on ethnographic work carried out between 2005 and 2008, they highlight the 'huge gulf' between the 'life expectation of becoming urban worker-citizens and their actual daily experiences which are characteristic of the dormitory labour regime and which involve serious exclusion from city life' (Pun & Lu, 2010, pp. 495–496). However, as with home-town associations, the dormitory regime imposed by capital is transformed by workers' conflictive behaviour. Chan and Pun (2009, p. 291) argue that both *hukou's* separation of production and reproduction and the generalised rural–urban chasm in China are recombined in a dormitory regime that generates a specific form of proletarianisation. Charting the organisational development of two strikes in 2004 and 2007 respectively, they find that the 'workers dormitory and urban communities, no matter how temporary, provide the potential to facilitate labour mobilisation and collective consciousness building' (Chan & Pun, 2009, p. 303). They conclude that the consequent struggles are part of an historic and long-drawn out formation of a 'class for itself' (Chan & Pun, 2009, p. 303).

While Friedman rarely uses these terms, his analysis of the separation of the impact of the 'specific process of proletarianisation of Chinese migrant workers' (Chan & Pun, 2009, p. 291) is likewise informed by spatial themes and their links to capital flows. But he is generally much less sanguine over the issue of class formation in general and the likelihood of a working-class against capital, in particular, in the context of migration. Migrant workers, argues Friedman (2012), 'do not refer to themselves as "workers," nor do they think of themselves as part of the "working class."' Furthermore, he argues that the spatial separation of production from reproduction means that 'migrants who are lucky enough to have employer-supported social insurance—a small minority—are paying into a system that they will never benefit from. If pensions are not portable, why would a migrant demand a better one?' (Friedman, 2012). We should not be surprised to learn that this argument was formulated prior to the shoe workers strikes over pensions that exploded in 2014! Thus the temporal realities of migrant workers' temporary presence in the cities dictate a rational focus on wages that is particularly relevant to young workers years off pensionable age. Friedman is more optimistic when he turns his attention to the recent increase in capital investment and urbanisation of the interior where the 'terrain of particularity' on which class struggles occur offers a more conducive set of conditions for the 'politicization of worker unrest' and 'more enduring forms of organization' (Friedman, 2012). Lower barriers to permanent residence in the second-tier cities of the interior offer the opportunity for migrant workers to 'demand all the things one needs for a decent life—housing, health care, education, and some protection against the risks of unemployment and old age' (Friedman, 2012). Friedman seems to juxtapose an underestimation of the potential for struggles beyond wages in the 'huge eastern megalopolises' with a sophisticated optimism regarding the emergence of what Marx would refer to as class for itself in the interior.

The Rising Forces of Labour

Our starting point for this section is the now landmark strike in a Honda-owned auto parts factory in Foshan, Guangdong. Viewed from a 'class in itself' perspective, the strike was not, in the main, conducted by what either Honda management or the Chinese legal system would term 'workers', even less, workers that form part of a class against capital. Although initially led by two full-time employees (Lyddon, Cao, Meng, & Lu, 2015, p. 140), the main block of strikers were so-called 'student workers' or interns from vocational colleges elsewhere in China that have become an important source of labour power over the last decade (Cole & Chan, 2015). The fact that most of the strikers were not regular employees rendered them outside the formal protection of the Labour Contract Law and local regulations that implement it—or perhaps not. As students, they were not members of the plant's trade union and were working in conditions inferior to regular workers (Chan & Hui, 2012, p. 659). Their labour power was disciplined by teachers whose leverage over them lay with the authority to withhold educational certificates on completion of the period of 'internship' thereby shutting off opportunities for more secure employment at the factory and likely elsewhere. Smith and Chan (2015, p. 311) argue that student workers form part of a strategy by both capital and local-level governments to fragment actual and potential class solidarities.

However, the direct and collective relationship of these workers with the means of production, in an auto parts supply chain that awarded them considerable 'structural power' (Lyddon et al., 2015, p. 148; Wright, 2000, p. 962), provided the material conditions for student and regular workers to organise a 17-day strike. The unrest concluded with the strikers' demands being largely met: a significant pay rise and the election of a re-organised trade union committee at the plant—although the higher level Guangzhou Federation of Trade Unions insisted that the incumbent chair be allowed another term to improve his performance.

We can see here the strength of Andrew's rejection of the class in itself formulation. Regardless of their administrative or legal status, the strikers found common interest 'against other men' (Thompson, 1963, p. 9) and combine around demands for effective trade union representation and improved wages. The 'other men' here are Honda's owners and managers and their state partners who, alarmed at the power of the strike, broke ranks and agreed to facilitate collective bargaining between capital and elected workers' representatives. Viewed solely as a class 'constituted by the economic structure ... rather than constituting itself in partisan combination and combat' (Andrew, 1983, p. 584), the role of the student interns and their significant contribution to China's labour movement would be logically downplayed, if not written out of the history books altogether—as I am sure the CPC will be happy to do. On the other hand, when viewed as a key—if not necessarily permanent—component of a class against capital, we are able to analyse the outcome of the strike for what it really represented: a negotiated class compromise premised on the withdrawal of labour power by a combination of migrant workers, student workers and local workers that overcame imposed fragmentation to act as members of a working class despite legal and bureaucratic constraints on such action. The strike and the sustained solidarity it generated was an expression of working class power that kick-started both copycat strikes as well as annual pay bargaining at the plant that has since spread to other auto sector plants in Guangzhou (Interview No. 1; Chen, 2013). Workers at the Honda plant struck briefly again in 2013 expressing discontent with the outcome of a collective wage bargaining round (Schmitt, 2013; Interview No. 1). Some workers and observers have interpreted the more recent strike as the outcome of management attempts to weaken the influence of the elected trade union committee at the plant (Interview No. 1 and Interview No. 8). While this is certainly a setback, it may also be regarded as a symbol of management's wariness of effective trade union activity and workers' capacity to organise it.

Honda's student workers overcame constraints and barged their way into a working class against capital via their own actions. Over a much longer period, the imposed concept of peasant worker (*nongmin gong*) has started to dissipate in the face of strikes by 'peasant workers' subject to its discriminatory power and divisive narrative (Pringle, 2013, p. 112). *Hukou* has nevertheless served as a valuable weapon of labour control for both state and capital (Lee, 2007, p. 207) underpinning a generalised narrative of victimhood (Chan, 1998, p. 3). Migrant workers in Guangdong, for example, were disregarded by the All China Federation of Trade Unions (ACFTU) due to their assigned status of peasant worker as opposed to urban worker or *zhigong* who constituted the union's traditional membership. In the vacuum, many migrants turned to labour NGOs (LNGO) for assistance with work-related grievances ranging from unpaid overtime to longer campaigns claiming compensation for industrial injury and disease. In recent years, strikes by so-called 'peasant workers' have driven a coach and horses through the victim scenario, none more so than the actions by dock workers at Yantian International Container Terminals (YICT).

YICT is a port terminal in Guangdong province that has expanded to form a crucial node in China's export-orientated economic growth (*South China Morning Post*, 11 April 1996, p. 2). Most YICT workers are migrants who have taken advantage of the relaxation of *hukou* restrictions resulting from labour shortages to establish long-term residence in the area. In 2007, YICT crane operators took strike action in pursuit of higher wages linked to the port's phenomenal growth and a recalculation of the lunch break as working hours. The strikers also demanded a trade union branch operated by elected representatives whose wages would be paid, according to the demands of the workers, directly out of their own wages (Case Study Reports, 2007). The structural power of these strikers derived from their position at a key logistical node of global production and supply chains. The strike produced an almost immediate backlog of ships waiting to be loaded with exports destined for Western markets (*South China Morning Post*, 9 April 2007, p. 1). This in turn focused the attention of the politically powerful Shenzhen Federation of Trade Unions (SFTU) with senior officials rushing to the scene at two o'clock in the morning. The SFTU facilitated talks between elected representatives of the strikers and YICT management in a bargaining process that won almost all of the workers' demands with the important exception of the workers' wish to fund their own trade union representatives directly. The SFTU refused to negotiate this demand on the grounds that it would constitute a violation of the Trade Union Law which stipulates that union dues are deducted by the employer and transferred directly to the higher union.

The strike settlement led to the establishment of a union branch based on check-off contributions administered by management; a system for electing union representatives and a substantial pay rise including a recalculation of the lunch hour. As with the Honda strike, annual pay bargaining was established at the port and has produced above inflation-rate pay rises all carefully documented by the SFTU (Interview No. 10). Significantly, a second strike occurred at the port in 2013 that involved most of the workers in the 2007 strike. The cause of the more recent strike was dissatisfaction with the outcome of collective wage negotiations (Interview No. 10). We see here what I have described elsewhere as an 'appropriation of associational power'. By this I mean that the city-level SFTU was forced to respond to the need for a functioning primary trade union in order to head off militancy that showed signs of developing towards the struggles of a class for itself across various ports in Guangdong (Interview No. 10) via demands for better representation and collective bargaining outcomes. However, in this formulation I part company with Andrew. In his view, a 'class in itself-class for itself' dichotomy is a 'Leninist constriction of Marxist politics and a doctrinal limitation to empirical application of class analysis' (Andrew, 1983, p. 584). However, my focus here remains on the emergence of a class against capital that is developing the capacity to constrain it via collective bargaining as was the case at YICT.

Dongguan's low-end manufacturing sector has been a key player in the Pearl River Delta's 'workshop of the world' story. The city is notorious for long working hours, poor health and safety, and wage-levels requiring extensive overtime for migrant workers to move beyond the most basic standard of living (*Financial Times*, 9 February 2009, p. 4). During the late 1990s, multinational brands that had taken advantage of these conditions responded to consumer-led pressure from the Global North for improved working conditions by introducing various versions of corporate social responsibility and accompanying codes of conduct in their supply chains. In China, these initiatives have failed to produce a sustainable impact on workers' pay and conditions (Yu & Pun, 2011, p. 70). On the other hand, the emergence of labour shortages combined with a knowledge of labour rights accumulated over three generations of rural–urban migration have provided the conditions for the development of short factory-based bursts of often intense labour unrest. These have included strikes defended by picket lines and the raising of interest-based demands—often considerably beyond the level stipulated by the minimum wage—settled via negotiation with the employer and varying degrees of state and official trade union interventions (CLB, 2014a, p. 38; Liu, 2010, pp. 30–52; Pringle, 2013, pp. 114–132). As the first generation of migrant workers have acquired seniority via up to 15 years of hard slog at the sharp end of global supply chains, demands have increasingly included adequate social security provisions based on the stipulations of the Social Security Law that came into force in 2010 or the regulations that preceded it. These latter strikes have been led by older workers whose connection with any form of agricultural work was severed in their late teens even though some family members still have access to land as a result of *hukou*-determined land-use rights. Nevertheless, the demands of these workers are working-class demands premised on a consistent relationship with the means of production that they neither own nor control and which constitute a means of survival and reproduction. But this is much more than a structural economic relationship.

Evidence of how far migrant workers have travelled towards 'proletarianisation' was provided by a dramatic strike at the Taiwanese-owned Yue Yuen (YY) during April 2014 (see Chan and Hui, 2012; Schmalz et al., 2016, in this issue). A massive 40,000 workers took part (*China Daily*, 30 October 2014, p. 5) in this extraordinary strike. The initial demand was for YY to pay full social insurance premiums and public housing fund payments as well as make up for the deficits resulting from underpayments dating back to 2005 (CLB, 2014b). According to posts on social media outlets such as *weibo*, workers' slogans included militant condemnations of the employer's 'illegal behaviour' (weibo.com/u.1266932233—account no longer accessible). An extended interview with a veteran YY worker conducted by an experienced activist and posted on the Worker View Point blog (Gong Ping She, 2014) illustrated the deep associations with long-term waged employment

> About 70 per cent of the workers have been here [i.e. at YY] for more than five years and between 10 to 15 per cent for ten—starting work at the factory as 18- and 19-year olds. There are levels of trust between senior workers that creates a sense of unity. Some even have [grown up] children working here. (2014)

The two-week strike was eventually broken by a heavy police intervention that saw riot police escorting workers back to YY assembly lines. This repressive behaviour was only partly offset by pay rise of renminbi (RMB) 230 per month with strikers' opinions diversifying over the issue of social insurance arrears (Gong Ping She, 2014). Nevertheless, the sheer scale of the strike and the fact that it was able to stop production by force of numbers have put enormous pressure on the Guangdong Federation of Trade Unions (GDFTU). In post-strike follow-up meetings, GDFTU Chairperson Huang Yebin organised meetings in Dongguan at which he urged local township- and enterprise-level trade unions in the city to pilot democratic methods in building up responsive trade union branches (GDFTU News Centre, 15 July 2014). While this strike was by no means a clear victory for the workers, its scale and character were the outcome of working-class formation generating demands that go beyond individualised rights and represent collectivised class interests that go beyond the pay packet and look towards retirement and social security. Labour activists with contacts inside the factory have predicted that there will be further labour unrest as the main issues of low pay and social insurance arrears have not been resolved (Interview No. 6). While collective bargaining has not emerged at YY or in the shoe sector in general, there is evidence that this is the direction the GDFTU wishes to proceed at least—albeit slowly and on its own terms. Moreover, the strike suggests that contrary to Friedman's expectations, the spatial separation of production and reproduction has not excluded demands that go beyond a focus on wages and is further evidence of a class against capital forged in conflictive behaviour. Both the strike at YY and the second strike at YICT included social reproduction-related demands over the pensions in the case of the former and housing provident scheme payments at YICT. There is also evidence from strike maps compiled by CLB and other organisations that more and more strikes include similar demands (CLB, 2015).

This section has presented a brief tour of strikes in Guangdong across three key industries: auto, logistical and shoe, respectively. I have hardly scratched the surface and make no claim on the representative credentials of these strikes. But I have picked examples that have either produced ongoing collective bargaining via elected representatives or demonstrated a clear need for it that has been at least partially acknowledged by the Party-led trade union. The key point is that the strikes demonstrate the emergence of a 'class against capital' rooted in class struggles. In the period under consideration, this has in turn generated a decisive shift in the balance of class forces in Guangdong that has seen both capital and state having to take part in forms of collective bargaining with workers' representatives who they would not have given the time of day to just a few years previously. This paper does not set out to examine the presence or otherwise of levels of class consciousness usually deemed a key factor in a 'class for itself' scenario. However, I and others have argued elsewhere that the copycat nature of strikes between 2008 and 2013 in Guangdong illustrates the first stirrings of a coherent class-based labour movement (CLB, 2014a, p. 5; Pringle, 2013, p. 195) although this view is certainly contested (Friedman, 2013, p. 303).

The next section examines the struggles of a section of Guangzhou's working class in a comparatively weaker bargaining position—sanitation workers (*huanwei gong*). In doing so, I will test my arguments that a class against capital has emerged in Guangdong between 2007 and 2014; and that future development of the collective bargaining that has formed part of response will be likely theoretically grounded on the premise that it is an instrument of class compromise that is, not revolution through which workers with common interests reach agreement with 'other men whose interests are different from (and opposed to) theirs' (Thompson, 1963, p. 9).

Sanitation Workers in Guangzhou

Usually in at least their late 40s and working alone for most of a day's shift, sanitation workers hardly fit the social media savvy, networked, consumer-orientated, well-dressed and modern image of '[T]he rising power of Chinese workers' as represented by the famous cover of the *Economist* in 2010 (*Economist* 29 August–6 September 2010). On the other hand, although subject to outsourcing, these were not informal workers in the ILO definition of the term. All but one had contracts that included deductions for all five aspects of labour insurance and, since 2012, contributions to a housing provident fund. By making use of the structural power they possessed in refusing to clean streets and the consequent implications for public health, Guangzhou's sanitation workers have won significant concessions. Neither the state nor capital in Guangdong deployed their almost certain capacity to organise sufficient numbers of scab labour to break the sanitation workers strikes. They opted to bargain directly with the representatives of a class against capital.

I selected this group of highly exploited workers as a case study precisely because their material conditions seem to support the arguments of unfinished proletarianisation and the separation of production from reproduction that I reject as insurmountable barriers to the formation of a class against capital rooted in class struggles resolved—at least partially—via collective bargaining. Subjected to segregation from above by outsourcing, and often migrant, older—my sample of 20 interviewees had an average age of 48 years—unskilled, female, and isolated by the labour process, this group would present enormous challenges to any organiser pretty much anywhere.

Sanitation workers were originally employed directly by the government across Guangzhou's districts. Between 2004 and 2006 the sector was deregulated and the work opened up to tender to hundreds of companies. The outsourcing has created a chain of financial transactions that involves private landlords, government agencies, neighbourhood and street management committees and private cleaning companies (Libcom.Org, 2014). In this system, government agencies collect fees from landlords and private residents that are then used to pay the private companies that have won street cleaning contracts. From the sanitation workers' perspective, the potential for late payment or worse is clear but more important to them is the frequent change in employer—sometimes every year—with each new company involved seeking to lower labour costs by reducing staff and increasing workloads. Some simply change the terms of contracts even—or perhaps especially—of workers who have been cleaning the same streets for up to 10 years (Interview No. 5). This system of outsourcing and frequent changes of contracts has been a key factor underlying recent strikes by sanitation workers:

> Yes, I took part in the strikes in 2013. There was a sit-in at Culture Park as a result of non-payment of welfare privileges we were entitled to. The strikes [started] back in 2007 resulting from a change in cleaning company that reduced our welfare entitlements. Back then we—hundreds of workers—went on strike, marched down the main road with big banners and shouted slogans. We blocked the road as a result. Then we marched to the government office demanding that they intervene [with the cleaning company]. There is a change in company every two or three years and this sparks a strike. (Interview No. 4)

The GZFTU responded to the fragmentation of sanitation workforce across tens of companies by setting up a sector-level Sanitation Workers Union. Its Luogang district branch apparently concluded a collective agreement with six companies in 2009 (*YangchengWanbao*, 21 July 2009). However, the initiative certainly did not prevent the increases in workload. As one interviewee from Yuexiu district explained:

> Take the rubbish bins on the main roads. Originally four people would be involved in the process of removing, washing and returning the bins. This was reduced to three, then two and now one person . . . I moved from work in a factory because I was getting too old for the pace of work. But it's becoming just as hard on this job. (Interview No. 3)

Despite the long hours of working alone in allocated streets, the label of 'peasant worker'—that sits well with the non-conflictual structural categorisation of a class in itself and misattributed to Marx (Andrew, 1983, p. 584)—was indirectly rejected during the interviews—especially by workers who had taken part in the strikes. This was sometimes quite explicit. One interviewee pointed out that as [W]ages are the source of income for all workers and therefore we sanitation workers are workers too. This 'peasant worker' business is government speak and I don't buy it ('zhengfu de hua') (Interview No. 2).

Most of the workers had little confidence in the trade union——and in four cases, no knowledge of it at all. Despite this many of the workers did take part in union elections although they were usually dismissive of the process. In most cases, views on the union were expressed in terms of it not being able to represent 'we sanitation workers' against the interests of capital that were overwhelmingly deemed as separate to their collective interests. Indeed, I would argue that in the context of the absence of freedom of association and protection of the right to strike, lack of faith in the ACFTU combined with participation in strikes is a clear—if indirect—indication of allegiance to a collective identity as a working class that is against capital well aware that demands of wages and pensions were against the interests of 'other men' (Thompson, 1963, p. 9) who preferred to fragment their interests across city districts.

Interviewees criticised the divisive wage system that resulted in workers being paid different amounts for the same work depending on the sub-district they worked in. In the Yuexiu district of Guangzhou this system was known as the '1 + 18' model (Interview No. 6). Further, a common—if minority—view was that sanitation work was a public service that should not be privatised as it essentially had been. As one street cleaner explained:

> This outsourcing to [private] employers and changing employers every year is not in anyone's interests except them. I think that the entire system should be brought back to how it was before and we should be directly employed by the government. This [street cleaning] is a public service. (Interview No. 7)

One of the most interesting challenges that emerged from my adoption of Andrew's rejection of class in itself lies in the conundrum that some of my data appeared to support Andrew's observation that 'Cohen's class in itself denotes a definitive structure underlying experience and behaviour' (1983, p. 582). Most of the quotes above seem to suggest a structural understanding of the position of sanitation workers in society but the recollections of strikes and struggle were fading. At times these memories seemed to concur with the idea that '[V]isible struggles are appearances or phenomena to be explained by the noumenal structure of class in itself' (Andrew, 1983, p. 582) and the solidarity they represented was fleeting. Although most of the sanitation workers interviewed expressed the view that their interests were essentially collective and certainly not the same as those of capital, the 'conception of a class against capital [that] suggests an empirical understanding of manifest opposition, struggle of conflict as definitive' (Andrew, 1983, p. 582) was at times qualified, to a greater or lesser degree, by time. This was in contrast to data from my research on the other strikes in Guangdong discussed in this paper.

But then came the explosion of sanitation worker unrest in the autumn of 2014. I was fortunate enough to be in a position to interview activists involved in organising this strike very soon after its successful conclusion and the data confirmed my inclinations towards Andrew's class against capital or rather his interpretation of Marx's approach. The 2014 strike took place in University Town district and was again sparked by the annual change of the employer (Interview No. 9). Sanitation workers began electing their own representatives in the last week of August and launched strike action on 26 August (Interview No. 9). Following protracted negotiations with the employers, the strikes won a RMB 3000 per year's employment as compensation for contract termination against the outgoing company's original offer of 1000 RMB. There was no suggestion of a structural confinement in the ideas expressed in interviews with sanitation workers leaders by LNGOs. On the contrary, the views of Wu Naiyang and Yu Wucang bristle with 'empirical understanding of manifest opposition' (Andrew, 1983, p. 582) as they call on the state to support their struggle against capital. As one sanitation worker and representative explained to an LNGO supporting the strike:

> The local government is the beneficiary of our hard work and it is in their interest to stand with us when the employer changes. We love the expression Yu [Wucang] proposed: "Steel-forged workers and ever-changing companies." This is our community, *and we are here to stay*. (CLB, 2014c—emphasis added)

Moreover, in the wake of the University Town strike, the incoming cleaning company largely failed in its attempts to divide local and migrant workers from Hunan by announcing a policy of only re-hiring local workers. Another sanitation worker and representative responded that 'there are no locals or non-locals, the striking sanitation workers at University Town are a big family, and we stand together' (CLB, 2014d). This does not look like unfinished proletarianisation. For China's foremost labour lawyer and collective bargaining expert, these words capture 'the courage, resilience and bargaining skills of the unofficial layer of workers representatives that has emerged in Guangdong' (Interview No. 11). These are the women and men at the forefront of Guangdong's class against capital.

Conclusion

The introductory words of the Rules of the International Workingmen's Association are clear enough: 'The emancipation of the working class must be conquered by the working classes themselves' (International Working Men's Association, 1867). In this task, their primary target is capital itself and a logical premise for its completion is the identification of capital as having interests antagonistic to their own. The capitalist state, as a relation of capital, is not on their side. A nominal workers' state with its particular narrative of struggle and domination is perhaps a trickier barrier than more familiar social formations of capital. Indeed the ideological barriers to the formation of a class against capital in this context should not be underestimated. Consider the impact of being reminded, as perhaps some of the currently detained labour activists such as Zeng Feiyang, He Xiaobo, Zhu Xiaomei, Meng Han, Peng Jiayong, and Deng Xiaoming are being reminded right now as I sit safely in my office far away, that the preamble of the Chinese Constitution is unambiguous on the issue of class power. Its preamble states that China is a 'people's democratic dictatorship led by the working class'. No need, they may be firmly told, to build up and train fully accountable workers' representatives in the arts of collective bargaining. The 'other men whose interests are different from (and opposed to)' yours are all subject to the people's democratic dictatorship and led by the working class. So back off—or else.

My paper here has attempted to provide evidence that this is not the case. By deploying a Marxist approach to class formation conceptualised, as Andrew reminds us, as a class against capital, I have tried to relocate the working class back where it belongs in emerging processes of collective bargaining—centre stage. My argument is temporally bound between 2007 and 2014 and spatially confined to Guangdong, a period in which a dramatic increase in class struggle in various sectors across the province constrained some of the worst excesses of rapid capital accumulation. Given the current levels of repression of LNGOs and activists, the further consolidation of Guangdong's class against capital may be held up by continued state interventions; or even reversed by industrial relocation (Butollo, 2014). And of course, attempts by capital to block improvements in labour's internal position will increase tension and challenge the state's capacity to mediate stable capital–labour relations—generating pressure on the ACFTU to up its game. Or the process may re-emerge on different terrains as Friedman (2012) suggests. Or all of this may happen. In the meantime, strikes continue to dominate industrial relations in Guangdong and beyond and strikes require the self-activity of workers and their supporters. This activity is not only inseparable from institutionalised and authentic collective bargaining. It is the key to the future of the labour movement itself.

Disclosure Statement

No potential conflict of interest was reported by the author.

References

Andrew, A. (1983). Class in itself and class against capital: Karl Marx and his classifiers. *Canadian Journal of Political Science*, *16*(3), 577–584.

Butollo, F. (2014). *The end of cheap labour: Industrial transformation and "social upgrading" in China*. Frankfurt-on-Main: Campus.

Case Study Reports. (2007). *Establishing a trade union for port workers*. Retrieved from http://web.warwick.ac.uk/russia/ngpa/cases.htm

Chan, A. (1998). *China's workers under assault: The exploitation of labor in a global economy*. London: M.E. Sharpe.

Chan, C. (2009). Strike and changing workplace relations in a Chinese global factory. *Industrial Relations Journal*, *40*(1), 60–77.

Chan, C., & Hui, E. (2012). The dynamics and dilemma of workplace trade union reform in China. *Journal of Industrial Relations*, *54*(5), 653–668.

Chan, C., & Pun, N. (2009). The making of a new working class? A study of collective actions of migrant workers in South China. *China Quarterly*, *198*, 287–303.

Chen, W. (2013). *Reform of the Trade Union System, towards wage consensus and sustainability between labour and capital: Investigation into the current situation of wage collective consultation in the Guangzhou auto sector*

(gaige he wanshan gonghui gongzuo tixi zujin gongzi laozi gongjue zhi ke chixu fazhan. Guangzhou qiche zhizao ye gongzi jiti xieshang xianzhuan de diaocha). Unpublished – on file with author.
China Labour Bulletin. (2001). *Reform or revolution: Discussions between Chinese workers and Han Dongfang*. Hong Kong: China Labour Bulletin.
China Labour Bulletin. (2014a). *Searching for the Union*. Retrieved from http://www.clb.org.hk/en/research-reports
China Labour Bulletin. (2014b). *More than ten thousand workers stage massive strike at Dongguan shoe factory*. Retrieved from http://www.clb.org.hk/en/content/more-ten-thousand-workers-stage-strike-massive-dongguan-shoe-factory
China Labour Bulletin. (2014c). *Striking sanitation workers seek new model of collective bargaining*. Retrieved from http://www.clb.org.hk/en/content/striking-sanitation-workers-seek-new-model-collective-bargaining
China Labour Bulletin. (2014d). *Unity is strength: The story of Guangzhou University Town sanitation workers' strike*. Retrieved from http://www.clb.org.hk/en/content/unity-strength-story-guangzhou-university-town-sanitation-workersE280%99-strike
China Labour Bulletin. (2015). Retrieved from http://strikemap.clb.org.hk/strikes/en
Clarke, S. (2014). [Review of the book ties that bind: Cultural identity, class, and law in Vietnam's labor resistance by Tran Ngoc Angie]. *Sojourn: Journal of Social Issues in South East Asia, 29*(3), 758–760.
Cohen, G. (1980). *Karl Marx's theory of history: A defence*. Oxford: Clarendon Press.
Cole, N., & Chan, J. (2015). *Despite claims of progress, labor and environmental violations continue to plague Apple, Open Democracy*. Retrieved from https://www.opendemocracy.net/beyondslavery/nicki-lisa-cole-jenny-chan/despite-claims-of-progress-labor-and-environmental-violatio
Friedman, E. (2012). *China in Revolt. Jacobin 7–8*. Retrieved from https://www.jacobinmag.com/2012/08/china-in-revolt/
Friedman, E. (2013). Insurgency and institutionalization: The polyanian countermovement and Chinese politics. *Theory and Society, 42*, 295–327.
Fu, D. (2009). A cage of voices: Producing and doing dagongmei in contemporary China. *Modern China, 35*(5), 527–561.
GDFTU News Centre. (2014). Retrieved from http://www.gdftu.org.cn/xwdt/ttxw/201407/t20140715_498842.htm
Gong Ping She. (2014). *In conversation with a Yue Yuen veteran (yu Yue Yuen yi wei lao gongren de shendu fangtan)*. Retrieved from http://blog.sina.com.cn/s/blog_ed2baf420101wdoo.html
International Workingmen's Association. 1867 (2015). Retrieved from https://www.marxists.org/archive/marx/iwma/documents/1867/rules.htm
Koo, H. (2001). *Korean workers: The culture and politics of class formation*. Ithaca, NY: Cornell University Press.
Lee, C. K. (2007). *Against the law: Labor protests in China's Rustbelt and Sunbelt*. Berkeley: University of California Press.
Libcom.org. (2014). *New Foundations for Struggle and Solidarity: The culmination of development and privatization on a Guangzhou Island*. Retrieved from http://libcom.org/blog/guangzhou-sanitation-strike
Liu, M. (2010). Union organizing in China: Still a monolithic labor movement? *ILR Review, 64*(1), 30–52.
Lyddon, D., Cao, X., Meng, Q., & Lu, J. (2015). A strike of "unorganised" workers in a Chinese car factory: The NanhaiHonda events of 2010. *Industrial Relations Journal, 46*(2), 134–152.
Marx, K., & Engels, F. (1976). *Collected works* (Vol. 11). New York, NY: International Publishers.
Mitchell, T. (2009). China's migrant workers face bleak outlook. *Financial Times*, 9 February.
Pringle, T. (2013). Reflections on labor in China: From a moment to a movement. *South Atlantic Quarterly, 112*(1), 191–202.
Pringle, T. (2011). *Trade Unions in China: The challenge of labour unrest*. Abingdon: Routledge.
Pun, N., & Lu, H. (2010). Unfinished proletarianisation: Self, anger and class action among the second generation of peasant-workers in present-day China. *Modern China, 35*(6), 493–519.
Schmalz, S. (2016). The Yue Yuen strike: Industrial transformation and kabour unrest in the Pearl River Delta. *Globalizations*, doi:10.1080/14747731.2016.1203188.
Schmitt, B. (2013). *Honda workers on strike in China, the truth about cars*. Retrieved from http://www.thetruthaboutcars.com/2013/03/honda-workers-on-strike-in-china/
Smith, C., & Chan, J. (2015). Working for two bosses: Student interns as constrained labour in China. *Human Relations, 68*(2), 305–326.
Thompson, E. P. (1963). *The making of the English working class*. Toronto: Penguin Books.
Wright, E. O. (2000). Working-class power, capitalist-class interests, and class compromise. *American Journal of Sociology, 105*(4), 957–1002.

Yu, X., & Pun, N. (2011). Walmartization, corporate social responsibility, and the labor standards of toy factories in China. In A. Chan (Ed.), *Walmart in China* (pp. 54–70). Ithaca, NY: ILR Press.

Interviews

Interview No. 1: Auto worker, Foshan/China, 24 July 2013.
Interview No. 2: Sanitation worker, Guangzhou, 10 August 2014.
Interview No. 3: Sanitation worker, Guangzhou, 10 August 2014.
Interview No. 4: Sanitation worker, Guangzhou, 14 August 2014.
Interview No. 5: Sanitation worker, Guangzhou, 15 August 2014.
Interview No. 6: Sanitation worker, Guangzhou, 19 August 2014.
Interview No. 7: Sanitation worker, Guangzhou, 19 August 2014.
Interview No. 8: Labour NGO officer, Hong Kong SAR, 26 October 2014.
Interview No. 9: Labour activist and former worker, Hong Kong SAR, 24 October 2014.
Interview No. 10: Academic, Capital University of Economics and Business, 16 December 2014.
Interview No. 11: Labour Lawyer, London, 14 September 2014.

The Labour Politics of China's Rural Migrant Workers

JENNY CHAN* & MARK SELDEN**

*The Hong Kong Polytechnic University, Hung Hom, Hong Kong
**Asian/Pacific/American Studies Institute, New York University, New York, NY, USA

ABSTRACT *This article analyses the Chinese rural migrant workers' collective struggles within a framework that highlights the deepening of contradictions among labour, capital, and the state. At times of labour crisis, aggrieved workers have taken legal and extra-legal actions to defend their rights and interests in the absence of leadership by trade unions. From 1 January 2015, Guangdong provincial government was compelled to enforce new collective bargaining regulations to regulate labour relations, when an increasing number of workers leveraged their power to disrupt production to demand higher pay and better conditions within the tight delivery deadlines. In addition to discussing the workplace bargaining power at the key nodes in global supply networks, we highlight the impact of demographic changes on the potential increase of the marketplace bargaining power of workers.*

Introduction

By early 2016, 277 million Chinese rural migrants had been drawn into industrialisation and urbanisation, an increase of 52 million from 2008, when the National Bureau of Statistics (2014, 2016) began to monitor the work and employment conditions of the rural migrant labour force in the wake of the global financial crisis. China's economy was hit hard, as exports had constituted one-third of gross domestic product in value, but it recovered quickly in the latter half of 2009 following the rollout of a 4 trillion yuan fiscal stimulus plan over 27 months (Wong, 2011, pp. 2–3). In 2014, by some measures, China surpassed the United States to become the world's largest economy (Morrison, 2015; Naughton, 2014; Whyte,

2014). Although its extraordinary growth rates have begun to slow, China's trade, investment, and construction will continue to have significant regional and global impact.

Over these past four decades, with a shift in manufacturing from the developed countries of North America, Europe, and East Asia to the emerging economies, China has become not only the workshop of the world, but also the epicentre of labour unrest. Yet, even as the size and complexity of China's working class grow, class contradictions sharpen, and social protest proliferates, the language of class has largely disappeared from Chinese discourse. As Lee and Shen (2009, p. 110) demonstrate, under dual pressure from the state and academic institutions, many scholars who study workers in post-Cultural Revolution China 'shun class analysis and define away labour issues as those of mobility, migration, and stratification'. In contemporary China, the word *jieji* (class) connotes antagonism and confrontation in the Marxist sense, eliciting dark memories of violent social struggles throughout China from the mid-1960s to the early 1970s. It is an image that is out of step with the 'harmonious society' and the 'Chinese dream' that contemporary China's leaders proclaim. Its replacement in social analysis, the concept of *jieceng* (strata) elides class conflict and highlights social mobility predicated on enhanced human resource capital through continuing education and skills training. Policy-makers and academics working in a social stratification paradigm analyse data on household income distribution, educational attainment, and occupational rankings to document the rise of a middle class, or various middle-class strata, while downplaying durable and deepening structures of class inequality (Anagnost, 2008; Andreas, 2012; Friedman, 2014; Goodman, 2014; Guo, 2016; Lee & Selden, 2008; Pun & Chan, 2008; So, 2013).

In this context, this article discusses the Chinese rural migrant workers, particularly their precariousness and collective struggles, within a framework that highlights the deepening of contradictions among labour, capital, and the state. With the influx of foreign direct investment and the relaxation of state restrictions on rural-to-urban migration since the late 1970s, successive cohorts of internal migrant workers have become the core of China's new working class. We examine the role of local governments in drawing in businesses and investments, and the specific conditions of rural migrants' production and reproduction in the contemporary political economy. At times of labour crisis, aggrieved workers have taken legal and extra-legal actions to defend their rights and interests in the absence of leadership or mobilisation by trade unions. What then are the prospects for Chinese labour to strengthen its power at the key nodes of transnational manufacturers? The answer will hinge not only on changing labour–capital relations, but also on the ways in which the government prioritises worker interests versus those of international and domestic capital, and on the impact of demographic changes on the growth of workers' marketplace bargaining power.

A New Generation of Chinese Rural Migrant Workers

China's economic rise spurs dreams of success from all walks of life. 'Wage work in the city', comments Sargeson (1999, p. 219), 'became the means for self-actualisation [of women peasant-migrants] in family and village'. For nearly all, however, it was transient; many among the first generation of rural migrants drawn to the urban labour market up to the 1990s returned to their villages to marry, settle, and raise children. The returned migrants and their families have access to village-allocated subsistence plots of land. The Rural Land Contracting Law, revised and implemented in March 2003, upholds the '30-year no-change rule' to household-contracted farmland for rural people, including those who have already migrated to work in earlier years. For rural migrants, agricultural land tenure is a form of insurance in the event of lay-offs or return to the home village, and a basis for subsistence for returned migrants whose access to health care and retirement benefits remains limited (Whyte, 2010). Given the precarious dependence on rural land, residents continue to draw on remittances from their (male) family members who have migrated to work in the city (Chuang, 2015a). Sporadic efforts towards cooperative rural construction and alternative development initiatives aside, sustainable farming, and lucrative non-farm work opportunities in the remote countryside are scarce.

Following China's accession to the World Trade Organisation in 2001, farm workers experienced ever more intense market pressures, one of the factors accelerating migration. Despite the elimination of agricultural taxes in 2005 and the extension of local insurance schemes (Chen, 2014; Frazier, 2014; Hsiao, 2014), much of the countryside has remained stagnant as youth have left en masse for the cities and jobs in industry, construction, and services. Some 'left-behind' villagers have leased or transferred their land-use rights to boost income. Others have no choice but to search for non-farm, low-wage, temporary jobs as a result of rural land grabs involving state–capital collusion resulting in windfall profits for cadres and loss of land rights for those who had tilled the land throughout their lives. They become new proletarians in the socialist market economy (Chuang, 2014, 2015b).

Still, the majority of Chinese rural migrants have experienced incomplete proletarianisation, in that they possess agricultural land-use rights as a birth right while working for wages as hired urban labourers to make ends meet (Chan & Selden, 2014; Friedman & Lee, 2010; Lee, 2016; Pun & Lu, 2010). Poverty alleviation officials have facilitated labour out-migration. The goal was to obtain remittances and ensure the development of marketable skills in young migrants while supporting China's export-oriented industrialisation. This cohort of officially registered 'rural migrants' includes tens of millions who were born, and even have spent their entire lives, in and around cities, yet retain 'rural household registration' in perpetuity. In effect, internal migrant workers are denied equal citizenship and welfare rights.

As of 2013, 46.6% of those classified as rural migrant workers were born after 1980, and the majority (60.6%) of these young people had completed nine years of formal education. An additional 20.5% are high school graduates (National Bureau of Statistics, 2014). They express a desire to broaden their horizons and experience a modern life and cosmopolitan consumption in megacities such as Shenzhen, Shanghai, and Beijing, as well as other fast-developing cities in inland provinces. A migrant worker in Beijing commented, 'If I had to live the life that my mother has lived, I would choose suicide' (Yan, 2008, p. 25). Growing corn and wheat on tiny parcels of land and keeping a few pigs and chickens may not leave her hungry, but getting ahead and moving upward is nearly impossible if she seeks to eke out a living on the small family plot. The second and third generations have their eyes firmly on the cities. 'Birds, don't be silly, no one cares whether you're tired from flying. People only care how high you fly', mused a 19-year-old migrant worker. Coming from a village in central China, she hoped to secure a better life for her mother and herself in Shanghai (Chan, 2013a). While some migrants are entranced by rosy dreams of entrepreneurial success, the high aspirations of these workers face acute problems in a society characterised by soaring income gaps, and the commodification of social services, such as housing, education, and medical care.

Capitalist Development, the Chinese State, and Global Capital

With the consolidation of profit-making state-owned enterprises, China's industrial system has been divided into three segments 'consisting of large, central-government firms; hybrid local and foreign firms; and small-scale capitalism' (Naughton, 2010, p. 441). To this, we add the dominance of gigantic, wholly owned foreign-invested manufacturers, which have access to cheap land, human resources, and numerous privileges from local governments across China. For a notable example, Taiwanese-based Foxconn Technology Group, founded in Taipei in 1974, has risen to become China's largest employer with more than one million employees. It is a leading player making possible China's emergence as the 'electronics workshop of the world', capturing over 50% of global market share in consumer electronics (Chan, Pun, & Selden, 2013, 2015a). As a leading Global 500 firm, Foxconn occupies a central place in transnational manufacturing, wherein workers can potentially achieve strong workplace-based power in collective bargaining. A labour strike at such a key point of globalised production may cause huge losses not only to the company, but also to brand buyers who are heavily dependent on it. Hence, these brands may push to settle in favour of workers. 'Workplace bargaining power', in the words of Silver (2003, p. 13), 'accrues to workers who are enmeshed in tightly integrated production processes, where a localised work stoppage in a key node can cause disruptions on a much wider scale than the stoppage itself'. China's manufacturing workers—most of them rural migrants in their late teens and 20s—have repeatedly used their structural workplace power to make primarily economic claims.

Foxconn's extraordinary growth is built on its cheap, big, fast, and efficient production model, and the subsidisation by the state at all levels. It manages production tasks and inventory logistics, resulting in ever-stronger interdependent relations between 'big buyers' and 'big suppliers' in the high-tech electronics supply chains (Appelbaum, 2008). In many cities throughout China, Foxconn runs multiple manufacturing facilities. In 2010, more than 500,000 employees worked in two Foxconn factories in Shenzhen city, on the northern border of Hong Kong (Foxconn Technology Group, 2010, p. 1). Subsequently, tens of thousands of workers were transferred to lower wage production sites in western, central, and northern China. By early 2016, Foxconn had 30-plus manufacturing complexes in all 4 provincial-level municipalities (Beijing, Tianjin, Shanghai, and Chongqing) and in 16 provinces throughout the country. From raw material extraction to processing to final assembly, Foxconn has built a network featuring vertical integration and flexible coordination across different facilities and 24-hour continuous assembly.

On the factory floor, the change in production requirements from iPhone 5c and 5s to iPhone 6 and 6 Plus, and the increase in output targets, placed Foxconn workers under intense stress. Thus far, Apple has refused to disclose to the authors the specifics of its iPhone contracts. Jacky Haynes, senior director of Apple's Supplier Responsibility Program, responded in a 18 February 2014 email concerning our question about the company's purchasing policies as they affect Chinese wages: 'Over the years, we have increased the prices we pay to suppliers in order to support wage increases for workers. Confidentiality agreements prevent us from providing the data you're requesting'.[1] Stated differently, Apple, the world's most profitable technology company, provided *no* evidence to substantiate its claim of increasing unit prices in order to facilitate higher wages at its independently owned suppliers. Although claiming to exercise corporate social responsibility in global supply chain management (Litzinger, 2013; Locke, 2013), Apple has never acknowledged its own culpability in squeezing suppliers and workers by imposing tight delivery schedules and high-quality demands at presumably ever lower prices.

Foxconn shocked the world when the '12 leaps', the suicides of rural migrant workers aged 17–25 who leaped from factory dormitories in Shenzhen, took place during the first five months of 2010 (Chan, 2013b; Chan & Pun, 2010; Pun et al., 2014; Pun & Chan, 2012, 2013). Foxconn union chairwoman Chen Peng, special assistant of CEO Terry Gou, not only failed to investigate the workplace factors responsible for worker depression but also made insensitive public comments that 'Suicide is foolish, irresponsible and meaningless and should be avoided' (*China Daily*, 2010). Not unlike their peers in other workplaces, and perhaps in an extreme form, the million-strong Foxconn workers are not collectively represented in a meaningful way. Five years on, in February 2015, the head of the All-China Federation of Trade Unions' (ACFTU) legal department Guo Jun criticised Foxconn, among other companies, for imposing illegal overtime of 'more than ten hours every day' on workers, in some cases resulting in 'deaths and suicides' (*China Daily*, 2015). But the practice of compulsory, illegal overtime labour on this scale was well known to government leaders throughout the years. If the central-level official union staff were really interested in building 'harmonious labour relations', they had failed to reform the management-dominated unions at Foxconn and other firms (Chan, Pun, & Selden, 2016a, 2016b). The dependence of the grassroots unions on management, and the limits on their activity posed by the state, severely undermines the capacity of enterprise unions to represent the workers. In the words of Anita Chan (2011, p. 42), the unions are 'an integral part of factory management' and 'worse than weak'.

Legal Activism

Corporate management has prioritised labour controls, with an emphasis on profit, organisational flexibility, and production efficiency, transforming China's industrial relations in the era of economic globalisation. Between 1978 and 1995, under the promotion of the 'rule of law', 49 labour laws and regulations were enacted, including the national Labour Law, which came into force on 1 January 1995 (Thireau & Hua, 2003, p. 85). The provisions of a written employment contract, minimum wages, overtime premiums, rest days, occupational health and safety, and social benefits have inspired citizens to file claims through fast-expanding labour dispute arbitration committees and courts. Lee (2010, p. 76) observes that, as the state seeks to channel labour conflict away from the street, 'the law has become the pivotal terrain of labour politics'. Arbitration committees are grassroots state organisations that bring together labour and management to resolve labour conflicts. In 1993, the State Council promulgated the Regulations on the Handling of Enterprise Labour Disputes, enabling employees of all kinds of enterprises to raise complaints to local labour dispute arbitration committees. The significance was that, while the 1987 Provisional Regulations on the Handling of Enterprise Labour Disputes in State Enterprises stipulated the rights to arbitration of state employees only, the 1993 Regulations for the first time granted workers in private and foreign-invested firms, the majority being rural migrants, equal access to arbitration (Harper Ho, 2003). But not all incidents of labour disputes fall within the domain of arbitration and the courts. Workers know that government arbitrators do not accept demands such as those for wage increases above the legal minimum.

Companies face increasing pressure to raise wages and improve conditions to retain workers, particularly a young cohort, who frequently change jobs in an attempt to get higher pay and benefits. Equally important, pressures from below together with state efforts to boost incomes between 2008 and 2012 led to average annual increases in statutory minimum wages of 12.6% (China Briefing, 2013). The government reported that average total income of rural migrant workers had risen steadily following the economic recovery in 2009, reaching 3072 yuan per month in 2015, a 7.2% increase from the previous year (National Bureau of Statistics, 2016). However, the high cost of living in large cities has remained a source of stress and frustration for low-income workers. Conflicts over non-payment or under-payment of wages, as well as inadequate compensation as workers were laid off following the shutdown, privatisation, or relocation of their factories, have become explosive.

Aggrieved workers 'mobilised the law' by quoting specific clauses of legal protection when their rights were violated (Chan, 2009; Gallagher, 2006; Hurst, 2009; Lee, 2007). Official statistics show that, in 1996, 48,121 labour disputes were accepted for arbitration, the total spiralling to 120,191 in 1999, involving more than 470,000 labourers as numbers soared in the context of massive lay-offs of state sector workers. The upward trend continued from 2000, reflecting widespread incidences of rights violations as the non-state and restructured state sector expanded. Labour cases further skyrocketed to 693,465, involving more than 1.2 million labourers nationwide in the economic crisis of 2008. Following the economic recovery and government intervention, newly accepted arbitration cases fell to 600,865 in 2010 and further to 589,244 in 2011. In 2013, however, the total number of labour dispute cases rebounded (665,760), despite greater responsiveness on the part of the government and its trade union offices to resolve problems at the grassroots level (China Labour Statistical Yearbook 2014, 2015).

In 2012, agency workers (also known as dispatched workers)—who engaged in labour relations directly with agencies but provided services to client companies—registered 17,000 cases to claim their social insurance benefits and wage payments as well as rights to labour contracts (China Labour Net, 2014). These contingent workers were long excluded from national legal protection prior to the implementation of the Labour Contract Law, effective from 1 January 2008. Under the new law, hiring agencies and client firms share joint legal responsibilities and agency workers are entitled to receive the same pay for doing the same work as directly employed workers. Moreover, they are assumed to take only 'temporary, auxiliary, and substitute' posts, thereby placing certain limits on informalisation while maintaining labour and organisational flexibility. However, huge discrepancies exist between workers' formal employment rights and the enforcement of these rights (Cairns, 2015; Gallagher, Giles, Park, & Wang, 2015; Xu, 2014; Zhang, 2015).

Research in 2009–2011 found that disgruntled workers again and again rejected arbitration decisions and appealed to higher courts when they perceived arbitrators' awards to be significantly below what they believed the Labour Law guaranteed them (Chen & Xu, 2012). Within 15 days of an arbitration ruling, workers have a right to apply for a trial of the original dispute. Such appeals have become increasingly common. If either side is dissatisfied with the verdict, it can appeal to a higher court, where a second trial is final. In recent years, governments at all levels have directed workers to resolve conflicts through mediation in order to reduce caseloads (Fu & Cullen, 2011). Outside of state-sanctioned dispute resolution paths, workers have also taken direct action to advance their rights and interests. The oscillation between legal and extra-legal avenues has at times fuelled activism by some, but others have become depressed and embittered.

Labour Challenges and Trade Union Reforms

As market reforms accelerated in the 1990s and thereafter, the fragmentation of labour and the diversification of ownership in the hands of Chinese and international capital profoundly challenged both workers and trade unions. In the three years from 1997 to 2000 alone, the ACFTU, whose strength had been centered in state-owned enterprises, lost at least 17 million members in the wave of privatisation or corporate restructuring (Traub-Merz, 2012, p. 28). In response, the government-run union bureaucracy targeted large foreign-invested companies such as Foxconn and Wal-Mart to unionise. By December 2009, 'unions had been set up in 92% of the Fortune 500 companies operating in China', and this trend has continued since (Liu, 2011, p. 157). By 2013, the centralised Chinese trade union organisation claimed a total membership of 288 million nationwide (Chinese Trade Unions Statistics Yearbook 2013, 2015)—surpassing the International Trade Union Confederation global membership of 176 million workers in 161 countries and territories excluding China. The number of union members is impressive, but in terms of the purpose of serving worker interests, we may ask: to what end?

In 2013, the government estimated that only 28.5% of 166 million rural migrant workers were covered by work-injury insurance, 17.6% by medical insurance, 15.7% by old age pensions, 9.1% by unemployment benefits, and 6.6% by maternity insurance (National Bureau of Statistics, 2014). A significant example of worker protest erupted in spring 2014 involving over 40,000 workers from all production departments at the world's largest footwear supplier, Taiwanese-owned Yue Yuen in Dongguan city, Guangdong, whose sneakers are sold to Nike, Adidas, Timberland, and other global brands. Workers demanded entitlement to employment benefits that the company had denied them. When worker–management negotiations broke down, a factory-wide strike closed the plant between 14 and 25 April, compelling municipal human resources and social security officials to mediate. On 1 May, senior management—under pressure from stability-obsessed higher level governments concerned about the blatant denial of state-mandated labour benefits—promised to provide insurance premiums in accordance with workers' current wages. They refused, however, to pay the 'historical debts', that is, unpaid welfare benefits owed to employees for previous work. In the absence of strong pro-labour government and union support for the full set of demands, workers accepted the partial victory and returned to work (Chen, 2015).

If large-scale strikes such as that at Yue Yuen sometimes win victories which could reverberate to the advantage of workers employed elsewhere, the critical question remains whether workers can secure the fundamental rights to collective bargaining and effective representation in the face of unified action by capital, the company unions, and the local state. Officials at the city and township levels have fostered a flexible labour regime wherein central government rules are bent to the investors' advantage. Gallagher and Dong (2011, p. 44) conclude that employers systematically 'ignored the law with impunity because of the lack of effective implementation and enforcement by local regulatory or supervisory organisations, including the trade union, the local labour bureau and the courts'. The state–capital nexus is indeed powerful even as specific, workplace-based grievances surface in lawsuits and collective protest of various kinds. Regional competition to secure and hold foreign investment in their domains—across the coastal provinces and between the interior regions—is very intense.

Local disruptions of global capitalism, however short-lived, enrich our imagination of possibilities for labour resistance. In May 2010, 1800 workers including a large number of 'student interns' at Honda participated in a factory-wide strike to demand an 800 yuan per month pay rise in Nanhai district, Guangdong. The worker representatives also insisted on reforming their union (Butollo & ten Brink, 2012; Lyddon, Cao, Meng, & Lu, 2015). In August 2010, Kong Xianghong, vice-chair of the Guangdong Federation of Trade Unions, presided over the direct election of shop-floor union representatives and subsequent collective wage bargaining in 2011. Many workers were disappointed, however, that the discredited factory union chair was permitted to remain as head of a partially reformed union and the two 'elected' vice-chairs were top-level managers, reflecting continued managerial control. Moreover, while the company was forced to yield on the important wage issue under pressure from the provincial trade union, in the name of restoration of 'industrial peace', it was able to ignore all other worker demands, including those for women's rights and improved welfare benefits (paid maternity leave and a one-hour meal break among them). As a result, the union committee quickly lost the confidence of rank-and-file workers.

Bargaining through workers' direct actions, in the form of strikes or demonstrations, has been and remains a viable way to address workers' shared grievances (Elfstrom & Kuruvilla, 2014). The official slogan of the ACFTU is 'When there's trouble, seek the trade union'. Worker leaders, again and again, only found company unions unresponsive to their plight. Indeed, worker solidarity frequently dissipated when leaders were intimidated, arrested, or bought off, or when state-brokered settlements provided workers with limited gains, while leaving the power structure and fundamental patterns of inequity and injustice intact. Tim Pringle (2011, p. 162), in assessing the future of Chinese union reforms in light of growing labour challenges, stresses the need not only for 'more accountable enterprise-level union chairpersons and committees' but also for 'more supportive, interactive and, at times, directive relationships between the higher trade unions and their enterprise-level subordinates'. To maintain governance legitimacy, the state continues to search for mechanisms for resolving labour conflicts and managing social discontent.

Mary Gallagher (2014, p. 87) stresses the role of 'the activist state' in which the Chinese government 'has struggled to maintain its labour system through more direct management of labour disputes'. As China's officials make extensive use of their discretionary power to resolve major labour disputes, rather than enabling workers to exercise fundamental rights to freedom of association, it is unclear how long this government interventionist strategy will remain viable, particularly when workers' basic rights and interests are routinely violated. The immediate result is that, in many cases, workers' individual grievances are partially addressed and collective actions broken up. Time and again, settlement of high-profile worker protests through direct government mediation is undertaken to restore 'social harmony' (Chen, 2012; Liebman, 2014). Indeed, officials have skilfully developed a wide array of 'protest absorption' techniques to settle labour disputes at the scene, with the goal of maintaining socio-political stability, such as lowering workers' 'realistic' expectation of claims to compensation, pressuring management to grant some economic concessions to adversely affected workers, and simultaneously manipulating workers' familial and social relations to silence the resistance (Deng & O'Brien, 2013; Lee & Zhang, 2013; Su & He, 2010).

The state–society relationships are contentious, requiring ever more legislative efforts, media advocacy, and direct involvement in labour management by government officials. Wang Tongxin, vice-chair of the Shenzhen Federation of Trade Unions, for example, called for 'power to the workers' and supported a municipal plan to facilitate union elections at 163 enterprises (each with more than 1000 workers) whose union committees were up for re-election in 2012 (Shenzhen Daily, 2012). This suggests the possibility that a directly elected union leadership could emerge in some localities within a 'Party-state-led model' of dispute mediation and unionisation in the workplace (Hui & Chan, 2015). In October 2013, the Guangdong Provincial People's Congress released for public discussion the Regulations on Enterprise Collective Consultations and Collective Contracts (Revised Draft). The overarching goal was to establish an effective negotiation system so as to harmonise labour relations or, to put it more directly, to reduce the incidence of strikes. The regulations specify that employees can initiate a 'collective consultation' process and management must present a point-by-point written reply within 20 days of receiving the notice. In response to strong opposition from major business associations, the provincial government weakened the critical provisions and, on 25 September 2014, passed the Regulations on Enterprise Collective Contracts in Guangdong, effective from 1 January 2015. Article 18 stipulates that over 50% of the workforce must endorse the formal call for compulsory talks to take place, a formidable obstacle to worker actions. Even if negotiations do happen, Article 24 prohibits workers from engaging in a work stoppage or slowdown. The long-term impact of the regulations on the role of trade union and workers' power is to be carefully observed (for an early bleak assessment of the Guangdong regulations, see Halegua, 2015).

Conclusion

China's emergence as a global economic power could not have occurred without the painstaking efforts of successive generations of rural migrant workers. A substantial number of rural (local) labourers are now being recruited from within or sent back to their home province, in some cases close to their hometowns, where they may draw on local social networks for support. With a greater sense of entitlement associated with belonging to a place, and perhaps greater social resources to bring to the fight for their interests, the result could be enhanced working-class power in factories and worker communities. At the same time, factories are relocating inland and offshore in the search for cheaper labour, land, and other resources, weakening further workers' generally short-term, localised solidarity actions. In these successive 'spatial fixes', the crisis of capitalist accumulation deepens. 'Realize the great Chinese dream, build a harmonious society', reads a government banner. To realise individual and national dreams, however, workers will have to secure justice and dignity, which in turn will require the institutionalisation of worker power.

Demographic changes have slowed the growth of the working-age population at a time of general ageing, potentially increasing the marketplace bargaining power of workers (Davis, 2014; Eggleston et al., 2013). Chinese fertility is presently 1.6 children per woman, down from more than 6 children in the 1950s and 2.5 in the 1980s. The number of labourers aged 20–24 is projected to decline from 125 million people in 2010 to around 80 million in 2020 (Gu & Cai, 2011). China's 2010 Population Census, moreover, showed that the age group 0–14 constituted 16.6% of the total population, down 6.3% compared with the 2000 Census data (National Bureau of Statistics, 2011). All of these indicators suggest a reduction in the labour supply in the coming decades. But employers are not going to sit idle. Recent research has shown that 'student interns', who are recruited from vocational schools and paid less than minimum wages in so-called 'internships', have become a new source of contingent cheap labour at the bottom of China's labour market (Chan, Pun, & Selden, 2015b; Martinez, 2015). As the backbone of the nation's export-oriented industrial development, young workers today have higher expectations than the first wave of rural migrants. They aspire to develop technical skills, earn living wages, enjoy comprehensive welfare, and hold the full range of citizenship rights in the towns and cities they inhabit.

At the key nodes of production, the integration of large manufacturers in transnational supply chains and tight delivery schedules for consumer products potentially enhance workers' bargaining power at the workplace level. With workers' growing awareness of the opportunities presented by the fact that giant corporations face pressures to meet quotas for new models and holiday season purchases, they have repeatedly come together at the dormitory, workshop, or factory level to voice demands or to stage protests. Access to internet and social networking technology also enables workers to disseminate open letters and to tweet urgent appeals for support. If suicide is understood as one extreme form of labour protest chosen by some to expose an oppressive production regime in which rural migrant workers are deprived of dignified work, many more workers are organising on their own, bypassing management-controlled trade unions. They call on wide-ranging policy changes at both industry and governmental levels amid the deep tensions being played out among labour, capital, and the Chinese state in global transformation.

Acknowledgements

We thank Andreas Bieler, Chun-Yi Lee, Barry K. Gills, Yingjie Guo, Tom Fenton, Ngai Pun, and two anonymous reviewers for valuable comments on earlier drafts.

Disclosure Statement

No potential conflict of interest was reported by the authors.

Funding

This publication arises from research funded by the John Fell Oxford University Press (OUP) Research Fund [ref. 152/015].

Note

1 Apple's five-page email correspondence dated February 18, 2014 is on file with the authors.

References

Anagnost, A. (2008). From 'class' to 'social strata': Grasping the social totality in reform-era China. *Third World Quarterly, 29*(3), 497–519.

Andreas, J. (2012). Industrial restructuring and class transformation in China. In B. Carrillo & D. S. G. Goodman (Eds.), *China's peasants and workers: Changing class identities* (pp. 102–123). Cheltenham: Edward Elgar.

Appelbaum, R. P. (2008). Giant transnational contractors in East Asia: Emergent trends in global supply chain. *Competition & Change, 12*(1), 69–87.

Butollo, F., & ten Brink, T. (2012). Challenging the atomization of discontent: Patterns of migrant-worker protest in China during the series of strikes in 2010. *Critical Asian Studies, 44*(3), 419–440.

Cairns, D. S. (2015). New formalities for casual labour: Addressing unintended consequences of China's Labour Contract Law. *Washington International Law Journal, 24*(1), 219–252.

Chan, A. (2011). Strikes in China's export industries in comparative perspective. *China Journal, 65*, 27–51.

Chan, J. (2009). Meaningful progress or illusory reform? Analysing China's Labour Contract Law. *New Labour Forum, 18*(2), 43–51.

Chan, J. (2013a, May 29). *Who speaks for China's workers*? Labour Notes. Retrieved from http://www.labournotes.org/blogs/2013/05/who-speaks-china%E2%80%99s-workers

Chan, J. (2013b). A suicide survivor: The life of a Chinese worker. *New Technology, Worker and Employment, 28*(2), 84–99.

Chan, J., & Pun, N. (2010). Suicide as protest for the new generation of Chinese migrant workers: Foxconn, global capital, and the state. *Asia-Pacific Journal, 37*(2). No. 10. Retrieved from http://japanfocus.org/-Jenny-Chan/3408

Chan, J., Pun, N., & Selden, M. (2013). The politics of global production: Apple, Foxconn, and China's new working class. *New Technology, Work and Employment, 28*(2), 100–115.

Chan, J., Pun, N., & Selden, M. (2015a). Apple's iPad city: Subcontracting exploitation to China. In K. van der Pijl (Ed.), *Handbook of the international political economy of production* (pp. 76–97). Cheltenham: Edward Elgar.

Chan, J., Pun, N., & Selden, M. (2015b). Interns or workers? China's student labour regime. *Asian Studies* (Official Journal of the Asian Studies Association of Hong Kong), *1*(1), 69–98.

Chan, J., Pun, N., & Selden, M. (2016a). Chinese labour protest and trade unions. In R. Maxwell (Ed.), *The Routledge companion to labour and media* (pp. 290–302). New York, NY: Routledge.

Chan, J., Pun, N., & Selden, M. (2016b). Labour protests and trade union reforms in China. In J. Drahokoupil, R. Andrijasevic, & D. Sacchetto (Eds.), *Flexible workforces and low profit margins: Electronics assembly between Europe and China* (pp. 205–222). Brussels: ETUI (European Trade Union Institute).

Chan, J., & Selden, M. (2014). China's rural migrant workers, the state, and labour politics. *Critical Asian Studies, 46*(4), 599–620.

Chen, A. (2014). How has the abolition of agricultural taxes transformed village governance in China? Evidence from agricultural regions. *China Quarterly, 219*, 715–735.

Chen, C.-J. J. (2015). Zhongguo weiquan zhengti xia de jiti kangyi: Taizichang dabagong de anli fenxi (Popular protest in an authoritarian regime: A wildcat strike in southern China). *Taiwanese Sociology, 30*, 1–53.

Chen, F., & Xu, X. (2012). 'Active judiciary': Judicial dismantling of workers' collective action in China. *China Journal, 67*, 87–108.

Chen, X. (2012). *Social protest and contentious authoritarianism in China*. New York, NY: Cambridge University Press.

China Briefing. (2013). *China initiates new round of minimum wage increases*. Retrieved from http://www.china-briefing.com/news/2013/01/04/china-initiates-new-round-of-minimum-wage-increases.html

China Daily. (2010, August 19). Foxconn rallies to end suicides by workers.

China Daily. (2015, February 3). Foxconn's long hours causing workers' deaths: Union. Retrieved from http://www.chinadaily.com.cn/china/2015-02/03/content_19477082.htm

China Labour Net. (2014). *Laodong zhengyi chuli tongji shuju* (Statistical data of labour dispute settlement). Retrieved from http://www.labournet.com.cn/ldzy/ckzl/ckzl2a.asp

China Labour Statistical Yearbook 2014. (2015). Beijing: China Statistics Press.

Chinese Trade Unions Statistics Yearbook 2013. (2015). Beijing: China Statistics Press.

Chuang, J. (2014). China's rural land politics: Bureaucratic absorption and the muting of rightful resistance. *China Quarterly, 219*, 649–669.

Chuang, J. (2015a). Factory girls after the factory: Female return migrations in rural China. *Gender & Society*. doi:10.1177/0891243215621718

Chuang, J. (2015b). Urbanization through dispossession: Survival and stratification in China's new townships. *Journal of Peasant Studies, 42*(2), 275–294.

Davis, D. S. (2014). Demographic challenges for a rising China. *Dædalus, 143*(2), 26–38.

Deng, Y., & O'Brien, K. J. (2013). Relational repression in China: Using social ties to demobilize protesters. *China Quarterly, 215*, 533–552.

Eggleston, K., Oi, J. C., Rozelle, S., Sun, A., Walder, A., & Zhou, X. (2013). Will demographic change slow China's rise? *Journal of Asian Studies, 72*(3), 505–518.

Elfstrom, M., & Kuruvilla, S. (2014). The changing nature of labour unrest in China. *ILR (Industrial and Labour Relations) Review, 67*(2), 453–480.

Foxconn Technology Group. (2010). *Foxconn is committed to a safe and positive working environment*. 11 October. Retrieved from http://regmedia.co.uk/2010/10/12/foxconn_media_statement.pdf

Frazier, M. W. (2014). State schemes or safety nets? China's push for universal coverage. *Dædalus, 143*(2), 69–80.

Friedman, E. (2014). *Insurgency trap: Labour politics in postsocialist China*. Ithaca, NY: Cornell University Press.

Friedman, E., & Lee, C. K. (2010). Remaking the world of Chinese labour: A 30-year retrospective. *British Journal of Industrial Relations, 48*(3), 507–533.

Fu, H., & Cullen, R. (2011). From mediatory to adjudicatory justice: The limits of civil justice reform in China. In M. Y. K. Woo & M. E. Gallagher (Eds.), *Chinese justice: Civil dispute resolution in contemporary China* (pp. 25–57). Cambridge: Cambridge University Press.

Gallagher, M. E. (2006). Mobilizing the law in China: 'Informed disenchantment' and the development of legal consciousness. *Law and Society Review, 40*(4), 783–816.

Gallagher, M. E. (2014). China's workers movement and the end of the rapid-growth era. *Dædalus, 143*(2), 81–95.

Gallagher, M. E., & Dong, B. (2011). Legislating harmony: Labour law reform in contemporary China. In S. Kuruvilla, C. K. Lee, & M. E. Gallagher (Eds.), *From iron rice bowl to informalization: Markets, workers, and the state in a changing China* (pp. 36–60). Ithaca, NY: Cornell University Press.

Gallagher, M. E., Giles, J., Park, A., & Wang, M. (2015). China's 2008 Labour Contract Law: Implementation and implications for China's workers. *Human Relations, 68*(2), 197–235.

Goodman, D. S. G. (2014). *Class in contemporary China*. Cambridge: Polity Press.

Gu, B., & Cai, Y. (2011). *Fertility prospects in China*. United Nations Population Division. Retrieved from http://www.un.org/esa/population/publications/expertpapers/2011-14_Gu&Cai_Expert-paper.pdf

Guo, Y. (Ed.). (2016). *Handbook on class and social stratification in China*. Cheltenham: Edward Elgar.

Halegua, A. (2015, February 25). China's new collective bargaining rule is too weak to ease labour conflicts. *South China Morning Post*. Retrieved from http://www.scmp.com/comment/insight-opinion/article/1723213/chinas-new-collective-bargaining-rule-too-weak-ease-labour

Harper Ho, V. E. (2003). *Labour dispute resolution in China: Implications for labour rights and legal reform*. Berkeley: University of California, Institute of East Asian Studies.

Hsiao, W. C. (2014). Correcting past health policy mistakes. *Dædalus, 143*(2), 53–68.

Hui, E. S., & Chan, C. K. C. (2015). Beyond the union-centred approach: A critical evaluation of recent trade union elections in China. *British Journal of Industrial Relations, 53*(3), 601–627.

Hurst, W. (2009). *The Chinese worker after socialism*. Cambridge: Cambridge University Press.

Lee, C. K. (2007). *Against the law: Labour protests in China's rustbelt and sunbelt*. Berkeley: University of California Press.

Lee, C. K. (2010). Pathways of labour activism. In E. J. Perry & M. Selden (Eds.), *Chinese society: Change, conflict and resistance* (pp. 57–79, 3rd ed.). London: Routledge.

Lee, C. K. (2016). Precarization or empowerment? Reflections on recent labour unrest in China. *The Journal of Asian Studies*, 1–17. doi:10.1017/S0021911815002132.

Lee, C. K., & Selden, M. (2008). Inequality and its enemies in revolutionary and reform China. *Economic and Political Weekly, 43*(52), 27–36.

Lee, C. K., & Shen, Y. (2009). China: The paradox and possibility of a public sociology of labour. *Work and Occupations, 36*(2), 110–125.

Lee, C. K., & Zhang, Y. (2013). The power of instability: Unravelling the microfoundations of bargained authoritarianism in China. *American Journal of Sociology, 118*(6), 1475–1508.

Liebman, B. L. (2014). Legal reform: China's law–stability paradox. *Dædalus, 143*(2), 96–109.

Litzinger, R. A. (2013). The labour question in China: Apple and beyond. *The South Atlantic Quarterly, 112*(1), 172–178.

Liu, M. (2011). 'Where there are workers, there should be trade unions': Union organizing in the era of growing informal employment. In S. Kuruvilla, C. K. Lee, & M. E. Gallagher (Eds.), *From iron rice bowl to informalization: Markets, workers, and the state in a changing China* (pp. 157–172). Ithaca, NY: Cornell University Press.

Locke, R. M. (2013). *The promise and limits of private power: Promoting labour standards in a global economy*. Cambridge: Cambridge University Press.

Lyddon, D., Cao, X., Meng, Q., & Lu, J. (2015). A strike of 'unorganised' workers in a Chinese car factory: The Nanhai Honda events of 2010. *Industrial Relations Journal, 46*(2), 134–152.

Martinez, N. J. (2015). Servants of servers: Rights violations and forced labour in the supply chain of ICT (Information and Communications Technology) equipment in European universities. *DanWatch*. October 5. Retrieved from https://www.danwatch.dk/en/undersogelse/servants-of-servers/

Morrison, W. M. (2015). *China's economic rise: History, trends, challenges, and implications for the United States* (Congressional Research Service (CRS) Report). September 11. Retrieved from https://www.fas.org/sgp/crs/row/RL33534.pdf

National Bureau of Statistics. (2011). *Press release on major figures of the 2010 National Population Census*. April 28. Retrieved from http://www.stats.gov.cn/english/newsandcomingevents/t20110428_402722237.htm

National Bureau of Statistics. (2014). *2013 nian quanguo nongmingong jiance diaocha baogao* (Investigative report on the monitoring of Chinese rural migrant workers in 2013). Retrieved from http://www.stats.gov.cn/tjsj/zxfb/201405/t20140512_551585.html

National Bureau of Statistics. (2016). *2015 nian nongmingong jiance diaocha baogao* (Investigative report on the monitoring of rural migrant workers in 2015). Retrieved from http://www.stats.gov.cn/tjsj/zxfb/201604/t20160428_1349713.html

Naughton, B. (2010). China's distinctive system: Can it be a model for others? *Journal of Contemporary China, 19*(65), 437–460.

Naughton, B. (2014). China's economy: Complacency, crisis & the challenge of reform. *Daedalus, 143*(2), 14–25.

Pringle, T. (2011). *Trade unions in China: The challenge of labour unrest*. Abingdon: Routledge.

Pun, N., & Chan, C. K. C. (2008). The subsumption of class discourse in China. *Boundary, 2 35*(2), 75–91.

Pun, N., & Chan, J. (2012). Global capital, the state, and Chinese workers: The Foxconn experience. *Modern China, 38*(4), 383–410.

Pun, N., & Chan, J. (2013). The spatial politics of labour in China: Life, labour, and a new generation of migrant workers. *South Atlantic Quarterly, 112*(1), 179–190.

Pun, N., & Lu, H. (2010). Unfinished proletarianization: Self, anger and class action of the second generation of peasant-workers in reform China. *Modern China, 36*(5), 493–519.

Pun, N., Shen, Y., Guo, Y., Lu, H., Chan, J., & Selden, M. (2014). Worker–intellectual unity: Trans-border sociological intervention in Foxconn. *Current Sociology, 62*(2), 209–222.

Sargeson, S. (1999). *Reworking China's proletariat.* Houndmills: Macmillan.

Shenzhen Daily. (2012, May 29). *Unions to promote direct elections.* Retrieved from http://szdaily.sznews.com/html/2012-05/29/content_2061431.htm

Silver, B. J. (2003). *Forces of labour: Workers' movements and globalization since 1870.* Cambridge: Cambridge University Press.

So, A. Y. (2013). *Class and class conflict in post-socialist China.* Singapore: World Scientific Publishing Company.

Su, Y., & He, X. (2010). Street as courtroom: State accommodation of labour protest in South China. *Law and Society Review, 44*(1), 157–184.

Thireau, I., & Hua, L. (2003). The moral universe of aggrieved Chinese workers: Workers' appeals to arbitration committees and letters and visits offices. *China Journal, 50*, 83–103.

Traub-Merz, R. (2012). All China federation of trade unions: Structure, functions and the challenge of collective bargaining. In R. Traub-Merz & K. Ngok (Eds.), *Industrial democracy in China: With additional studies on Germany, South-Korea and Vietnam* (pp. 11–51). Beijing: China Social Sciences Press.

Whyte, M. K. (Ed.). (2010). *One country, two societies: Rural–urban inequality in contemporary China.* Cambridge: Harvard University Press.

Whyte, M. K. (2014). Soaring income gaps: China in comparative perspective. *Dædalus, 143*(2), 39–52.

Wong, C. (2011). The fiscal stimulus programme and public governance issues in China. *OECD Journal on Budgeting.* Retrieved from http://www.oecd.org/gov/budgeting/49633058.pdf

Xu, F. (2014). Temporary work in China: Precarity in an emerging labour market. In J. Fudgeand & K. Strauss (Eds.), *Temporary work, agencies, and unfree labour: Insecurity in the new world of work* (pp. 143–163). New York, NY: Routledge.

Yan, H. (2008). *New masters, new servants: Migration, development, and women workers in China.* Durham, NC: Duke University Press.

Zhang, L. (2015). *Inside China's automobile factories: The politics of labour and worker resistance.* New York, NY: Cambridge University Press.

Dockworkers' Resistance and Union Reform within China's Globalised Seaport Industry

XUEBING CAO* & QUAN MENG**

*Keele Management School, Keele University, Staffordshire, UK
**School of Labour Economics, Capital University of Economics and Business, Beijing, People's Republic of China

ABSTRACT *This study examines the prominent 2013 Yantian dock strike in China and analyses the main factors contributing to the dockers' successful campaign. It finds that the dockers' capacity to take strike action mainly derives from their bargaining power, including structural power such as workplace bargaining power and logistical power, and their institutional power such as workers' sense of moral power. More importantly, the event shows that the extent of dockworkers' resistance, workplace union reform, and employers' response were shaped by the globalisation of production in China's seaport industry and the transformation of political economy in East Asia.*

Introduction

On 1 September 2013, hundreds of gantry and tower crane operators lodged a non-union strike in Yantian International Containers Terminal (YICT) and paralysed the world's biggest single-site container handling port, in Shenzhen, China (CLB, 2013; T. Wang, 2014). After two days' mediation and negotiation, the dispute was settled with the workers' victory against their employer, Hutchison Port Holdings (HPH), one of the biggest global port operators, demonstrating the dockworkers' impressive bargaining power. Coincidentally, the event happened only four months after the end of a bitter and lengthy dispute in nearby Hong Kong International Terminals, which is also owned by HPH (Cheng, 2014, p. 218). The strike showed Yantian dockworkers' persistent struggles against transnational capital within China's globalised seaport industry, adding to the recent wave of collective unrest protesting the labour regime in China (Gray, 2015). It is surprising, however, that there was not adequate media coverage on the 2013 dispute, or in-depth academic studies.

Following China's dramatic economic development, including the expansion of the transport industry, Chinese workers have enjoyed more employment opportunities, but many have also experienced low pay and poor working conditions. Yet the labour movement has been hindered by the country's unitary industrial relations system and the malfunctioning official union organisation, the All-China Federation of Trade Unions (ACFTU), which remains 'categorically opposed to worker mobilisation' (Friedman & Lee, 2010, p. 524). Often Chinese unions can only manoeuvre between the government and labour, because they must balance their dual institutional identity—as government affiliates on the one hand and workers' organisations on the other (Chen, 2010, p. 108).

Despite the lack of organised labour movements, Chinese workers' unorganised collective resistance is not uncommon as industrial conflicts have grown significantly in recent years. Labour unrest, supported by workers' growing awareness of rights protection, is based on their disruptive capacity in response to globalised capital relocation and restructuring (Silver, 2003; Wright, 2000). Yet Chinese workers' resistance, such as the 2013 Yantian dispute that reflects dockers' bargaining power and the state of labour organisations, is also grounded in the development of labour agencies that are shaped by national and international environments. As Gray (2015) states, labour relations in East Asia are characterised by workers' resistance against global capitalism and subordination in various processes of 'passive revolution' both within and beyond workplaces. Meanwhile, it is important to acknowledge the essence of cultural, organisational, and political dynamics for the formation of workers' class consciousness (Koo, 2001). In this context, the 2013 Yantian strike poses a number of interesting questions: How did the strike break out? What did the dockers' workplace union and management do during the strike? What are the main factors contributing to the dockers' successful campaign? How was the strike linked with the dockers' capacity to disrupt production? How should we elucidate the Yantian workers' bargaining power and the state of workplace union organisation?

To respond to these queries, two fieldwork visits were undertaken between August 2014 and May 2015. Access was obtained through trade unions, so the researchers were able to conduct interviews with three union officials and seven workers. All the workers interviewed experienced the 2013 dispute, with the union officials being involved with the mediation and negotiation process. Data have also been drawn from secondary sources, namely printed and online reports from both foreign and Chinese media. To maintain confidentiality, all the interviewees are anonymous and their names are coded.

The rest of the paper consists of five parts. First, it discusses theories of dock strike by analysing the cultural explanation and dockers' workplace bargaining power, as well as the impact of technology and globalisation. Second, it briefly introduces the organisational context of the 2013 Yantian dispute. The third and fourth parts evaluate the 2013 strike process, with detailed discussion of management's response, workers' bargaining power and mobilisation, and the role of the trade union. The paper concludes by highlighting the dispute's implication for the transformation of the Chinese labour movement, and the impact of changing political economy on industrial conflicts in China's globalised seaport industry.

Dockworkers, Strikes, and Bargaining Power

Industrial Conflict at the Docks

Ports and shipping are central to the economic globalisation process, as more than 80% of global trade (by weight) with origins or destinations in developing countries is waterborne (Turnbull, 2000, p. 376). The degree of industrial peace is vital to docks because workplace conflict can significantly disrupt the transportation of goods within the global shipping line. However, historically, dockers are among those 'strike-prone' occupations that are featured with strong union organisations and frequent mass industrial actions (Hamark, 2013; Hyman, 1984). In Britain, for instance, docks stood out up to the 1980s as 'the most strike-prone sector', with 50% of dockers on strike each year compared with 5% of other non-coal workers (Edwards, 1995, p. 451).

The traditional debate about dockers' strike proneness hinged on the extent to which this is associated with dockers' occupational, cultural, and organisational characteristic, recurrent grievances, and effective union mobilisation. Kerr and Siegel (1954, pp. 203–204) attributed this to dockers' isolated mass status, strong sense of closed community, higher degree of internal cohesion, and unique identity detached from the external society. Dock work was said to require heavy, physical effort, and dangerous operation, with their accident rate being one of the highest in all industrial occupations (Miller, 1969, p. 306). Doing physically demanding and dangerous jobs made dockers tough and combative workers who were more likely to strike (Kerr & Siegel, 1954, p. 195).

The isolated mass thesis has been questioned by many commentators. As Edwards (1977) puts it, the main reason for frequent conflict in the docks is the changing management practices that have generated more grievances. Dockers are not usually exclusively separated from other communities, and the model of workplace relationship should not be a static and isolated one for such claim 'fails to explain variations over time and also within industries' (Edwards, 1995, p. 449). Nonetheless, this is not to dismiss the idea of community and the sense of common purpose that can help understand the dynamic character of workplace relations, and dockers' ability to mobilise and sustain collective solidarity (Blyton & Turnbull, 2004, p. 345).

However in recent years, docks around the world have become a relatively quieter arena where the frequency of strike has been much less than before (Silver, 2003, pp. 99–100). Part of the change is linked to technological innovation largely resulting from the increasingly globalised sea port industry worldwide. In particular, the containerisation and the growing volume of global freight logistics have reshaped the scale of port infrastructure, accompanied with the intensification of global capital investment and the use of labour-saving technology (Hall, 2009, pp. 68–69). The deregulation of employment schemes, together with new work practices such as just-in-time and casualisation (Turnbull & Wass, 2007, p. 587), has dramatically downsized the historically militant dock labour force and in large part accounts for the dramatic decline in labour unrest (Silver, 2003, p. 111). Yet dockers still possess a strong sense of solidarity and collectivity (Turnbull, 2000, p. 375). While some unions have found it harder to protect members' interests against multinational corporations, many other unions' resistance is more successful (Turnbull & Wass, 2007, p. 609). As dockers strive to 'retain control of traditional dock work' (Edwards, 1995, p. 452), bitter disputes continue to emerge in the waterfront where dockers keep resisting the threats of job removal and wage squeeze in an increasingly globalised industry.

Bargaining Power, Globalisation, and Technological Innovation

Another powerful account of dockers' capacity to strike is the notion of bargaining power, including associational power and structural power (Wright, 2000, p. 957). Associational power is supported by unions and political parties, while structural power includes market bargaining power that comes from the tight labour market and workplace bargaining power that comes from 'workers' strategic position of a particular group of workers within a key industrial sector' (Wright, 2000, p. 962). Associational power can also be moral or symbolic power, involving 'the struggle of "right" against "wrong", providing a basis for an appeal both to the public and politicians, as well as to allies in civil society' (Webster, Lambert, & Bezuidenhout, 2008, p. 12). Workplace bargaining power refers to dockers' bargaining advantage and disruptive potential ability to 'harm distribution, production and profit' (Hamark, 2013, p. 279), and their 'remarkable degree of autonomy and control' (Turnbull, 2001, p. 367). Dockers are among some jobs that are 'central to the production process, with a high disruptive potential' (Martin, 1992, p. 36). Because the disruption caused by transport workers' struggles can usually have a high level of deterrence as it will go beyond the transportation and logistics network, they 'have possessed and continue to possess relatively strong workplace bargaining power' (Silver, 2003, p. 100). In addition, dockers may also possess another type of structural power, logistical power, which can take 'matters out of the workplace and onto the landscape where workplaces are located' (Webster et al., 2008, p. 13).

For docks around the world, the economic globalisation and technological advancement have had profound influence on the changing dynamics of workplace labour relations. Since the 1950s, containerisation, the foremost port labour-saving technology, has radically altered port-cargo-handling methods across the world (Schwarz-Miller & Talley, 2002, p. 529). But its impact on dockers' capacity to strike is not a straightforward picture. On the one hand, dockers' bargaining power is threatened by improved productivity, increased automation, and reduced demand for dock labour force, mainly casual and periphery workers (Martin, 1992, p. 170). For instance in the USA, due to the use of new machinery, by the mid-1980s dockworker jobs declined 60% compared with the level in the 1970s at most ports (Schwarz-Miller & Talley, 2002, p. 529). Job losses and increased substitutability of labour can directly lead to dockers' decreased market bargaining power, union membership, and associational power. Moreover, the automated operation means most dockworkers are increasingly working in isolated small units, making it harder for them to develop collegiate spirit and solidarity. It also makes the defence of workers' collective interests more difficult due to the increased flexibility of work (Martin, 1992, p. 170).

On the other hand, new technologies may enhance core dockers' bargaining power, because now the operation of modern ports, closely integrated with global production and supply chains, is more vulnerable and these skilled dockers could find it easier to disrupt production than before thanks to higher cost related to disruption. First, the expansion of containerised cargo ports has increased the demand for skilled dockworkers that can handle the modern machinery, and reinforced their market and workplace bargaining powers that are derived from their strategic position within the production process. Port employers, meanwhile, are more reluctant to see industrial disputes due to 'the rising costs from disruptions in the utilization of expensive port infrastructures and container ships' (Schwarz-Miller & Talley, 2002, p. 529).

Second, dockworker unions have renewed their mobilisation strategies to respond to the changing political and economic environments. For example, after the 1980s, American dock unions increased their campaigns for negotiating work conservation schemes and securing pay rises, and made some gains through these activities (Schwarz-Miller & Talley, 2002, p. 528). But meanwhile employers have updated their counter-strategies that are also empowered by technological fixes (Silver, 2003, p. 101). Third, modern technology is influential for empowering workers' logistical power. For instance during the 1995–1998 Liverpool dock dispute, dockers used the internet to call for international unions' support (Carter, Stewart, Hogan, & Kornberger, 2003, p. 302). Such logistical power is important as it 'takes structural power outside the workplace and into the public domain' (Webster et al., 2008, p. 13). This is not to deny, of course, that the success of a dispute relies on many other factors, such as the employers' strategy, labour market conditions, and public support.

Industrial Relations in Yantian

The Development of YICT

The proliferation of China's container port industry, the world's fastest growing one in recent decades, has been dramatic since the early 1980s. As one of the major destinations for global foreign direct investment and a manufacturing powerhouse, China needs a significant logistic system, such as shipping and ports, to support the economic advancement (Thun, 2014, p. 302). Between 1982 and 2000, the annual increase rate of seaport container throughput was more than 10%, with the importance of container cargos to China's sea ports jumping from less than 5% in 1980 to nearly 60% in 1998 (Cullinane, Fei, & Cullinane, 2004, p. 35). Now China is a dominant player in the international ocean transport sector, and there has been a huge amount of investment, including foreign capital, being poured into the country's container transport industry (Cullinane et al., 2004). One of the most prominent ports is Yantian port (YICT), the country's largest single-site container terminal and the only major seaport controlled by a foreign company.

YICT was established in 1994 as a joint venture, and has been since controlled by Hong Kong-based HPH. Yantian port is within a cluster of giant seaports along China's southern coast line that encompasses over 60% of the country's total container throughput (Cullinane et al., 2004, p. 39). In only 20 years, YICT developed 16 large deep-water container berths, becoming the busiest container cargo port in China and a main hub for international shipping in the region (K. Wang, 2014). The company's leading position is reinforced by its location in South China, which is the so-called 'world factory' region offering huge flow of import and export cargoes, making YICT an important part in the global supply chain. On the other hand, YICT's business is often constrained by China's cumbersome customs procedures and 'anything else involving substantial government input' (Cullinane et al., 2004, p. 52).

YICT directly employs 2300 staff, 800 of whom are crane operators (HPH, 2013). In addition, there are 3000 sub-contracted employees working around the port to provide peripheral and support services. Within its management team is the well-known YICT union (affiliated to the ACFTU) that is branded by the authorities as a 'model workplace union' (T. Wang, 2014). The union distinguishes itself by a 'democratic' direct election system, one of the very few such types in contemporary China as its chair person is elected every three years (Interview 7); although in fact, this was pushed by Yantian dockworkers in the first place after a high-profile dispute in 2007. Nevertheless, the state mediation, in this case a relaxation of the strict labour regime in a foreign-invested port, seems to provide some room for workers' collective resistance and some (limited) degree of union democracy.

The 2007 Dispute and Union Election

The 2007 Yantian union direct election was not a voluntary experiment; rather it was a tentative attempt triggered by the workers' spontaneous strike, which was the result of dockers' grievances over low pay and the lack of employee voice mechanism. A non-union firm at the time, YICT had already been very successful in its expansion, achieving a profit increase of nearly fivefold in the past 10 years (Wang, 2013). But employees did not get a corresponding pay rise for a number of years and their discontent accumulated gradually until a number of crane operators started the strike on 7 April 2007 (CLB, 2013). The walkout resulted in an immediate stoppage of the port operation and serious disruption to the regional supply chain. Dockers' demands included not only better wages, but also the 'somewhat unusual demand to set up their own union, an indication of their desire to exercise greater control over their own workplace' (Friedman & Lee, 2010, p. 520). The strike was settled promptly, and workers were soon offered a wage increase and immediate union establishment through election.

As a turning point in China's contemporary labour history, the 2007 YICT union election reform signalled that grassroots union reform became possible. Workers in the nearby region's companies started to follow this model and asked for establishing union organisations, including the high-profile 2010 Nanhai Honda strike (Lyddon, Cao, Meng, & Lu, 2015). Despite its shortcomings such as the controlled nomination, YICT reform has been regarded as a landmark event (Wang, 2013) and a significant step forward for the ACFTU since never before had any union officials been directly elected in China's transport industry. Yet workers' growing consciousness was not accidental; rather it was deeply rooted in the transformation of the political economy of the region, especially the Chinese government's changing dispute resolution method used to sustain globalised capitalist production (Gray, 2015). After the election the Yantian workplace union played a key role in helping establish wage collective consultation mechanisms and maintain regular union elections. In the following 6 years, through annual wage consultations, employees had a 'steady and continuous pay rise', contributing to what the ACFTU regarded as 'more harmonious labour relations' and 'increasingly higher working enthusiasm' among dockworkers (Workers Daily, 2011). It seemed that the reform was able to bring in industrial peace, which was kept until September 2013 when a new strike broke out again in YICT.

The 2013 Yantian Strike Process

The September 2013 Yantian dispute was another unorganised sit-in strike, as workers exercised their bargaining power again through spontaneous and collective action. It is important to note that in early 2013, dockers in Hong Kong Terminals (HIT) held a 40-day strike, which featured intense collective bargaining from beginning to end and independent unions that played a leading role. During the event, over 400 dock crane operators demanded a 20% pay rise and better working conditions, paralysing the world's third-busiest container port (wsj.com, 2013). A wide range of societal demonstrations, rallies, and donations offered significant political and financial support to the dockers who had been undermined by the limited political space for the labour movement (Cheng, 2014, p. 218). The strike was eventually settled with a 9.8% pay rise after the employer endured considerable political and economic pressures. With a 'half-victory' (SCMP, 2013), the Hong Kong dock strike made workers better understand their labour rights and bargaining power. On the other hand, despite YICT and HIT being both operated by HPH, Yantian dockers were not directly connected with their Hong Kong counterparts working only 50 miles away, because they worked in two completely different systems (labour market, industrial relations climate, and legal environment). But the Hong Kong dispute was widely reported by China's official media, including Xinhuanet (2013), which looked at the strike and negotiation processes. The Hong Kong dockers' fight against the city's richest tycoon and his sub-contractors was inspirational for colleagues around the world, certainly including those in Yantian, many of whom had suffered serious pressures from globalisation and intensification of work.

Hiller (1969) pointed out that strikers usually needed to have justifications for their behaviour. To this end, YICT workers' demand for a 2000–3000 Yuan pay rise was linked with their grievance over the company's changes in housing benefits and education subsidies, something that would see 'workers' net income being cut' (Interview 6). The stoppage happened during the shift change at 8:00 on the Sunday morning, 1 September 2013, initiated by a group of day-shift gantry crane operators, who refused to operate their machinery (T. Wang, 2014). These operators' action was soon followed by more tower crane operators, who also stopped working (CLB, 2013). Admittedly it was not a well-coordinated event since there was no union involvement in the beginning, nor did any striking workers ask the union to step in. Soon the action spread to the majority of the workforce and workers marched around the office building and then gathered in the dining hall discussing their tactics (Interview 7). Despite the union's non-involvement, the dockers were able to stand together with their collective demand, as many of them had experienced the spontaneous strike in 2007.

Over the years, due to management's dominance during the wage consultation process, Yantian dockers' real concerns were rarely taken into account by the company. The 500 Yuan allowance, given to crane operators after the 2007 dispute, gradually lost its importance as employees in other positions were also awarded similar allowances. In addition, the 9-grade pay structure, being set up after 2007 to reflect a widened gap between different grades, caused many workers' complaints of 'unequal distribution' between similar jobs. For instance, tower crane operators could only be paid about 6000 Yuan, but gantry crane operators received 9000–10,000 Yuan. Furthermore, in 2013 YICT implemented a new housing fund policy that saw most employees' net income reduced, and this resulted in grievances among most workers who believed that the company was too mean (T. Wang, 2014). Despite the company' successful business achievement and steady pay rise, workers still felt they were being unfairly treated and some, especially crane operators, believed that YICT was not generous in paying its employees (Interview 6). The company was said not to care about workers' real concerns. As one crane operator said:

> This housing fund (in 2013) led to a pay cut in real terms compared with our increased contribution. We could only get 5,000 Yuan net income each month and how could you buy property in Shenzhen with such a low income? We have to live and raise our families, especially children. The company should seriously listen to our concerns. (Interview 2)

The stoppage was initiated by gantry crane operators who were deeply worried about the loss caused by the housing fund change, although they were paid higher than some other staff in the port. Just half an hour later, the workplace union officials were called back to the company to help solve the situation and act as mediator. It was a peculiar bargaining scene because managers and workers did not talk face to face, with the union acting as the middle agency, passing messages between the two parties (Interview 7). As the company tried, but failed, to persuade workers to resume work, soon the whole Yantian port production stopped and cargo lorries started to form a long queue along the road outside the port (Chinaworker.org, 2013).

The first day's negotiation lasted until two o'clock in the morning, with little progress being made because management refused to make substantial concessions and workers also had different ideas from time to time. Dockers were unable to agree with a clear and consistent target, and it was difficult for strikers to carry on mobilising collective interests when there was no institutional organisation and proper leadership. By the next morning the senior official from Shenzhen municipal union came and helped the mediation. Meanwhile, more port employees joined the strike, including most support and control room staff (Interview 6). While the operation was stopped, huge numbers of containers were left in the port without being inspected or loaded/unloaded (Interview 7). The company was also under pressure from the local government, which was 'deeply concerned' about the impact of the strike (CLB, 2013). After a few rounds of intensive talks, a deal was finally struck, and workers ended the strike at 4 p.m. in the afternoon. The settlement was to offer all workers an equivalent 30% pay rise, about 1700 Yuan increase per month (T. Wang, 2014).

YICT, Dockworkers, and Workplace Union During the Strike

What Made the YICT to Compromise Again?

YICT quickly settled the dispute mainly because the company was worried about the economic and political impact. Economically the company needed to maintain a steady operation and competitive advantage (K. Wang, 2014), and a stable employment relationship is vital for retaining such a position. For YICT, it was sensible to settle the strike swiftly, because in an industry where there is worker flexibility, high capital investment, and tightly coupled supply chains, firms tend to prioritise the avoidance of disputes (Martin, 1992, p. 181), and this is even more so in globalised container ports (Turnbull & Wass, 2007).

Politically the government and ACFTU did not want any workplace conflict escalated, and the transport industry is a sensitive area for foreign investment (CLB, 2013). The government's key concern was to avoid the domino effect of wider social unrest. For YICT, maintaining a good relationship with the authorities was vital, and a quick settlement could pacify such concern and avoid further loss.

The Role of the Workplace Union

Prior to the walkout, the dockers' secretive mobilisation was unknown to union officials, and the union's intervention was initially resisted by strikers. However, the union did play a key role during the negotiation process after the union was able to be accepted and trusted by both the dockworkers and management. As one of the union officials said

> Obviously we were under pressure when we were given such an important role to convince workers to resume production. But we were also proud of the fact that the union was the only organisation that was trusted by both the staff and the company senior management; . . . for the company, we are very important. (Interview 7)

The union was accepted by workers because they 'didn't want to stand out by themselves as they might worry about job security; . . . so by the end they agreed that the union could represent them in negotiations' (Interview 7). With workers needing formal leadership the union acted as a mediator and coordinator to look after strikers' opinions. It was acknowledged by some workers that the union chair was popular because 'he is a great guy who has helped us a lot' (Interview 2). The final negotiation and settlement were also facilitated by the union as well.

The contribution of the YICT union demonstrates the fact that union intervention can help to institutionalise conflict (Mills, 1948) and, in the case of China, to defuse conflict (Chen, 2010, p. 105). As one union official suggested, collective bargaining could happen during the dispute 'when both management and workers accepted us as the formal "middle man" in negotiations' (Interview 7). Nevertheless, this was only a one-off process, and since the end of the 2013 dispute, the union has not been given any official role to represent workers in collective bargaining.

Yantian Dockers' Bargaining Power

The dispute shows Yantian dockworkers' great courage and capacity to defend their interests through unorganised action. It is likely that what workers learned in the 2007 dispute helped them to start another strike. As Edwards (1995) argues, 'there is an established habit to the use of strike, and once it has become accepted as the means to resolve disputes, its use becomes taken for granted' (p. 450). But more importantly, it was dockworkers' bargaining power that was able to help their successful campaign. Such power came from their jobs as the key operators in a busy container port, the extended support from more fellow colleagues, and their effective mobilisation tactics.

First, Yantian dockers' high degree of disruptive capacity is based on their structural power, mainly workplace bargaining power, relevant to the particular nature of the dock labour process and the use of modern cargo-handling technology that has made the port operation more vulnerable to disruption. In 2012, YICT made a historical breakthrough by achieving 100 million TEUs (twenty-foot equivalent unit) annual throughput, a threshold marking the port's world-class status (T. Wang, 2014). Such improvement in productivity and efficiency does mean that any disruption of production will cause significant damage to the company. Dockers believed that they were very important because 'most operation positions are not easy to be immediately substituted in the local labour market' (Interview 6), and once the strike started, the disruption 'could cost the company a lot of money in a very short period of time' (Interview 9).

Dockers' structural power also includes their logistical power. Although much of Yantian dockers' mobilisation process was not known to the public, and nobody has been identified as the strike leader, the dockers effectively utilised social media, especially mobile phones and the internet, to communicate and mobilise. Their job did not allow them to gather often, but they found opportunities to be together when they were off work and exchanged ideas by using online chatrooms such as QQ and Wechat, through which some important conversations could be undertaken to determine the time and actions of the first stoppage (T. Wang, 2014). As one docker remembered:

> Concerned with the housing fund policy, crane operators felt deep pressure because their net income reduced more significantly . . . So before the strike started many colleagues spoke up about their feelings in the QQ chat rooms. The housing fund problem suddenly escalated the conflict . . . . (Interview 6)

This type of logistical power strengthened dockers' preparation, as the cyberspace communication can 'provide the opportunity to create new networks' that help workers to reconfigure space and coordinate campaigns (Webster et al., 2008, p. 192).

Second, Yantian dockworkers did have a certain level of associational power, although such power was limited. Despite the absence of union organising, there was a sense of collectivism among strikers, demonstrated by the extended strike participation, increasing from about a few hundred operators in 2007 to nearly the entire workforce in 2013. In addition, the union network was used by workers as many strikers were also workplace union committee members. During the dispute, dockers used the union office space as their base to discuss demands and negotiation strategies. As described by a senior union official, 'the small union meeting room was stuffed with the union committee members who were also on strike; ... our first meeting took one hour before we could get a closer sense of workers' demand' (T. Wang, 2014).

Another type of associational power is dockers' moral power. Although dockers might have a lower degree of collectivity at work due to separated operation system, the discontent regarding pay and job intensification did strengthen their determination to unite together (Interview 6). As one operator said:

> The crane job is not easy as we all have back injuries. We are concerned about the consequences of working high above the ground, but this has not been taken care of by the company. We cannot work too long and we might have to retire earlier, or transfer to another job. (Interview 4)

Such sentiment was shared by many dockers in Yantian. One tower crane operator admitted that he was deeply concerned about his health, as a doctor had recommended him not to continue doing such a dangerous and heavy job as crane operation. He said: 'I definitely cannot continue this job until 60 [when I retire]. It is not about income but the company must care about our health' (Interview 1). With common interests relating to pay and working conditions, the sense of injustice and grievance made Yantian workers focus on finding the way in which these could be changed. When dockers had a common sense of grievance it was easier to form a united and powerful alliance.

Conclusion

The 2013 Yantian strike demonstrates Chinese dockers' collective resistance, just like their Hong Kong counterparts a few months earlier, against multinational capital in a globalised waterfront. Despite the absence of strong institutional support from official unions, Yantian dockers used alternative methods to mobilise themselves, showing the extent of Chinese workers' defiance of the labour regime and subordination (Gray, 2015). In many respects it reflects the strength of dockers' capacity to mobilise due to traditionally strong community and occupational culture, and the dynamics of job control and workers' bargaining power, especially the strong structural power at the point of production (Silver, 2003). Such power came from the dockworkers' position within the production process and the vulnerability of the container port operation that is shadowed by technological innovation and globalised supply chain. Social media offered the dockers alternative means of logistical power, which was helpful for the campaign because it was less hindered by workplace management. The unorganised dockers were supported by large numbers of colleagues and the negotiations were assisted by the workplace union, offering a sense of associational power although such power was delicate and limited.

On the other hand, Yantian workers' bargaining power would not easily be materialised if the internal and external contexts were different, as the transformation of the labour movement in East Asia is not isolated from historical, cultural, and political dimensions (Gray, 2015). Like Korea's labour movement in the 1980s and 1990s (Koo, 2001), Chinese workers' struggle is shaped by globalisation that has complex consequence for the formation of a new generation of working class, and the status of labour organisations is also adjusted by particular experiences of the country's changing labour regime (Gray, 2008, p. 28). More importantly, because economic globalisation has made container terminal operators extremely cautious about 'the high cost of any disruption to shipping in ports' (Turnbull & Wass, 2007, p. 589), Yantian workers were able to succeed in this instance; in contrast to the 2013 Hong Kong dock strike which became a public event and drew world-wide attention, the Yantian strike was not widely known due to the authority's censorship on media coverage. However, the two cases share a common feature, as they both helped workers to further understand the importance of collective action in protecting their rights. The Yantian case recapitulates the fact that the development of Chinese industrial relations is pertinent to unorganised workers who 'have imposed great pressures on employers' (Liu & Li, 2014, p. 86). As Gray (2015, p. 151) highlights, the recent labour unrest in the country represents 'a qualitative shift towards a militant workers' consciousness capable of challenging Chinese labour subordination'. Yet like most collective disputes in contemporary China, such a victory can be momentous because workers' protests are still 'constrained by existing political conditions' (Friedman & Lee, 2010, p. 521). The headway of China's labour movement, like what has been happening in Yantian, will primarily depend on the unpredictable development of the region's political economy.

The event also manifests the dilemma of the highly praised 'Yantian union model' in sustaining industrial peace. It may be plausible to claim that direct elections are generally positive, but they 'cannot solve everything' (Wang, 2013) since the so-called democratic election is hindered by political, institutional, and structural problems (Howell, 2008, p. 861). Yantian workers have not been given substantial democratic rights after the 2013 dispute and their workplace union, like those affiliated to ACFTU, has not changed much. Ironically just a few months later, in May 2014, YICT was 'honoured' with the 'May 1st Labour Medal', the ACFTU's highest award, for its 'excellent maintenance of the harmonious workplace labour relations' (Chinaports.org, 2014). At the same time, it was rumoured that a few strike activists had been quietly sacked by YICT after the dispute (Interview 6). Again, it is the political economy of Chinese labour that plays a major role in influencing the extent of worker resistance and union reform, as well as employers' response (Gray, 2015). Hence Yantian workers may need the workplace union that can help enhance their bargaining power. Despite the dockers' strength to take collective action, such compromise and corporation are necessary, since there are always 'harsh realities of employment relationships' in the dockyard (Turnbull, 2001, p. 372).

Acknowledgements

The authors wish to thank Dave Lyddon, the editors of the journal, and three referees for their very helpful comments on earlier drafts of this article.

Disclosure Statement

No potential conflict of interest was reported by the authors.

References

Blyton, P., & Turnbull, P. (2004). *The dynamics of employee relations* (3rd ed.). Basingstoke: Palgrave MacMillan.

Carter, C., Stewart, C., Hogan, J., & Kornberger, M. (2003). The polyphonic spree: The case of the Liverpool dockers. *Industrial Relations Journal, 34*(4), 290–304.

Chen, F. (2010). Quadripartite interactions of strike settlement in China. *China Quarterly, 201*, 104–124.

Cheng, J. Y. (2014). The emergence of radical politics in Hong Kong: Causes and impact. *The China Review, 14*(1), 199–232.

Chinaports.org. (2014). *YICT was awarded 'May 1st Labour Medal'*. http://shenzhen.chinaports.org/News_info.htm?id = 174748

Chinaworker.org. (2013). *HPH Shenzhen Yantian workers struck again*. Retrieved from http://chinaworker.info/ccn/2013/09/03/3935/

CLB. (2013). Labour unrest in China: The absence of collective bargaining. *China Labour Bulletin*. Retrieved from http://www.clb.org.hk

Cullinane, K., Fei, W. T., & Cullinane, S. (2004). Container terminal development in mainland china and its impact on the competitiveness of the port of Hong Kong. *Transport Reviews*, *24*(1), 33–56.

Edwards, P. (1977). A critique of the Kerr-Siegel hypothesis of strikes and the isolated mass: A study of the falsification of sociological knowledge. *The Sociological Review*, *25*(3), 551–574.

Edwards, P. (1995). Strikes and industrial conflict. In P. Edwards (Eds.), *Industrial relations: Theories and practices* (pp. 434–460). Oxford: Blackwell.

Friedman, E., & Lee, C. K. (2010). Remaking the world of Chinese labour: A 30-year retrospective. *British Journal of Industrial Relations*, *48*(3), 507–526.

Gray, K. (2008). *Korean workers and neoliberal globalization*. New York, NY: Routledge.

Gray, K. (2015). *Labour and development in East Asia: Social forces and passive revolution*. London: Routledge.

Hall, P. (2009). Container ports, local benefits and transportation worker earnings. *Geojournal*, *74*(1), 67–83.

Hamark, J. (2013). Strikingly indifferent: The myth of militancy on the docks prior to World War II. *Labor History*, *54*(3), 271–285.

Hiller, E. T. (1969). *The strike: A study in collective action*. New York, NY: Arno Press.

Howell, J. (2008). All-China Federation of Trades Unions beyond reform? The slow march of direct elections. *The China Quarterly*, *196*, 845–863.

HPH. (2013). *Handling vessels any size any time*. Hutchison Port Holdings Trust 2013 annual report. Retrieved from http://hphtrust.listedcompany.com/misc/ar2013/ar2013_l.pdf

Hyman, R. (1984). *Strikes* (3rd ed.). London: Fontana.

Kerr, C., & Siegel, A. (1954). The inter industry propensity to strike: An international comparison. In A. Kornhauser, R. Dubin, & A. M. Ross (Eds.), *Industrial conflict* (pp. 189–212). New York, NY: McGraw Hill.

Koo, H. (2001). *Korean workers: The culture and politics of class formation*. Ithaca, NY: Cornell University Press.

Liu, M., & Li, C. (2014). Environment pressures, managerial industrial relations ideologies and unionisation in Chinese enterprises. *British Journal of Industrial relations*, *52*(1), 82–111.

Lyddon, D., Cao, X., Meng, Q., & Lu, J. (2015). A strike of 'unorganised' workers in a Chinese car factory: the Nanhai Honda events of 2010. *Industrial Relations Journal*, *46*(2), 134–152.

Martin, R. (1992). *Bargaining power*. Oxford: Clarendon Press.

Miller, R. (1969). The dockworker subculture and some problems in cross-cultural and cross-time generalizations. *Comparative Studies in Society and History*, *11*(3), 302–312.

Mills, C. W. (1948). *The new men of power*. New York, NY: Harcourt Brace.

Schwarz-Miller, A., & Talley, W. K. (2002). Technology and labor relations: Railroads and ports. *Journal of Labor Research*, *23*(4), 513–520.

SCMP. (2013, May 8). Everyone a loser after Hong Kong dock strike ends. *South China Morning Post*. Retrieved from http://www.scmp.com/news/hong-kong/article/1232519/strike-end-sees-all-involved-losers

Silver, B. J. (2003). *Forces of labor: Workers' movements and globalization since 1870*. Cambridge: Cambridge University Press.

Thun, E. (2014). The globalization of production. In J. Ravenhill (Eds.), *Global political economy* (pp. 283–305). Oxford: Oxford University Press.

Turnbull, P. (2000). Contesting globalisation on the waterfront. *Politics and Society*, *28*(3), 367–391.

Turnbull, P. (2001). Rethinking dock work [Book Review]. *Labour History Review*, *66* (3), 367–380.

Turnbull, P., & Wass, C. (2007). Defending dock workers: Globalisation and labor relations in the world's ports. *Industrial Relations*, *46*(3), 582–612.

Wang, K. (2014). An introduction of the development experience and future prospect of Shenzhen Yantian International Container Terminals. *Technological Innovation and Application*, *29*, 13–14.

Wang, T. (2013). Pass the power back to workers. *Chinese Worker*. Retrieved from http://www.chineseworkers.com.cn/_d276227433.htm

Wang, T. (2014). The unbearable lightness of the collective consultation system: The process and reflection of the Yantian 9.1 strike. *Chinese Workers*. Retrieved from http://www.chineseworkers.com.cn/_d276640243.htm

Webster, E., Lambert, R., & Bezuidenhout, A. (2008). *Grounding globalizations: Labour in the age of insecurity*. Oxford: Blackwell.

Workers Daily. (2011, July 25). *YICT's wage collective consultation has led to 'two highs'*.

Wright, E. O. (2000). Working-class power, capitalist-class interests, and class compromise. *American Journal of Sociology*, *105*(4), 957–1002.

WSJ.com. (2013, April 8). Hong Kong strike hits tycoon's image. *Wall Street Journal*. Retrieved from http://www.wsj.com/articles/SB10001424127887323550604578410233885297880

Xinhuanet. (2013, March 29). *Strike broke out in Li Ka-Sing's dock*. Retrieved from http://news.xinhuanet.com/gangao/2013-03/29/c_124519064.htm

Interview List

Interview 1, YICT tower crane operator, May 2015
Interview 2, YICT gantry crane operator, May 2015
Interview 3, YICT gantry crane operator, May 2015
Interview 4, YICT gantry crane operator, May 2015
Interview 5, YICT coach driver, May 2015
Interview 6, YICT engineer department, May 2015
Interview 7, YICT union official, August 2014
Interview 8, YICT union official, August 2014
Interview 9, YICT port security department, May 2015
Interview 10, YICT union official, May 2015

The Yue Yuen Strike: Industrial Transformation and Labour Unrest in the Pearl River Delta

STEFAN SCHMALZ*, BRANDON SOMMER** & HUI XU*

*Friedrich Schiller-University Jena, Jena, Germany
**International Institute of Social Studies, The Hague, The Netherlands

ABSTRACT *In April 2014, approximately 40,000 workers stalled production at Yue Yuen (YY) Gaobu, a shoemaker, in Guangdong, China. We identify three reasons for the strike: First, China's rise is leading to a wave of capital relocation to lower wage countries. Accordingly, YY Gaobu faces increasing pressure, which contributes to a deterioration of working conditions to save costs. Second, the Chinese Communist Party's anti-corruption campaign is creating new spaces for YY workers to push their demands. Third, there are increased worker protests regarding social insurance payments. Therefore, the strike is paradigmatic, because class composition (middle-aged migrant workers) and demands (social insurance) differ from earlier conflicts. Drawing on the theoretical framework of World-Systems Analysis and in-depth field research, we conclude that the strike will have a lasting effect on Chinese labour relations, because of its focus on social insurance.*

This article is based on 68 interviews and 4 focus groups with experts, managers, and migrant workers, conducted by the authors between June and September 2014 in Guangdong and Hong Kong on labour relations, precariousness, and industrial conflict in the Pearl River Delta. We conducted five interviews and one focus group at the Yue Yuen plant in Gaobu. Seven more interviews were carried out with experts in Guangzhou, Shenzhen, and Hong Kong directly referring to the strike, with one of the interviewees being an NGO activist involved in the strike. We are grateful to two anonymous reviewers for their comments and to the DFG Research Group on Post-Growth Societies at Friedrich Schiller-University Jena for financial support.

Introduction

In April 2014, more than 40,000 workers halted production at an important factory of the Yue Yuen (YY) group, a Taiwanese shoemaker, in Gaobu, Dongguan, Guangdong province, China. The workers' main demand was a reimbursement of embezzled social security payments. The strike lasted about two weeks and caused losses of tens of millions of US dollars. Plant operations were finally restored through intensive state intervention in the bargaining process between YY management and striking workers. State intervention included massive police repression against the workers. Negotiations eventually led to a promise to pay missing social benefits.

The YY strike was one important event in a series of strikes between 2013 and 2015 that affected many industries in Guangdong including electronics, textiles, and plastics (China Labor Bulletin, 2015). The YY strike was not only the largest industrial conflict in the last decade in the Pearl River Delta (PRD); it also spread to other factories in Dongguan as well as to other YY production sites in China. However, it was not the first surge of labour unrest in the PRD, which is the heartland of manufacturing in Guangdong. Strikes in Guangdong previously culminated in a particularly large strike wave in the spring of 2010, when workers stopped the assembly lines at Honda Auto Parts Manufacturing Co., Ltd. (CHAM) in Foshan and bargained for a wage increase of 800 RMB (at that time around US$120) and better representation of their interests at the plant level. Most scholars agree that the protest at Honda marked a watershed for the Chinese labour movement, because since 2010, workers have more assertively claimed wage increases and the organisation of strike actions has improved (Chan & Hui, 2014; Elfstrom & Kuruvilla, 2014).

In this paper, we argue that the YY conflict was a paradigmatic strike for Chinese labour relations. It stemmed from a generational change: Today, middle-aged and older migrant workers are actively involved in labour struggles. This is surprising in many respects, as this social group was often considered less assertive, because of their perceived ties to the countryside (Pun & Lu, 2010). Yet, because of the precarious position many workers face as they approach retirement and a host of recently introduced social insurance laws, they are now willing to strike for social insurance benefits, which was hitherto a marginal issue in labour struggles in the PRD. Furthermore, these conflicts are becoming increasingly influential: whereas in the past local officials and entrepreneurs tended to disregard legal standards, especially around social insurance to increase competitiveness, they must now respond to growing pressure from this increasingly assertive group of older workers.

In what follows, we situate our argument within a framework of World-Systems Analysis and, thus, within a global–historical understanding of the industrial transformation in Guangdong. We argue that China's rise is leading to a restructuring of global commodity chains, as wages grow and competitive pressure increases. Correspondingly, we identify three main reasons for the YY conflict. First, we explore how in light of these changes, the YY plant faced increasing competition, which led to a gradual deterioration of benefits and working conditions to save costs. Second, we examine how the political conflict between the central government and the Dongguan government over legal standards and corruption opened a window of opportunity for YY workers to push their demands. Third, we analyse the individual motivations of middle-aged and older workers stemming from their precarious positions after retirement, which is creating an increasing need to claim social insurance as promised to them within the law. We conclude with an overall analysis of the timeline and results of the strike. We argue that the strike will likely have far-reaching consequences for Guangdong's and China's industrial relations as pressure to put into practice existing rules in labour-intensive export industries is intensified.

China's Rise and Labour Unrest in Guangdong

Guangdong province was the laboratory for Chinese reform and opening-up policy, which began with Deng Xiaoping's 'Four Modernizations' in 1978. The government created China's first Special Economic Zones in Shenzhen, Zhuhai, and Shantou. After Deng Xiaoping's 'Southern Tour' in 1992, where he visited the special economic zones in the PRD, the region became a model for other provinces. In the early 1990s, Guangdong province contributed more than one-third of China's exports and received nearly one-third of all foreign direct investment (FDI) to China (Coughlin & Segev, 2000, pp. 7ff.). Low wages were the basis of this 'workshop of the world'. Entrepreneurs from Hong Kong and Taiwan contributed significantly. As rising labour costs and real estate prices in Hong Kong and Taiwan made businesses unprofitable, they relocated to the mainland. The result was not only fast economic development, but also a large inflow of rural migrant workers from poorer provinces. Today, more than 35 million people without urban residence live in Guangdong.

Consequently, export industries play an important role in Guangdong's economy. In their analysis of Chinese industrial relations, Lüthje, Luo, and Zhang (2013, pp. 24ff.) identify five different regimes of production; state bureaucratic, corporate bureaucratic, corporate high performance, flexible mass production, and low wage classic. The latter two regimes are characterised by low wages, extremely long working hours, a lack of collective agreements, and routine violations of legal standards. Additionally, mainly rural migrant workers are employed in these factories (Lüthje et al., 2013, pp. 27f.). For a long time, the Chinese Communist Party (CCP) did not question the PRD's economic model, which is particularly prevalent in the East of the Delta (e.g. Dongguan) and based on the aforementioned two regimes. Instead, it was considered successful in generating foreign exchange, jobs, economic growth, and for transferring technology.

However, the global financial crisis of 2008/2009 and the subsequent deep recession in the USA and Europe, exposed the fault lines that exist in China's current growth model, whereby the PRD's exports fell sharply by about two-thirds (Pettis, 2013, pp. 21ff.; Schmalz & Ebenau, 2012, pp. 496f.; Yu, 2010, p. 90). The global recession was a catalyst, highlighting pre-existing structural problems such as China's one-sided export orientation and overinvestment that magnified the crisis. In late 2008, the government approved a stimulus package of 4 trillion RMB (US$586 billion). Significant parts of these investments went into infrastructure. As only a fifth of the total expenditure went into measures to increase consumption, Chinese exports in 2010 hit pre-crisis levels, which demonstrates that the crisis did not substantially transform the Chinese economy (Naughton, 2010). Already before the crisis, important initiatives such as the new minimum wage legislation (2004) and the Labour Contract Law (2008) had been implemented, but these failed to significantly improve consumption. Therefore, additional reform initiatives followed. In 2011, the Chinese social security system for migrant workers was organised as a public insurance system. Employers and employees contribute money to a public welfare system, which includes pension insurance, health insurance, unemployment insurance, accident insurance, maternity leave, and a housing fund. The central government's Twelfth Five-Year Plan (2011–2015) went further including both targets to raise consumption through measures including an expansion of welfare systems, public wage increases, and investment projects in advanced technology. Other reforms were implemented by Guangdong's then-party secretary, Wang Yang. He coined the slogan that it is time to 'empty the cage to exchange the birds' to replace labour-intensive low-tech export industries with more technologically advanced industry. Accordingly, the provincial government identified high-tech enterprises as key priorities which are subsidised through tax breaks.

However, it is highly controversial whether the government's policy was successful. Since the crisis, China's high current account deficit decreased from 10.1% of GDP (2007) to 2.9% (2013), but most studies show that the low consumption share of GDP remains stable (e.g. Pettis, 2013, pp. 45ff.). And although export industries still dominate Guangdong's industrial structure, there is growing pressure to raise wages and growing state support to increase the consumption share. This pressure results in a restructuring and relocation of value chains, thus, industrial upgrading in Guangdong involves a relocation of low value-added industries to other low-wage locations (Butollo, 2014, pp. 83ff.; Zhu & Pickles, 2014). It is yet unclear if industrial upgrading will succeed and how it will affect working conditions. Despite aggregate real wage increases by one-third between 2007 and 2013 in Guangdong, industrial upgrading in some industries such as the garment industry has not seen a proportionate increase in wages and social benefits (Butollo, 2014, pp. 343ff.).

The rise of China and particularly Guangdong as a major export hub of global capitalism also led to labour protests. Most observers agree that in the 2000s, the character of protests changed, as labour struggles increasingly erupted in the coastal 'sunbelt' of Chinese private capitalism and were no longer limited to the effects of privatisation and restructuring of state-owned enterprises in the Northern 'rustbelt' (Lee, 2007, pp.157ff.). However, up to now, there is no effective institutionalised collective representation of interests to push workers' claims. The *All-China Federation of Trade Unions* (ACFTU) is a bureaucratic state institution that is not engaged on the shop floor level to represent workers or even to organise strikes (Friedman, 2014). Even though the ACFTU in Guangdong has begun to implement some reform measures (elections of delegates at the company level, etc.), the overall character of the union has not changed and workers frequently go on strike to push their demands without participation of, or even explicitly against, the official union. Recent economic instability has reduced the profitability of China's labour-intensive export industry and the emergence of new lower cost production sites in Southeast and South Asian countries has led to pressure to reduce labour costs resulting in layoffs in Guangdong's export industry. As a consequence, new struggles in the export sector such as the YY strike emerge in this process (China Labor Bulletin, 2015).

From a theoretical perspective, this restructuring can be seen as part of a larger process of historical capitalist development, as Silver (2003) argues in her study on labour unrest since 1870, which is inspired by a specific variety of World-Systems Analysis (Arrighi, 2011; Arrighi & Silver, 1999). Accordingly, the capitalist world-system is epitomized by a spatially uneven three-layered structure of core, semi-periphery, and periphery (Arrighi & Drangel, 1986). The trade of goods and services between core and periphery is characterised by unequal exchange. Therefore, in each zone, different economic activities prevail: today, core activities refer to the production of capital goods, specialised services, and R&D, while peripheral activities are mainly characterised by the export of commodities, agricultural goods, and labour-intensive manufacturing. Correspondingly, semi-peripheral countries such as China are identified by a mixture of both.

Moreover, the capitalist world-system tends to cyclical reorganisation. Hence, since the rise of historical capitalism in the fifteenth to sixteenth century, the centre of global capital accumulation and political power cyclically shifts from one nation state to another (Arrighi, 2011). Since the 1980s, China is moving to the centre of global capitalism, challenging US hegemony and leading to a reorganisation of global commodity chains. Silver (2003, pp. 74ff.) found that each such wave of geographical relocation of production in global capitalism also leads to a relocation of labour struggles. For instance, in late-industrialising countries such as Brazil or South Korea, labour movements emerged in the 1970s and 1980s alongside economic development.

Consequently, China as a large recipient of FDI and a global industrial centre is predicted to be the 'emerging epicentre of world labour unrest' (Silver & Lu, 2009).

Also, World-Systems Analysis considers actors and activities involved in global production part of global commodity chains, which are defined as 'networks of labour and production processes whose end result is a finished commodity' (Bair, 2005; Hopkins & Wallerstein, 1986, p. 159; Silver, 2003, pp.75ff.). Consequently, global commodity chains are crucial to understand the mechanism of unequal exchange, as most of the profits generated are captured in the high value-added links of commodity chains. Drawing upon Vernon's product lifecycle theory, Silver (2003, pp. 77ff.) observes a process of 'product fixes', in which formerly innovative production activities become standardised and are finally relocated to the semi-periphery or the periphery, whereas design and R&D activities remain in the core. Thus, as production disperses geographically, commodity chains are restructured such that profitability in lower value-added links of commodity chains is comparatively low and, if wages in these links rise, new waves of relocation begin. In Silver's terms, the current round of geographical relocation of production, new 'spatial fixes' put China's export industry under pressure (Silver & Lu, 2009, pp. 178f.), as factory owners in labour-intensive industries tend to seek lower cost production sites, countries such as Vietnam or Bangladesh.[1] One of the key reasons for the conflict at YY is this restructuring process of historical capitalism and the limits of social upgrading in the low value-added links of the shoe commodity chain.

The Case of YY: The World's Largest Athletic Shoemaker

The first reason for the strike, we argue, is due to the CCP's efforts to rebalance China's growth model, which directly affects the YY group by increasing competition, leading to a deterioration of benefits and working conditions. YY is part of Pou Chen (PC) group, a large Taiwanese conglomerate. Besides shoe manufacturing, PC is engaged in the electronics industry, retail services, and the real estate sector. YY is the most important part of PC, as it is the largest athletic shoemaker in the world. Although YY is attempting to capture larger shares of the value added in the commodity chain by becoming a shoe retailer for the Chinese domestic market (Appelbaum, 2009, p. 74), YY is primarily a contract manufacturer. Important brands in the athletic shoe business such as Adidas and Nike are among YY's customers. Design and expertise come mostly from their customers in the core; YY is responsible for production. YY therefore is embedded in the lower part of a buyer-driven global commodity chain, in which designers and retailers capture a large part of the added value (about 25–50%, respectively). The company has produced in Mainland China since 1988 where they began investing exclusively in Guangdong, later diversifying to other regions (Merk, 2008, p. 86). In the following decade, new production sites were established: for market access (the USA and Mexico) and for labour savings (Vietnam, Indonesia, Bangladesh and Cambodia). In 2003, YY had a turnover of US$7.6 billion with a profit of 5.7% (Yue Yuen Industrial Holdings Limited, 2014, pp.2ff.), whereas branded companies often realise double-digit profits; 29.3% of YY's turnover came from the US market and 20.2% from the Europe. YY is reorienting towards new growth markets; in 2013, 42.3% of YY's sales were made in Asia.

YY has a large factory in the industrial town of Gaobu in Dongguan with more than 40,000 workers. The factory comprises six production facilities, onsite dormitories, and social infrastructure. The Gaobu factory mainly produces athletic shoes, but also casual shoes and intermediate products such as shoe soles. Each production facility is divided into lines sorted by brands, in which components or shoes are produced (Adidas, Nike, etc.). The branded companies bring knowledge (design, etc.) of the production process, and also their own sophisticated machinery and executive staff. YY's production model is close to what Lüthje et al. (2013, p. 27) calls a regime of 'flexible mass production', based on flexible low-wage production and advanced machinery (Merk, 2008, p. 87). However, the best days of the Gaobu factory seem to have passed. The factory has seen several waves of downsizing, from a peak of 100,000 employees in 2006, because of lower labour costs at other YY sites and growing competition with Mainland Chinese producers (int61o). Due to these 'technological' and 'spatial fixes', the importance of the Gaobu factory within the company has declined. YY Gaobu and Ho Chi Minh City used to be the company's largest production sites, but now the Vietnamese factory's workforce is much bigger. At the end of 2013, YY employed about 413,000 workers, with one-fourth working in Mainland China of which about one-tenth were in Gaobu, and more than a fifth in Ho Chi Minh City.

The overall economic situation of the company restricted negotiation for wage increases and became a breeding ground for conflict. However, only a few years earlier, YY had been perceived by some managers of branded companies as a comparatively successful case of Corporate Social Responsibility. Besides having implemented some codes of conduct (no forced labour, compensation of overtime work, etc.), YY provided many social services including a kindergarten, a hospital, English courses, and leisure activities (Appelbaum, 2009, p. 74; Chang, 2009, p. 99f.; Merk, 2008, p. 90f.). The factory's social services were known as a best practice model in the region. In her bestseller 'Factory Girls', Chang quotes a worker who had left several factories owing to bad working conditions and had finally returned to YY: 'I've moved here and there, and I always seem to end up in this factory' (2009, p. 105). However, YY's work environment deteriorated before the strike. Social services no longer compensated for sluggish wage development. For instance, minimum wage increases were often lost through cuts to bonuses (China Labor Bulletin, 2014). Before the strike, wages were about 2200 to 3000 RMB, including overtime and piecework, which was relatively low in comparison to the 2012 average wage in Dongguan of 4750 RMB. Equally, the 37 migrant workers in our sample, who mostly worked in SMEs with a 'flexible mass production' or 'low wage classic' regime of production, earned wages of between 3000 and 3500 RMB, thus, usually receiving a higher wage than YY workers. Additionally, there is significant production line pressure (int66w). Thus, the first reason for the strike was increasing competitive pressures due to the structural situation at YY, which led to a shrinking space for social compromise.

Political Conflict in the Party State

The second reason for the strike was that YY does not simply face economic pressure, they also face political pressure, which we argue has opened up space for YY workers to push their demands. Several reform initiatives of the central government aim at industrial upgrading and target low-wage production in the export industry. Yet, it is complicated to push reforms at the local level, as close ties exist between local governments and entrepreneurs. Dongguan is a popular location for export industries, regulation of business by the city government is poor and dubious ties between party state and export capital are particularly striking (int0r). Many officials are thought to be corrupt and legal standards are implemented ineffectually. For instance, there is a substantial illegal red light district with more than 300,000 sex workers, which contributes about one-tenth of the city's revenues (*South China Morning Post*, February 13, 2014). However, in recent years, Dongguan has seen drastic changes as state officials in Beijing clamp down on local corruption. The party leadership of Xi Jinping is using Dongguan as a testing ground for its anti-corruption campaign. This campaign aims at rooting out 'tigers' and 'flies' referring to officials big and small, to ensure respect for the rule of law and the survival of the CCP. The state media framed the city as a kind of Chinese 'Sodom and Gomorrah'. Newspapers frequently publish articles about prostitution, corruption, and drug trade in 'Sin City' (*China Daily*, February 11, 2014). Moreover, the state uses large-scale police operations to discipline local officials and (Taiwanese) entrepreneurs in order to enforce the law.[2]

Political pressure by the central government opened a window of opportunity for YY workers to point out deficits and illegal practices at the factory, which the Dongguan local government had ignored or even supported (int0r, int68r). Most workers knew about close ties between the local government and YY management, and after the issue of missing social insurance payments became public, there were rumours about corruption, suggesting that local government officials had taken the worker's money as bribes from YY (int66w). Corruption was routed in the way pensions payments were calculated, whereby workers found out that YY had not contributed enough money to social insurance because the company did not use the gross wage; instead, they calculated remittances based on the local minimum wage (approximately 1300 RMB) (Chan & Hui, 2016). It is also reasonable to assume that the main activists of the strike knew about a strike's potential political impact as they framed the social insurance issue as their main claim (int0r, int68r). The situation therefore resembled what scholars of social movements have called a 'political opportunity structure' (see Tarrow, 1994, pp. 85f.). The discourse of missing social insurance payments worked well to pressure the local government and YY management because it contained the potential of revealing corruption at multiple levels. Notably during the strike, the central government directly intervened to force YY Gaobu to repay missing social insurance payments, thus, openly attacking the local government for being complicit in inhibiting the full implementation of the workers' rights. The YY strike thus rose out of a particular situation, whereby political tensions played a crucial role.

The Fear of Insecurity: Generational Priorities and the Importance of Social Insurance

Besides the structural framework presented so far, the composition of the workforce and workers' personal incentives to go on strike are crucial for a comprehensive understanding of the development of the YY conflict, which we will argue is the third reason for the strike. At first glance, YY appears to be a typical case of a regime of 'flexible mass production'. For example, most employees are migrant workers from Hunan, Hubei, Jiangxi, and Sichuan; about three-quarters are women. Workers receive very little training—only a three-day crash course. The factory is organised hierarchically such that about 200 Taiwanese managers and supervisors are at the top of the hierarchy; between 300 and 400 Mainland Chinese have lower management positions; and the remaining, approximately 40,000 Mainlanders are workers. The ACFTU does not play a role in the plant. In a survey of workers at YY Gaobu conducted by the NGO China Labour Watch in 2010, about 36% of workers did not even know whether there was a union (China Labor Watch, 2010, pp. 38f.).

However, some characteristics of the plant do not resemble a regime of 'flexible mass production'. Even though worker turnover is high, approaching 6% monthly, the plant has a comparatively large permanent staff. The composition of the core staff is made up of mostly middle-aged and older migrant workers; many have worked in Gaobu for more than 10 years and these workers receive seniority payments of up to 290 RMB monthly. There are just a few agency workers in the plant. Consequently, the YY workforce does not follow the patterns of strike mobilisation that scholars have identified in other cases (e.g. Elfstrom & Kuruvilla, 2014;

Pun & Lu, 2010). These studies assume that, in the last few years, a 'second generation of migrant workers' were the dominant force in strike actions. The members of this group do share some characteristics with the first-generation migrants; however, unlike their parents, they grew up in urban areas and tend to have better social networks and increased knowledge about legal rights and the urban labour market. Equally, they do not have knowledge of farming as they left the countryside early in life and many do not have access to land or enough land to make a simple living. Hence, unlike their 'half proletarianised' parents, they are more dependent on wage labour (Pun & Lu, 2010). Additionally, it is argued that young workers also have higher demands concerning wages and working conditions and, thus, tend to get involved in offensive strikes for wages more often than older and middle-aged workers. For instance, young apprentices organised the paradigmatic strike at Honda (Chan & Hui, 2014).

The YY strike does not fit this general picture. The immediate cause of the protest was unpaid social insurance payments. This particularly affected middle-aged and older migrant workers who were more willing to go on strike for these important social protections. Accordingly, the relationship between age groups and strike issues is different. In our interviews with migrant workers in the PRD,[3] we were able to grasp this relationship, as we found that throughout their working life, both the reasons and readiness to go on strike changed. The work biographies can be divided into two loosely identifiable stages and a transition period. YY workers fit into these stages, as they seem to be generalisable across industries and locations in the PRD. The first stage is a relatively new phenomenon and perhaps a sign of China's tighter labour market. Today, young workers switch jobs quite quickly for a small increase in salary or marginally better working conditions. However, this should not be perceived as unreasonable behaviour, as most stereotypes in the Chinese media about the so-called 90s generation suggest. Rather, the workers often follow a rational short-term strategy to improve their living standard. In one of our interviews, a 30-year-old female bottle factory worker told us that after she had worked in an electronics factory for about three years, she had changed her job voluntarily six times. She did so 'because the working conditions of those jobs were bad and the salary was low', 'the rules were too strict', and it was 'too exhausting to work overtime until late at night every day' (int15w). Such strategies are only feasible because of the labour shortage and the workers' comparatively high knowledge of urban labour markets, that is, their growing workplace bargaining power. Consequently, today's young workers tend to find employment relatively quickly. When we asked young workers how long it would take to find a new job, we overwhelmingly received answers of 'less than 10 days' (int14w). As already mentioned, scholars identified this 'second generation of migrant workers' as the main actor in recent collective struggles (Chan & Hui, 2014; Pun & Lu, 2010).

During their work life, most migrant workers reach a turning point. When pondering having a family (around mid-twenties in China), a transition period begins. This period is marked by a turn towards stability whereby factors such as a stable, reliable job, and social insurance become increasingly important. For instance, the same worker who changed her job six times in the past decade explains why she finally decided to work and stay in the bottle factory: 'There is no overtime, even if we have to do overtime, it won't be too late so I can go home to my son. It also pays social insurance and there is not too much working pressure' (int15w). The transition period resembles a scrambling stage as workers either find stable long-term employment while their value on the labour market is still high or develop realistic strategies to save enough money to return home.

Finally, in their late-thirties, a second phase begins. In most cases, the dreams of returning to the countryside in order to open a small business becomes more difficult as life pressures take over. Stability is highly coveted in this stage as economic and social demands of parenting increase. Additionally, workers begin to think more seriously about retirement (50 years for women and 60 for men in China), which means that pensions become increasingly important. Furthermore, their workplace bargaining power shrinks continuously, because older workers are not as attractive on the labour market. The relative position of older migrant workers depends on the choices they made before and the skills, which they have collected on the way. The stability stage is extremely important, as workers must contribute at least 15 years of social insurance to receive social insurance payments upon retirement. In our interviews, several workers expressed their worries about social insurance and the problems of their children not being able to support them in their advanced years. Such problems also exist at YY: 'I have worked here for thirteen years and I have three more years before I retire. I don't know what to do without social insurance after that', explained a YY worker (int66w). The reform of the welfare system in 2011 (implementation of an insurance system for migrant workers) and 2013, where the government made it possible to transfer pension claims to other provinces, increased the readiness of workers to stand up for their rights to ensure that they receive social insurance and to protect their jobs.

Development and Results of the Strike

The catalyst for the strike was missing social insurance payments. For weeks, information about missing payments had spread among line supervisors and white-collar workers and caused major discontent. A larger number of employees and line supervisors even threatened to resign if YY did not pay compensation (int61o, 64r, 66w) and some of them started to organise before the strike. Confirming many of the rumours, one employee, about to retire, found out that after having worked 18 years at YY, he would not be able to transfer his pension to his hometown and that his pension was less than expected. From the perspective of the workers, the missing pension payments were another form of shirking the full cost of employees. This resulted in a loss of trust, since workers felt cheated by the management; additionally, rumours about corruption were repeatedly discussed (int66w).

The last straw was a worker being beaten in sole plant no. 3, which led, on 5 April 2014, to a spontaneous strike. Although the initial strike action was limited to sole plant no. 3, 2000–6000 workers joined the strike (China Labor Bulletin, 2014). Even in the initial stages, most workers argued for compliance with legal standards and, thus, a repayment of the missing social insurance payments. In response to the workers' claims, YY management announced that they would find a solution for the problem before 14 April. Until then, there were no more strike actions, but some workers began to organise themselves more efficiently. A group of activists met on 12 April with a labour NGO, which had experience advising striking workers. Together, they defined the main objectives of the strike as repayment of the missing social insurance payments, public housing fund, a wage increase of 30% and a re-election of the company's union delegates (int67r).

On 14 April, the assistant General Manager Li Lujia submitted the management's offer to a large crowd of workers. It did not include a repayment of the missing social payments for past working years. The YY manager told workers that the local government did not agree to that stipulation (China Labor Bulletin, 2014), as it feared that compensation could lead to similar claims at other factories in Dongguan. On the same day, the conflict spread to the entire YY site at Gaobu. Workers in four YY plants went on strike under the slogan 'Compensate our social insurance, increase our income, make a buyout offer'. The following day, 40,000 workers were on strike. The police mobilised thousands of officers from different cities of the PRD to Gaobu and began to arrest several workers.

The strike had a strong impact, which led production to a near standstill. The entire town was crowded with protesters and police. At the same time, a first round of state-led collective bargaining was initiated. Management, delegates of the strikers and members of the local government participated in negotiations. The trade unions had no role. The strike also spread to other factories. On 18 April, YY workers in Anfu in Jiangxi province laid down their tools as well. After one week of striking, the local ACFTU branch sent a task force to investigate the strikers' allegations. The union issued a statement, in which it supported collective bargaining, but called on the workers to go back to work. Simultaneously, owing to an open intervention of China's Ministry of Human Resources and Social Security, the YY management issued a new plan (*The Wall Street Journal*, April 25, 2014). It included a wage increase of 230 RMB, implementation of social insurance according to the law and a reimbursement of missing benefits for the social insurance and housing funds (Chan & Hui, 2016). Many workers were not satisfied, however. The situation got worse. The police temporarily arrested workers and two NGO activists. On 23 April, YY management, the union and the local government issued a statement that workers should return to work. On the same day, management announced that workers who continued to strike would be fired after three days. The announcement came alongside further police violence. On 29 April, through police repressions and YY concessions, order had been re-established at YY.

The results of the strike were ambivalent. The workers achieved some of their objectives. Additionally, the ACFTU began establishing a directly elected company union. Due to YY's huge size and the minimal role the union played during the strike, the project has been rather unsuccessful (int58r). As of August 2014, only 1500 workers joined the union. The strike left its mark. In 2014, the company's profits went down by US$27 million because of the strike. Additional costs for wages and social insurance payments were around US$31 million, and the repayment of the employers' portion of their missing contributions for social insurance amounted to US$37 million. The strike action also led to new 'spatial fixes': some of YY's main customers, key international brands, reacted to the strike by relocating orders to other YY plants or to its competitors. For instance, Adidas relocated some machinery to Wanbang (Fresh) Shoes Industry in Qingyuan, which was mainly motivated to prevent higher production costs and losses due to further strikes. The decrease in orders resulted in reduced overtime work and, thus, in falling wages. In addition, the full implementation of social insurance led to a rise in workers' contributions, which were deducted from wages. Consequently, workers' wages decreased significantly. Therefore, quite a few workers criticised the results of the negotiations. Asked whether the strike was helpful to solve existing problems at YY, a worker responded:

> Help? Not at all. Before the strike, we had a salary of more than 3000 Yuan. In the past, the insurance cost us 20 to 30 RMB but now it is 300 Yuan, [. . .] and we even have to pay the tax! For young workers they deduct about 400 Yuan altogether every month, for old workers 500 to 600 Yuan. I only received 1900 last month not reaching 2000! Before I often had 3000 Yuan. I didn't work overtime last month. Workers get less and less but the output remains at the same low level. [Management] said, 'No output, no bonus'. (int66w)

Thus, the events point out the 'social contractions of semi-peripheral success' (Silver & Lu, 2009, p.183), as the space for social compromise in China's shoe industry seems to be rather limited because of competitive pressures. Also, the strike damaged YY's reputation and, therefore, many young workers left the factory. Today, employees even receive a bonus if they help to recruit new workers (int60w). However, older employees who were already preparing for retirement can take advantage of a rationalisation of the social insurance system at YY but at a higher cost. A lawyer, who had assisted the workers at the beginning of the strike thinks that further conflicts are likely: 'YY may have another strike within two years, because there are still a lot of unsolved problems' (int56r). The lawyer should be proven correct.

Changing Labour Conflict, Changing Labour Relations?

The overall influence of the strike on labour relations in China should not be underestimated. The events at YY have already had a lasting impact simply due to its sheer size. The strike was the largest one in China in the last decade and received a huge media response. More importantly, it helped to spur reform efforts of some CCP officials, as social insurance has become an important issue for industrial conflict. A trade union official told us: 'According to the statistics, in Guangdong, from April to August 2014, there were more than 10 strikes, which were caused by the social insurance problem. They were all influenced by the YY strike' (int58r). Afterwards, there were a number of large strikes that followed the example of YY. For instance, in December 2014, about 2500 workers went on strike at Guangzhou Panyu Lide Shoes Co. Like the YY workers, they demanded a reimbursement of missing social insurance payments. In March 2015, 5000 workers went on strike in a dispute over housing fund payments at Stella Shoe Co. in Dongguan (*Financial Times*, March 11, 2015). The conflict also had a boomerang effect: About 4000 workers in plant 3 at YY Gaobu, who felt threatened to lose their housing fund through a plant restructuring, went on strike again. Both strikes were caused by a new regulation of the Dongguan government that would have limited the circumstances when worker can access the funds and would have restricted their use.

The YY conflict and subsequent struggles also indicate that strike actors and conflict issues have changed. Most of these strikes were organised by middle-aged and older workers and, therefore, a group that was perceived to be less assertive has now become an important force in industrial conflict in Guangdong. For these employees, the stakes are high: they fear the potential loss of their pensions, especially if the minimum contribution time is not reached or if the company does not remit contributions according to the law. As well, they fear job losses in the event that plants shut down. This new 'age precariousness' results from hyper-flexible low-wage production in the PRD during the last decades and is aggravated by the fear of dismissals in the current wave of industrial restructuring and near-zero vertical job mobility. It is the result of a new round of geographical relocation of production, where capitalists relocate labour-intensive production to lower cost and lower regulation zones in South East and South Asia. From a theoretical perspective, this development can be seen as an ongoing cyclical restructuring of the capitalist world-system (Arrighi, 2011; Silver & Lu, 2009). In this process, new 'spatial fixes' put China's export industry under pressure and show the limits of social upgrading in the low value-added links of the shoe commodity chain.

This paper has demonstrated that new issues shape labour relations in Guangdong since 2013 whereby social insurance (11.9%) and plant relocations and mergers (11%) are increasingly becoming important motivations for worker action (China Labor Bulletin, 2015). Accordingly, besides offensive wage struggles, today, struggles about the protection of potential losses from the process of economic modernisation appear. The implications of this new dynamic are not clear yet. However, it is likely that missing social insurance payments will lead to more strikes. The result of a study by the NGO China Labor Watch (2014) that 'among the more than 400 factories' that it inspected, 'not one bought workers all of the social insurance items required by Chinese law' indicates the issue's relevance. The strikes will likely exert additional pressure on Chinese policy-makers and entrepreneurs to put social security laws into practice.

Consequently, social security will play an important role in the bottom regimes of production (flexible mass production and low wage classic). If this trend becomes prevalent in other regions in China, it would equal a noticeable re-regulation of Chinese labour relations, and would speed up a further wave of capital relocation to South and South East Asia.

Disclosure Statement

No potential conflict of interest was reported by the authors.

Notes

1 In an interview with the president of a Hong Kong industrial federation, he stated that 'rising labour costs for the past five or six years' are forcing Hong Kong's industrialists to seek further investment possibilities for 'a second factory abroad' (int25r); some of our interviewees in the PRD's export industry made similar statements.

2 A number of respondents who are entrepreneurs in Dongguan reported that state control has increased significantly and that quite a few local businesspersons are afraid of the central government's anti-corruption campaign.

3 This section refers to 37 biographical interviews with workers from Shunde (21) and Dongguan (16) from our sample. In these interviews, we focused on the workers' experiences with precariousness.

References

Appelbaum, R. (2009). Big suppliers in greater China: A growing counterweight to the power of giant retailers. In H. Hung (Ed.), *China and the transformation of global capitalism* (pp. 65–85). Baltimore , MD: Johns Hopkins University Press.

Arrighi, G. (2011). *The long twentieth century: Money, power, and the origins of our times* (2nd ed.). London: Verso.

Arrighi, G., & Drangel, J. (1986). The stratification of the world-economy: An exploration of the semiperipheral zone. *Review, 10*(1), 37–96.

Arrighi, G. & Silver, B. (Eds.). (1999). *Chaos and governance in the modern world system.* Minneapolis: University of Minnesota Press.

Bair, J. (2005). Global capitalism and commodity chains: Looking back, going forward. *Competition and Change, 9*(2), 153–180.

Butollo, F. (2014). *The end of cheap labour in China? Industrial transformation and social upgrading in China.* Frankfurt/M.: Campus.

Chan, C., & Hui, E. (2014). The development of collective bargaining in China: From 'collective bargaining by riot' to 'party state-led wage bargaining'. *The China Quarterly, 217*, 221–242.

Chan, C., & Hui, E. (2016). Bringing class struggles back: A Marxian analysis of the state and class relations in China. *Globalizations.* doi:10.1080/14747731.2016.1207935

Chang, L. T. (2009). *Factory girls. From village to city in a changing China.* New York, NY: Spiegel & Grau.

China Labor Bulletin. (2014). *Defeat will only make us stronger: Workers look back at the Yue Yuen shoe factory strike.* Retrieved from http://www.clb.org.hk/en/content/defeat-will-only-make-us-stronger-workers-look-back-yue-yuen-shoe-factory-strike

China Labor Bulletin. (2015). *China Labour Bulletin strike map.* Retrieved from http://www.numble.com/PHP/mysql/clbmape.html

China Labor Watch. (2010). *A case study: Adidas and Yue Yuen. Focusing on the Corporate Code of Conduct of International Corporations.* Retrieved from http://www.chinalaborwatch.org/upfile/2010_11_2/20101130143496.pdf

China Labor Watch. (2014). *Statement on large strike at the Yue Yuen shoe factory.* Retrieved April 14, 2014, from http://www.chinalaborwatch.org/newscast/232

Coughlin, C., & Segev, E. (2000). Foreign direct investment in China: A spatial econometric study. *World Economy, 23*(1), 1–23.

Elfstrom, M., & Kuruvilla, S. (2014). The changing nature of labor unrest in China. *Industrial and Labor Relations Review, 67*(2), 453–480.

Friedman, E. (2014). *Insurgency trap. Labor politics in postsocialist China.* Ithaca, NY: Cornell University Press.

Hopkins, T., & Wallerstein, I. (1986). Commodity chains in the world-economy prior to 1800. *Review, 10*(1), 157–170.

Lee, C. K. (2007). *Against the Law: Labor protests in China's rustbelt and sunbelt.* Berkeley: University of California Press.
Lüthje, B., Luo, S., & Zhang, H. (2013). *Beyond the iron rice bowl: Regimes of production and industrial relations in China.* Frankfurt/M.: Campus.
Merk, J. (2008). Restructuring and conflict in the global athletic footwear industry: Nike, Yue Yuen and labour codes of conduct. In M. Taylor (Ed.), *Global economy contested: Power and conflict across the international division of labour. Rethinking globalizations* (pp. 79–97). London: Routledge.
Naughton, B. (2010). Reading the NPC: Post-crisis economic dilemmas of the Chinese leadership. *China Leadership Monitor, 32.* Retrieved from http://media.hoover.org/sites/default/files/documents/CLM32BN.pdf
Pettis, M. (2013). *Avoiding the fall: China's economic restructuring.* Washington, DC: Carnegie Endowment for International Peace.
Pun, N., & Lu, H. (2010). Unfinished proletarianization: Self, anger and class action of the second generation of peasant-workers in reform China. *Modern China, 36*(5), 493–519.
Schmalz, S., & Ebenau, M. (2012). After neoliberalism? Brazil, India, and China in the global economic crisis. *Globalizations, 9*(4), 487–501.
Silver, B. (2003). *Forces of labor. Workers' movements and globalization since 1870.* New York, NY: Cambridge University Press.
Silver, B., & Lu, Z. (2009). China as an emerging epicenter of world labor unrest. In H.-F. Hung (Ed.), *China and the transformation of global capitalism* (pp. 174–187). Baltimore, MD: Johns Hopkins University Press.
Tarrow, S. (1994). *Power in movement: Social movements, collective action, and politics.* Cambridge: Cambridge University Press.
Yu, H. (2010). Impact of the global economic crisis on the Pearl River Delta and Yangtze river delta regions. In Y. Zheng & S. Y. Tong (Eds.), *China and the global economic crisis* (pp. 89–112). Singapore: World Scientific.
Yue Yuen Industrial Holdings Limited. (2014). *2013 annual report.* Retrieved from http://www.yueyuen.com/index.php/en/about-us-7/investor-annos/902-2014-04-24-annual-report-2013
Zhu, S., & Pickles, J. (2014). Bring in, go up, go west, go out: Upgrading, regionalisation and delocalisation in China's apparel production networks. *Journal of Contemporary Asia, 44*(1), 36–63.

Interviews

Int0r. (2014, July 4). 'Chinese Labour Relations Scholar'. Interviewed by Stefan Schmalz.
Int14w. (2014, July 9). 'Bathroom Fitting Worker'. Interviewed by Stefan Schmalz and Brandon Sommer.
Int15w. (2014, July 9). 'Bottling Company Worker'. Interviewed by Stefan Schmalz and Brandon Sommer.
Int25r. (2014, July 21). 'Industrial Association Hong Kong'. Interviewed by Stefan Schmalz and Brandon Sommer.
Int56r. (2014, August 13). 'Labour Lawyer'. Interviewed by Stefan Schmalz, Brandon Sommer and Hui Xu.
Int58r. (2014, August 18). 'Union Official Guangdong'. Interviewed by Stefan Schmalz, Brandon Sommer and Hui Xu.
Int60w. (2014, August 20). 'Café Worker in Gaobu'. Interviewed by Stefan Schmalz and Brandon Sommer.
Int61o. (2014, August 20). 'Yue Yuen Manager'. Interviewed by Stefan Schmalz and Brandon Sommer.
Int64r. (2014, August 20). 'Yue Yuen Line Supervisor'. Interviewed by Stefan Schmalz and Brandon Sommer.
Int66w. (2014, August 27). 'Yue Yuen Worker'. Interviewed by Brandon Sommer.
Int67r. (2014, September 5). 'Labour NGO Activist'. Interviewed by Stefan Schmalz and Hui Xu.

The Makings of Subaltern Subjects: Embodiment, Contradictory Consciousness, and Re-hegemonization of the Diaosi in China

NGAI-LING SUM

Lancaster University, Lancaster, UK

ABSTRACT *This article examines the emergence since 2011 of the 'Diaosi' (loser) identity among second-generation migrant workers in China. This subjective identification of a new social category with little hope can be contrasted with the hopeful policy constructions of a strong China eager to promote the civilizing 'suzhi' (population quality) of its population nationally and internationally. Yet, as this article shows, in four steps, these phenomena are intertwined. First, it locates the emergence of this 'Diaosi' subject in the global and national dialectics of hope in China since the global financial crisis. Second, drawing on neo-Foucauldian and neo-Gramscian scholarship, Diaosi marginality is related to the interactions among global capitalist production, the socialist market economy, continuous state domination via a household registration system (hukou), and the civilising discourse of 'suzhi'. Third, it shows how the Diaosi embody their multiplex loser identity and marginality affectively and expressively in their everyday demeanour. Fourth, it examines recent efforts by state/corporate capital and the party-state to re-make and re-hegemonize Diaosi life in the name of consumption, civility, and social stability. The article ends with some neo-Gramscian remarks on the complexities and contradictory consciousness of marginal social categories, such as the Diaosi, and their openness to passive revolution and (re-) hegemonization.*

Introduction

This article examines the emergence of Chinese second-generation migrant workers who have been narrating and presenting themselves as 'Diaosi' (losers) since 2011. This self-identification of a new subject category with little hope can be juxtaposed to the concurrent policy constructions of China as an object of hope and strength eager to promote the civilizing 'suzhi' (population quality) of its people on (inter-)national levels. Yet these two phenomena are intertwined. This article has four sections. First, it locates the emergence of this 'Diaosi' subject in the dialectics of China as hope object since the global financial crisis. With the fear of recession in the US and Europe, emerging markets, especially China, have been constructed as objects of hope and sources of demand by transnational policy and business actors. This was articulated to China's own hope, evident since the 1990s, of building national strength, improving the 'suzhi' of its population, etc. This dialectics of hope was a central feature of the conjuncture in which the Diaosi subject emerged.

Second, drawing on neo-Foucauldian and neo-Gramscian scholarship, Diaosi marginality is analysed in terms of a co-governance by global capitalist production, the socialist market economy, continuous state domination via a household registration system (*hukou*), and the civilizing discourse of 'suzhi' (Anagnost, 2004; Pun, 2005; Yan, 2008). Focusing on suzhi-hukou discourses and practices, the article examines them as a biopolitical population management mechanism in which less value is attached to migrant workers' lives and their labour-power receives lower wages. This suzhi-hukou way of reproducing and managing inequalities means that migrants live in marginal conditions. Their marginality and subalternity are popularized through terms such as 'Dwelling Narrowness', 'ant tribe', and 'rat tribe' and, most recently, the *Diaosi* subject. Third, the article focuses more on the Diaosi's subjective embodiment of marginality in their everyday affective and expressive demeanour. Their experiences of exclusion, devaluation, unfulfilled consumer, and romantic desires are central to the Diaosi-loser system of signification. This is far from consistent but involves what Gramsci terms 'contradictory consciousness', which comprises resistance and resignation. Fourth, it considers current efforts by state/corporate capital and the party-state to re-make and re-hegemonize Diaosi life in the name of consumption, civility, and social stability. The article ends with remarks on the potential of (neo-)Gramscian insights on subalternity and subalterns for examining the complexities of marginal social categories such as the Diaosi and their embodiment of contradictory consciousness as well as the passive revolution and (re-)hegemonization that are involved.

Financial Crisis and the Dialectics of China Hope

The 2007 financial crisis in North America and Western Europe prompted fears of recession, rising debts, and growing austerity. In response, transnational capitals sought new sites of demand and investment outside these regions. Emerging economies such as China were discursively constructed as dream sites that could contribute towards a global recovery (Sum, 2013a). More specifically, until its economic slowdown began in 2013, some (inter-)national policymakers, think tanks, consultancy firms, bankers, and economic journalists (e.g. Jager, 2008; O'Neill, 2013) represented the 'BRIC' economies, especially 'China', as global hegemonic 'hope' objects that could 'drive' global growth. Narratives such as 'China as the big BRIC', 'China as the second largest economy in the world', 'China has an 8% GDP growth rate', 'China has a large middle-class consumer market', etc. were circulated transnationally (for dissenting views, see Chanos, 2011; Pettis, 2011).

This hegemonic hope for global recovery is articulated to the Chinese Communist Party's hope for national glory through modernity (Yang & Lim, 2010), consumer citizenship (Ren, 2013), and a neo-Confucian 'civility' (Bell, 2010) conducive to 'social harmony' (later in terms of the 'China Dream'). Discourses on 'harmony' and 'suzhi' are prevalent in policy and everyday life since the 1990s (Anagnost, 2004; Yan, 2008). This approach to the art of governing has many manifestations but one particular expression is the discourse of middle-class 'suzhi' (Tomba, 2009). This new class, comprising urban professionals and entrepreneurs, is constructed as 'suzhi' bearers. Their embodiment of population quality includes education, lifestyle, civil dispositions, and the ability to capacitate themselves to appreciate the 'finer things in life' (Ren, 2013, pp. 34–44; Zhang, 2010, p. 19). This embodiment of 'suzhi' is especially pronounced in the middle-class consumer subjects whose actions are seen as stimulating the market without challenging the social order (Tomba, 2009).

This co-identification of global China and its domestic middle class as hope objects was materially grounded in the rolling out of neoliberal measures/techniques in China under socialist state rule/guidance (Pow, 2009, pp. 38–39). Focusing on middle-class housing as symbolic of these changes, this middle-class hope for 'suzhi' life is intertwined with the desire for housing and homeownership in urban metropoles (Zhang, 2010, pp. 52–78). From a political economy perspective, this remaking of neoliberal personhood has depended on the marketization of land and housing markets from the 1990s onwards. This allowed for the institutionalization of a land-use rights market as well as the purchase of commercialized housing (Wu, Xu, & Yeh, 2007, p. 50). It allows local governments (and their investment arms), land/property developers, and state-owned banks to: (i) derive income from selling land-use rights, obtaining land-based loans, collateralizing land/property, and building/selling/speculating commodity housing for profit; and (ii) pursue GDP growth rates (as GDPism) (Sum, 2013b) that help cadres and those with connections to rise up the bureaucratic ranks (Sum, 2013a). This land- and property-based mode of accumulation and its related home consumption form one of the avenues in which the middle-class can demonstrate and realize wealth, status, 'suzhi', and exclusivity. 'Finer things in life' include home ownership, housing choice, home wealth generation, home décor, living in a gated community, quality family, quality husband/wife/children, etc. (Xiao, 2010; Zhang, 2010). The hope of creating a good life and social distinction is also reflected in the culture of marriage. The dream of 'living happily ever after' is to self-capacitate (with extended family support) to buy property, find a partner with matching qualities, and improve on one's future 'suzhi' and aspirations. There is a patriarchal folk saying of 'no car, no house, no bride' (Offbeat China, 2011) that aptly captures these aspirations as well as the unevenness of the consumer, marriage, love, and intimacy markets in China.

This mode of land- and property-based accumulation was reinforced by the onset of the 2007 financial crisis. Worried about falling exports and rising unemployment, the Chinese leadership proposed a four-trillion Renminbi stimulus package in 2008 to reflate the economy. Up to 2011 this was reinforced by US quantitative easing and related financial inflows to China (Cho & Rhee, 2013).These policy measures were well-received by the international policy and business communities, but they have aggravated the deep-rooted central-local fiscal tensions and local governments' efforts to appropriate and use land as collateral and to raise revenue. This intensified real estate inflation and fears of a 'property bubble' in China since 2009 (Huang, 2013). During the peak boom period from 2003 to 2012, property prices in major cities such as Beijing and Shanghai rose 3.65 and 3.41 times, respectively (Xianhuanet.com, 2013). As for rents, the average unit rose three times in the same period (Baidu.com, 2013).[1] These bubble tendencies have accentuated the impact of uneven development on the material standards of urban dwellers and migrant workers labouring under poor conditions. Social unrest in terms of labour, land, and housing activism (Hsing, 2010; Leung, 2015; Zhang, 2010) began to rise. Apart from activism, marginality was expressed through terms such as 'Dwelling Narrowness' (Hung, 2011; Yu, 2011), 'ant tribe' (Zhang, 2013), and 'rat tribe' and, more recently, the *Diaosi* subject. The latter (self-)narrate as 'loser' subjects with 'little hope' (see below). Their 'lack of hope' is dialectically intertwined with the global hegemonic construction of China as a 'hope' object and its own modernity hope of national strength and a quality population.

Exclusionary Practices in China's Biopolitical Population Management Mechanism: 'Hukou' and Suzhi'

This dialectics of hope in the changing cultural political economy (Sum & Jessop, 2013) of China is a central feature of the conjuncture in which the Diaosi subject emerged. Affected by rising housing prices, bad living conditions, and unequal access to powerful connections, young migrant workers feel that they have been left behind by these neoliberal commodification drives—made worse by the targeting of these workers in state-sponsored modes of devaluation. Drawing on neo-Foucauldian scholarship (e.g. Legg, 2005; Miller & Rose, 1990), this section considers how the exclusionary household registration (hukou) and 'suzhi' systems (Anagnost, 2004; Kipnis, 2006; Pun, 2005; Yan, 2008) co-constitute China's biopolitical management mechanism to create cheaper migrant-labour bodies.

First, the purpose of the hukou system, established in the 1950s, has changed from preventing peasants from leaving their land to allowing them to 'float' into urban areas since the Deng era. Being a peasant in China is not an occupation but a status tied to one's birth (Zhang, N., 2014). Under the hukou system, rural migrants can move to cities, work and reside there but are not entitled to urban resources such as schooling and hospitals. This discourse of hukou targets the migrant population once they move to the cities. It operates as a governmental technology of classification and categorizes them as 'nongmin gong' (peasant workers). The policy space then excludes them from full entitlement to subsidized housing, education, medical care, and welfare. This functional discrimination is deployed to deny migrants urban citizenship. Although the *hukou* system has undergone several reforms, it is still hard to convert from rural to urban status and, where it occurs, the privileges of the urban elite and China's costs of production are challenged in fundamental ways.

Since the 1990s, the exclusionary nature of hukou practices has been exacerbated by the modernity discourse of 'suzhi', which posits a hierarchy of civility. This not only denies the rural population access to urban resources but also devalues it as having 'lower quality'. Thus migrants are judged/labelled as transient and secondary. This technology of judgement assigns them a lower status more suitable for undesirable employment (e.g. factory work, construction industry, low service sector, etc.) at lower wages (Zhang, F., 2014). These practices can be seen as part of a state-based biopolitical population management mechanism that marked migrants out as rural-inferior bodies to be assigned lower value in the urban environment. Once they migrate from the countryside, such exclusionary practices downgrade the value of their life as well as the market value of their labour-power. They become the source of cheap and flexible labour serving national development and China's insertion into global capitalism. These hukou-suzhi ways of constructing and governing inequalities mean that migrants must resort to living in marginal and sub-citizen conditions. Their sub-citizenship plights, together with the rising housing prices and rents, mean that industrial and service migrants must rely on employer-provided dormitories (Pun, 2005), rent sub-standard accommodation in villages at the peripheries of towns (Wu, Webster, He, & Liu, 2010, pp. 114–184), or reside in liminal spaces (e.g. balconies, roof tops, or underground accommodation) in central urban conurbations of global cities. In Beijing, some migrants rented/shared small rooms at around US$ 65 per month in 2014 in underground air raid shelters/storage spaces with communal toilets/

kitchens and no natural light. About a million low-wage service workers (e.g. waiters, hairdressers, janitors, shop assistance, street peddlers, chefs, security guards, construction workers, etc.) occupied this subterranean housing in 2014 (Pulitzer Centre, 2015). This facet of subaltern life is dubbed as 'rat tribe' and has been captured photographically by Sim (2015).

Diaosi Embodiment of Marginality and Contradictory Consciousness

These uneven macrosocial and biopolitical developments also affect their urban labouring and vulnerable body. Amongst many forms of expression, since the end of 2011, young migrants, who were users and makers of Internet pop culture and social media, increasingly self-narrate their marginality and subalternity as 'Diaosi'. Young migrant workers feel that they have been left behind and express their marginality affectively through their self-identification as Diaosi. This making of the Diaosi subject can be captured by three inter-related moments with regards to bodily representations.

This first started in online fan clubs when they debated about a Chinese soccer player called Li Yi. This player once compared his football skills to the celebrated French player Thierry Henry (nicknamed 'Emperor Henry' in China). On this basis, his fans dubbed him 'Li Yi the emperor' (da di). This set the scene for the Diaosi online wordfest. Thus the term 'fans' was transliterated as 'fe-si' which means 'vermicelli' kind of noodle. When discussing their football hero, Li Yi's fans started to call themselves di-si (fans of the emperor); and, in return, their critics parodied 'di' into 'diao' which is a slang word for 'dick' (penis). Through this transposition from 'di' to 'diao', Li Yi's fans were no longer 'fans of emperor' but 'fans of penis' (diao-si).

This metonymic transposition via the body set the stage for the second moment of this collective wordplay. Li Yi's fans, instead of being offended, appropriated this as a self-mocking label within their proud fandom. They took pride in this derogatory label that resonated with subaltern migrants caught up in the dialectics of hope and frustration in China's development. This label soon went viral, escaping its original social base. Within two months after its coining in 2011, it generated 41.1 million search results and 2.2 million blog posts on Google and China's Twitter-like Weibo, respectively (Lui, 2015). Young subalterns started to proclaim themselves as 'Diaosi' and there are all kinds of chat rooms and social media set up for this purpose (e.g. YY and QQ chats).

A third moment began as the label gained popularity and Diaosi expressed their new system of signification in the public arena. They use their body to express exclusion, devaluation, frustration, hardship, social pain, as well as unfulfilled consumer and romantic desires. They self-represent Diaosi marginality in corporeal terms and sceptically and ironically mapped themselves as 'poor, short and ugly' losers (Marquis & Yang, 2013, p. 3). They visibilize themselves as coming from an underprivileged background earning a meagre wage, consuming little, and having no social connections.[2] Their meagre income/consumption and low social standing are coupled with the social-emotional side of living a devalued life of long working hours, poor housing, uncertain career, living away from family, guilt towards parents at home, and empty emotional life with little love/romance/intimacy. This emptiness and loneliness are often highlighted in Diaosi narrations of how they spent Valentine's Day, Christmas, festive seasons, and the small hours of the night looking for Internet companions. Such affective discourses from the margins are not purely personal; they also express collective social experiences that are embedded in unequal access to state-based urban resources/status as well as inequalities generated by neoliberal policies in everyday economic and social life.

This everyday making of Diaosi subalternity is expressed through a binary trope that depicts two main body types based on their unequal access to power networks, consumption, love, romance, and intimacy. First, male Diaosi self-deprecate as 'poor, short and ugly'. With meagre income and unattractive physiques, they construct themselves as unable to impress girls by showering them with material gifts and/or charm. They have 'no house, no car and no bride/girlfriend' and spend most of their time at home, use cheap mobile phones, surf on the Internet, and play media games such as DotA. This male-oriented Diaosi construction has gradually spread to female subalterns, who also self-narrate as Diaosi. It was estimated that around 500 million people self-identify as Diaosi (Gao, 2013). The popularity of this identity is partly reinforced by the mutual imbrication of the activities of the social media and their users. By February 2013, it was even widely circulated on these media (e.g. *Weibo.com, sina.com, qq.com, tianya.cn; nbweekly.com*) what constitute male and female Diaosi 'standards' (see Table 1).

Second, this Diaosi subject is juxtaposed with another body type, characterized as: (i) Gaofushuai who are 'tall, rich and handsome' and (ii) 'princelings', who are 'second-generation officials'/'second-generation rich' with special party and family connections. In this Diaosi's system of signification, this second group are 'superior' and privileged with 'three treasures' (iPhone, sports car, and designer watch) (Marquis & Yang, 2013, p. 9) and also attract beautiful girls (see later). This juxtaposition of opposing body types constructs a Diaosi–Gaofushuai binary based on economic and social inequalities. Drawing on Scott's concept of 'hidden transcripts' (1992), this performative and narrative modern folklore about unevenness contains a mix of latent critique, self-mockery, self-protection, and self-entertainment (Yang, Tang, & Wang, 2015). It is a mundane way of protesting and relieving pressure in a system where exclusion is highly institutionalized and freedom of speech involves guerrilla tactics. The gaps between these two groups are further highlighted online via satirical cartoons, everyday photographs, TV shows, fantasy talks, etc. These include comparing their diverse modes of transport (bus vs. BMW), brands of smartphones (Nokia vs. Apple iPhone); eating places (side-street stores vs. expensive restaurants), and romantic encounters.

Table 1. Mapping of male and female Diaosi standards in 2013

Typical male Diaosi	Typical female Diaosi
1. Have less than 1000 RMB (USD 150) cash on you	1. Never bought bikinis
2. Wear shoes costing less than 800 RMB (USD 130)	2. Never wear bright nail vanish
3. Have fewer than three girlfriends before marriage	3. Never have a matching set of lingerie
4. Receive less than 1000 RMB (USD 150) in annual bonuses	4. Never wear high heels over 5 cm
5. Use pirated smartphones or those under 2000 RMB (USD 300)	5. Have not changed hairstyle for the last 6 months
6. No powerful friends	6. Have dieted for more than 5 months
7. Smoke cigarettes that cost less than 20 RMB	7. Never guffaw in public
8. No car or use cars costing less than 100 000 RMB (USD 15,000)	8. Walk behind men
9. Drink only beer and cheap liquor	9. Never look at or over-indulge in a mirror
10. Did not travel long-distance in the last 3–5 years	10. Never remove body hair

Source: Weibo.com http://www.weibo.com/p/100808303d2e61b631b1f41af0887a9590ada2?pids=Pl_Third_App__9&feed_sort=timeline&feed_filter=timeline#_rnd1428440459949

Apart from framing inequalities via body and consumption types, Diaosi also construct themselves as 'romantically unlucky' as their ideal girlfriends (named 'goddesses') are 'Bafumei' (fair-skinned, rich and pretty) and not 'Heimu'er' ('Black Fungus' women who are overly sexually experienced) (Li, Spotti, & Kroon, 2014). Given their meagre income, unattractive physique and the existence of a match-making industry catering mainly for rich men (Larmer, 2013), Diasoi imagine that they will be out-competed by Gaofushuai/princelings and the Bafumei girls only belong to these rich and powerful men. This trope was vividly captured in a set of popular remarks first posted on *ifeng.com*:

> Diaosi have no money, no background, no future; they love playing DotA, ...love 'moving bricks' [signifying themselves as workers in construction industry]. . . . . In front of Guofushuai, their fate is to kneel before them; gathering all their courage to chat up a 'goddess', what they get in return is a mocking 'hal-hal'[3] . . . . They share low status, a boring life, a hopeless future, and an empty emotional life, they are not accepted by society. (http://news.ifeng.com/opinion/special/diaosi/)

These ironic remarks reveal the subaltern-Diaosi common sense that contains a mix of precarious life with little money and no background; the self-mockery of a fate with no future/hope; the emotional emptiness of being shunned/mocked by 'goddesses', the latent hostility towards social elitism embodied by Gaofushuai and princelings; and the despair of not being accepted; but these tropes are concurrently subordinated to the hegemonic norms of sexual stereotypes and the unfulfilled dream of consumerism and entrepreneurialism for socio-economic advancement. Such ironic identities (Szablewicz, 2014, p. 268) and contradictory consciousness (à la Gramsci) involves self-deprecating critiques towards social inequalities but also submitting to the seduction of neoliberal consumerism and entrepreneurialism.

Re-hegemonization of Diaosi's Contradictory Consciousness

This contradictory consciousness could be developed into a more critical consciousness and/or be re-hegemonized by dominant forces to provide new hope. As the Diaosi identity becomes more popular, celebrities—especially youth icon bloggers and technology entrepreneurs—begin to appropriate this identity (Gu, 2014). In addition, it seems that Diaosi identity is partly being mainstreamed and re-hegemonized in two ways.

First, with the fall in GDP growth rate from 8 to 7.5% and an official anti-corruption campaign, (trans-)national capitals are looking afresh at the subaltern-Diaosi as a consumer market that could compensate for falling demand in the luxury goods market. Thus a popular article first posted on the US-based *Tea Leaf Nation* highlighted that 'while the high-end market is weak, the Diaosi market prospects are bright' (Zhang & Barreda, 2013). This article was translated and re-posted on numerous Chinese business websites (e.g. *business.sohu.com*) and was widely regarded as the first Diaosi market report. Riding on this Diaosi tide, Gu (2014) from *Wall Street Journal* further mapped them as a consumer group as follows:

> What they lack in spending power compared with Western teens or rich Chinese, diaosi make up for in sheer numbers. Some of China's most successful companies, including Tencent Holdings Ltd., Alibaba Group and YY.com, have built multibillion-dollar businesses targeting them. (Source: *Wall Street Journal*, 13 February 2013)

In short, they are re-evaluated by (trans-)national capital as a specific target consumer group with unfulfilled dreams of being Gaofushuai. Within China, the cultural industries wasted no time in capturing the Diaosi subject via mobile-phone games such as 'Diaosi Spring', Diaosi fictions/love music, and *Sohu*'s TV drama on 'Diaosi Man'. Other creative Internet-based groups such as *Alibaba, YY.com and Tencent Holdings Ltd.* have designed different virtual products and pleasurable experiences to capitalize on their desires for counter-attack, wealth, consumption, enjoyment, entertainment, and companionship/love/romance/sex.

In Diaosi's mode of signification, 'counter-attack' is a term borrowed from online war games where the losing side regains control and finally wins. Transposing this online imagery to the Diaosi–Gaofushuai relationship, counter-attack becomes a way to catch up with Gaofushuai in material terms. For example, some financial websites (e.g. *yunxindai.com*) urge Diaosi to launch 'beautiful counter-attacks' by purchasing peer-to-peer (or P2P) financial products targeting lower-income groups. Their starting point could be as low as RMB 100. Once they subscribe, they are said to be 'investors' and destined to catch up with Gaofushuai in terms of their possession of wealth management products. Thus framed, 'counter-attack' is not an act of resistance towards structural inequalities; rather it is a hope-based self-responsibilizing technology (Foucault, 1988) to encourage them to constitute themselves as 'investors' and to work on themselves to improve their conditions in an imagined 'P2P' environment. It thus confirms individualized consumption and competitive entrepreneurialism oriented to suzhi improvement rather than challenging them. These products are appropriated differently with many joining the ranks of the millions of users who generate substantial revenues for the providers (e.g. see Table 2); whilst many others are cautious and, in some cases, financially literate Diaosi offer critical advice through websites such as *diaosibaoliao.cc* and *p2peye.com.*

The acts of incorporation of Diaosi into the circuit of consumer and financial capitalism take other forms too. Retail and cultural industries draw them into their orbits by providing fun, pleasure, and entertainment to their suffering bodies. For example, China's largest online shopping site, *Alibaba*'s *Taobao*, created a *Diaosi Fashion Club* selling goods based on value, quality, and fun. Concurrently, global mid-range fashion chains such as *Zara* and *H&M* are also attracting this group of online consumers. The German car magazine, *AutoBild*, has announced three 'cheap branded cars' to target the Diaosi market (Zhuayoukong.com, 2014).

China's cultural-entertainment industry is also joining the Diaosi market by providing pleasurable group entertainment as a 'cure' of loneliness. For example, *YY.com* and *9158* are both video-based networks. They feature virtual gift systems in which performers can earn credits through activities such as providing chat shows conducted by cute/sexy girls, karaoke singing, or conducting tutorial videos. Participants can convert these virtual credits into real cash. This kind of affordable entertainment allows Diaosi to act out Gaofushuai-like lifestyle and even dating fantasies. The *QZone*, which is run by *QQ.com*, is popular as migrants can use a mobile phone (and not computer) to access the Internet. It is free but charges for value-added services such as online games, avatar-based social networks with their own currency and products, and a virtual pet portal. On average, users spend about USD 20 per month on these products (see Table 2). These sites are popular ways of keeping in touch with families/friends and their services/products are heavily used, possibly as 'cure' for loneliness in their devalued life.

Second, complementing this capitalist subsumption of the Diaosi identity (in other words, its re-hegemonization) is the re-assertion of party-state leadership over their contradictory common sense. Diaosi's spontaneous critiques towards social inequalities and self-mocking 'subversive laughter' have not gone unnoticed by those in power. This creative use of slang and body tropes captures the social pain, frustration, and exclusion of the subaltern migrants. It also touches and highlights some political sore points with potentials to challenge existing power configurations. Recognizing such potentials, there are tendencies since March 2013 to disrupt, de-politicize, and re-hegemonize this contradictory identity to become more consistent with the 'socialist spiritual civilization', 'improve suzhi', 'social stability', and, more recently, the 'China Dream'. Cultural actors such as linguists and film directors spearheaded this process of de-politicization via a civilizing mission. For some linguists, Diaosi's insinuation of the 'male genitalia' was regarded as 'rude' and 'vulgar'. More specifically, *HaoMingkam*, a prominent linguist, a party member, and founder of the influential Language Scrutiny book series, considered it as linguistically corrupted and too crude and uncivilized for public consumption. In his explanation for why the term Diaosi failed to make it into the *2012 Ten Most Popular Phrases* in China, he stated that:

> .... the extensive use of these words may allow some people to become psychologically and morally shameless; they think they can say anything. If a person uses vulgar language, his/her behaviour is far from being civilized. (culture.people.com.cn, 2013)

In the same period, this civilizing mission was echoed by Feng Xiaogang, who is a commercially successful film director/writer/actor. He claimed that he had difficulties in explaining Diaosi to his counterparts abroad. In his microblog, he recorded that this identity is not so much self-deprecating as 'self-destructive' and even 'brainless' (Chinanews.com, 2013). This piece was forwarded tens of thousands of times. This has attracted agreement from Hao, the linguist, but this disruption generated resentments from within the Diaosi community (Sina.com, 2013). Nonetheless, language and identity monitors of this kind continue to scrutinize and even sanitize the term by morphing it from its original version of Diaosi (meaning 'fans of penis') to a homonym of 'Dil-si' (meaning 'hanging wire'). Major websites such as *Wikipedia* (in Chinese) and *Baidu* even posed these two terms as being interchangeable with some even claiming that 'Dil-si' is more suitable for 'female Diaosi'. This focus on the sanitization of its scatological aspects (Yang, Tang, & Wang, 2015) depoliticizes the social claims of Diaosi and weakens its critical edge. By the end of December 2014, the official presses also jointed in this civilizing mission. Official newspapers were posting critiques of Diaosi and their identity. On 2 December 2014, the *People's Daily* posted an article on 'Assessing Diaosi: When will Self-Deprecation End?' This column highlighted that Diaosi is a self-denigrating label and its ' .... cultures neither allow young people to be more independent nor transmit a more positive force to the society'. It 'should be denounced and abandoned, because it can cause serious harm to the spirit of youth' (wenweipo.com, 2014). This piece was reprinted in other official newspapers such as *China Youth Daily.* These ways of monitoring and civilizing the Diaosi identity do not destroy critical consciousness but affect how its contradictory character is played out online in representational struggles.

This marginality is rejected by some subalterns and accepted by others. Some indulge in consumption and/or seek pleasure from the culture industries; others live in hope and assume personal responsibility to fulfill these entrepreneurial-consumerist dreams by improving 'suzhi', obtaining better qualifications, finding good jobs, meeting good marriage partners, and moving over-ground to more comfortable housing. These entrepreneurial self-hopes coexist with experiences of social inequalities, suffering bodies, self-mocking irony, frustrated sexuality, and hopeless future as part of their system of signification. This system is by no means consistent or coherent. It contains 'contradictory consciousness' and fragmentation (Crehan, 2002, pp. 191–193). The resulting political struggle is embedded in the contradictory ensemble of state-mediated capitalist-consumerist social relations that produce hope, devalued life, marginality, and exploitation in China's cultural political economy. Such contradictory locations are reflected in a common sense that contains hegemonic forms of thinking as well as modes of critical insight. It interlaces agreement with the dominant consumerist/entrepreneurial

Table 2. Major Internet-based groups and their Diaosi-targeted sites and products

Name of corporations	Nature of sites and products	Sales and user volumes
Alibaba Group		
	• *Taobao* • On-line shopping • *Diaosi Fashion Club* for clothing and accessories • Hosting *Zara* goods • *Single's Day* for shopping • *Yu'ebao* • P2P money-market fund started since 2013 • Users can start with RMB 1 • Offer higher interest rates and instant liquidity • Mainly small clients with an average deposit of RMB 3300 (USD 532) • Aggregated amount then invested in Zenglibao money-market fund run by Tianhong (a Tianjin-based private-run asset management firm)	• *Single's Day* sales volume • RMB 35 billion (USD 5.7 billion) 2013 • RMB 19.1 billion (USD 3.1 billion) 2012 • RMB 5.2 billion (UDS 0.8 billion) 2011 • RMB 554 million (USD 90 billion) in assets and 81 million investors in 2014
YY.com		
	• Social communication platform • Provide group video sessions on concerts, education, fashion, sports, and personal finance • Sessions are hosted by stars and can be rewarded by paying for their virtual gifts (e.g. lollipop; flowers)—a way of living the imagined life of Gaofushuai • Virtual dating service	• 310 million registered users and 60 million monthly active users • Active users spend on average RMB 200–300 (USD 32–48) per month
Tencent Holdings Ltd.'s QQ.com		
	• QZone • Social messaging service and e-commerce • Provide online/mobile-phone games with cute/sexy girls • Sell virtual goods (e.g. funny images, pets, clothing and accessories to customize online avatars, etc.)	• 89 million customers spent on average USD 20 each per month

Source: Author's own compilation based on information on the three corporate websites.

ideology and precariousness, loneliness, self-mockery, frustrations, and latent critical thinking as part of the subaltern conditions and languages.

Two Sets of Concluding Remarks

This article ends with two sets of remarks. First, regarding the Diaosi, it examined the dialectical intertwining of a loser/little hope subject with the global imagination of China as a 'hope' object since the financial crisis. This is the conjuncture in which the Diaosi subject emerged. Their marginality is co-governed by global capitalist production, the land- and property-based mode of accumulation, and continuous state domination via a hukou-suzhi biopolitical population management policy mechanism. With increasing inequalities and the making of a devalued life, younger second-generation workers self-narrate as Diaosi and express such identity affectively. They embody their marginality via a body discourse that builds on the everyday unevenness regarding power networks, consumption, marriage, love, and intimacy. This self-representational struggle of Diaosi is fragmented and they remain at best a 'class against the dominant order' rather than becoming, as a primarily class-theoretical analysis might anticipate, a unified class for itself that could effectively resist hegemony/domination. Indeed, at the time of writing, dominant market actors are providing consumer and entrepreneurial hope and state forces are seeking to remake, rehegemonize, and disrupt the Diaosi subject with variable resonance. From a Gramscian viewpoint, it is worth asking whether the fragments of Diaosi could create an autonomous sphere of action that would enable them to overcome subalternity in the absence of the full consciousness of their alleged class identity and interests?

Second, by asking these questions inspired by neo-Gramscian insights, this paper has also addressed labour/subaltern studies on China. Some Marxist/Weberian scholars sought to understand second-generation migrant workers in terms of their class position and consciousness (e.g. Chan & Pun, 2009; Chan, Pun, & Seldon, 2013; Chan & Siu, 2012, pp. 79–160; Leung & Pun, 2009). These arguments are often linear. They assume that conditions of exploitation will either lead to proletarianization and identification with the working class or, where this is not fully developed, it is explained in Weberian terms concerned with limits on organizational and/or representational capacities. Conversely, those interested in the subaltern consciousness of migrant labour often focus on their cultural communicative practices (e.g. new media, urban cinemas, and literature) and their speaker-abilities (e.g. Pun, 2005; Sun, 2014; Yan, 2008). Inspired by first-generation Indian subaltern studies, especially Spivak, they hardly mention Gramsci, who discussed the subaltern in *Notebook* 25 in 1934. Indeed, this prompted Marcus Green (2002), a Gramscian subaltern scholar, to claim 'Gramsci Cannot Speak'.

To give Gramsci a voice, this article suggests three (re-)entry points. First, examine the production of class consciousness not as automatic but as a culturally mediated lived experience with diverse expressions (Zene, 2011). The latter shifts attention from the working class (proletariat or sub-proletariat) to 'subaltern classes/groups' that encompass more components of society (Buttigieg, 2013, p. 36). This allows an examination of different types of subaltern groups beyond their labouring identity (e.g. Diaosi's love life). Such marginal groups are fragmented with diverse expressions of critical consciousness and contradictory common sense (Green and Ives, 2010, p. 304).

Second, neo-Gramscian insights also question the Marxist/Weberian focus on organizational and representational factors affecting the ability of labour to mobilize in China. For Green (2002, p. 19), improving these factors will not overcome group marginalization because this has deeper roots in exploitation and contradictions grounded in the overall ensemble of social relations with their various kinds of social exclusion (Green & Ives, 2010, p. 305). Third, we can examine how subaltern agency is positioned between the politics of silence/invisibility dominated by elite discourses (cf. Spivak, 1988) and the potentials of gaining their own voice and negotiating within and in relation to domination (cf. second-generation subaltern studies, e.g. Green, 2002, p. 18; Nilsen & Roy, 2015, pp. 1–5; Zene, 2011, pp. 96–98).[4] Apart from focusing on the ability to speak, neo-Gramscians such as Green and Ives (2010, pp. 302–307) stress the importance of 'language and imaginations from the bottom up' that allow for the visibilization of the varieties of subaltern agencies with diverse locations (Liguori, 2015). Sun's work on *Subaltern China* (2014) is moving in this direction. However, if we seek to go beyond first-generation subaltern studies and return to the Gramscian tradition, we should also focus on language/imaginations/discourses (not only communication practices), contradictory consciousness of the subaltern, as well as the concurrent processes of re-hegemonization that involve diverse realignments of subaltern knowledge/practices with hegemonic principles (Vahabzadeh, 2008, p. 108).

In short, a neo-Gramscian entry point extends the examination of working-class consciousness to different types of subaltern classes/groups. The marginal and fragmentary elements of these groups have not become a class for itself; but exist as 'multiplicity' of elements of 'consciousness construction' (Green & Ives, 2010, p. 292; Modonesi, 2014, p. 2). In this regard, movement beyond first-generation subaltern studies discloses a range of subaltern experiences of subordination and insubordination and the affective languages and imaginations that contains critical and contradictory insights that can be re-grounded diversely in hegemonic principles. These constitute parts of the 'passive revolution' that depoliticizes and disrupts critical insights and alternative thinking among subaltern groups (Thomas, 2009, p. 147).

Disclosure Statement

No potential conflict of interest was reported by the author.

Notes

1 Worried about social instability, central government took steps between 2010 and 2013 to dampen the property market (e.g. tightening credit, raising deposits for purchase of new land to 50%; restricting the purchase of second and third homes, etc.) with only moderate effects upon housing prices and rents.

2 The Market and Media Research Centre of Beijing University conducted a survey on the 2014 Living Conditions of Diaosi. Of 210,000 youths interviewed, more than 60% described themselves as Diaosi. This survey showed that they earned RMB 2917.7 (USD 479). From this, they spent RMB 500 (USD 81) on rent, RMB 39 (USD 6) per day for 3 meals, RMB 1076 (USD 174) to send to parents, and RMB 500 (USD 81) on vacations.

3 'Hal-hal' is a popular Chinese term used by social networks and QQ groups. It has various meanings that range from communicating self-mockery through helplessness to don't know what to say. For details, see http://nx.shangdu.com/news/72-16463-0.html

4 This article draws on but goes beyond first-generation subaltern studies especially Spivak's post-Marxist-Derridean conception of the communicative process between subalterns and elites (Zene, 2011, p. 94). Whereas Spivak examines this in terms of speech acts, this article directs attention to the contradictory consciousness and self-representation of the subaltern and everyday struggles. This more Marxist–Gramscian analysis draws on Green (2002) and second-generation subaltern scholars (e.g. Zene, 2011; Nilsen & Roy, 2015).

References

Anagnost, A. (2004). The corporeal politics of quality (Suzhi). *Public Culture*, *16*, 189–208.

Baidu.com. (2013). *Housing market observer: Difficult to break the law of housing prices do not fall and rent can only rise*. Retrieved from http://house.baidu.com/guangyuan/scan/0/5908764472327346505/

Bell, D. (2010). *China's new confucianism*. Princeton, NJ: Princeton University Press.

Buttigieg, J. (2013). Subaltern social groups in Antonio Gramsci's Prison Notebooks. In C. Zene (Ed.), *The political philosophies of Antonio Gramsci and B.R. Ambedkar* (pp. 35–42). Abington: Routledge.

Chan, A., & Siu, K. (2012). Chinese migrant workers: Factors constraining the emergence of class consciousness. In B. Carrillo & D. Goodman (Eds.), *China's peasants and workers* (pp. 79–101). Cheltenham: Edward Elgar.

Chan, C., & Pun, N. (2009). The making of a new working class? A study of collective actions of migrant workers in South China. *China Quarterly*, *198*, 287–303.

Chan, J., Pun, N., & Seldon, M. (2013). The politics of global production: Apple, Foxconn and China's new working class. *New Technology, Work and Employment*, *27*(2), 100–115.

Chanos, J. (2011). Chanos Interview on 'China's property bubble is hitting the wall. *Business Insiders*. Retrieved from http://www.businessinsider.com/chanos-china-european-kind-of-numbers-2011-9?IR=T

Chinanews.com (2013). *Expert's assessment of Feng Xiaogang's comments on 'Diaosi': Giving obscene connotations to buzzwords*. Retrieved from http://www.chinanews.com/cul/2013/03-06/4621699.shtml

Cho, D., & Rhee, C. (2013). *Effects of quantitative easing on Asia: Capital flows and financial markets*. Asian Development Bank Economics Working Paper Series, 350. Retrieved from http://www.adb.org/sites/default/files/publication/30283/ewp-350.pdf

Crehan, K. (2002). *Gramsci, culture and anthropology*. London: Pluto Press.

Culture.people.com.cn. (2013). *Linguist agrees with Feng Xiaogang view: The term 'Diaosi' should not be abused*. Retrieved from http://culture.people.com.cn/n/2013/0308/c22219-20717662.html

Foucault, M. (1988). The political technology of individualism. In L. H. Martin, H. Gutman, & P. H. Hutton (Eds.), *Technologies of the self: A seminar with Michel Foucault* (pp. 145–162). Amherst: University of Massachusetts Press.

Gao, J. (2013). *The "Diaosi" social class: Presage of impending social changes in China*. Retrieved from http://www.ministryoftofu.com/2013/06/the-diaosi-social-class-presage-of-impending-social-changes-in-china/

Green, M. (2002). Gramsci cannot speak. *Rethinking Marxism*, *14*(3), 1–24.

Green, M., & Ives, P. (2010). Subalternity and language: Overcoming the fragmentation of common sense. In P. Ives & R. Lacorte (Eds.), *Gramsci, language and translation* (pp. 289–312). Lanham: Lexington Books.

Gu, W. (2014). China's self-described losers play a winning role: Consumer underclass may be where the real money is. *Wall Street Journal*. Retrieved from http://www.wsj.com/articles/SB10001424052702304703804579380683402958724

Hsing, Y.-T. (2010). *The Great Urban transformation: Politics of land and property in China*. Oxford: Oxford University Press.

Huang, Y. (2013). Lack of affordable housing threatens China's urban dream. *China Dialogue*. Retrieved from https://www.chinadialogue.net/article/show/single/en/6365-Lack-of-affordable-housing-threatens-China-s-urban-dream

Hung, R. (2011). The state and the market: Chinese TV serials on the case of Woju (Dwelling Narrowness). *Boundary*, *38*(2), 157–187.

Jager, M. (2008). BRIC as international investors: China in a class of its own. *Deutsche Bank Research, Talking Point*. Retrieved from http://www.slideshare.net/soniabess/china-as-an-international-investor-in-a-class-of-its-own-presentation

Kipnis, A. (2006). Suzhi: A keyword approach. *The China Quarterly*, *186*, 295–313.

Larmer, B. (2013, March 9). The price of marriage in China. *The New York Times*. Retrieved from http://www.nytimes.com/2013/03/10/business/in-a-changing-china-new-matchmaking-markets.html?_r=0

Legg, S. (2005). Foucault's population geographies: Classifications, biopolitics and governmental spaces. *Population, Space and Place*, *11*(3), 137–156.

Leung, P. N., & Pun, N. (2009). The radicalization of the new Chinese working class: A case study of collective action in the gemstone industry. *Third World Quarterly*, *30*(3), 551–565.

Leung, P. P. (2015). *Labor activists and the new working class in China*. London: Palgrave.

Li, K., Spotti, M., & Kroon, S. (2014). *An e-ethnography of Baifumeion the Baidu Tieba: Investigating an emerging economy of identification online*. Tilburg Papers in Culture Studies, 120, Tilburg University. Retrieved from https://www.tilburguniversity.edu/upload/c7982626-e1a6-40a8-9334-9fba945ac568_TPCS_120_Kunming-Spotti-Kroon.pdf

Liguori, G. (2015). Conceptions of subalternity in Gramsci. In D. McNally (Ed.), *Antonio Gramsci* (pp. 118–136). London: Palgrave.

Lui, J. (2015). *China's disaffected Diaosi tribe*. Retrieved from http://gbtimes.com/life/chinas-disaffected-diaosi-tribe

Marquis, C., & Yang, Z. (2013). *Diaosi: Evolution of a Chinese meme*. Retrieved from http://www.civilchina.org/2013/07/diaosi-evolution-of-a-chinese-meme/

Miller, P., & Rose, N. (1990). Governing economic life. *Economy and Society*, *25*(3), 327–356.

Modonesi, M. (2014). *Constructing the political subject*. London: Pluto Press.

Nilsen, A., & Roy, S. (2015). Introduction. In A. Nilsen & S. Roy (Eds.), *New subaltern politics* (pp. 1–10). New Delhi: Cambridge University Press.

Offbeat China. (2011). *Leftover women in China speak their hearts out 'no car, no house, no bride'*. Retrieved from http://offbeatchina.com/leftover-women-in-china-speak-their-heart-out-no-house-no-car-no-bride

O'Neill, J. (2013). *The growth map: Economic opportunity in the BRICs and beyond*. London: Portfolio Penguin.

Pettis, M. (2011). China: No hard landing, but no solution. *Financial Sense*. Retrieved from http://www.financialsense.com/contributors/michael-pettis/2011/08/01/no-hard-landing-but-no-solution

Pow, C.-P. (2009). *Gated communities in China: Class, privilege and the moral politics of the good life*. London: Palgrave.

Pulitzer Centre. (2015). *Beijing's rate tribe*. Pulitzer Centre of Crisis Reporting. Retrieved from http://pulitzercenter.org/project/asia-china-beijing-rat-tribe-migrant-workers-poverty-service-poor-housing

Pun, N. (2005). *Made in China*. Durham, DC: Duke University Press.

Ren, H. (2013). The middle-class norm as responsible consumption in China's risk society. In A. Anagnost, A. Arai, & H. Ren (Eds.), *Global futures in East Asia: Youth, nation, and the new economy in uncertain times* (pp. 29–52). Stanford: Stanford University Press.

Scott, J. (1992). *Domination and the arts of resistance*. New Haven, CT: Yale University Press.

Sim, C. Y. (2015). *Meet the million migrant workers living beneath Beijing's streets*, Creative Time Reports. Retrieved from http://creativetimereports.org/2015/01/24/sim-chi-yin-rat-tribe-beijing-underground-apartments/

Sina.com. (2013). *Language experts agree with Feng Xiaogang: The Diaosi term should not be abused*. Retrieved from http://ent.sina.com.cn/s/m/2013-03-08/05393872334.shtml

Spivak, G. (1988). Can the subaltern speak? In C. Nelson & L. Grossberg (Eds.), *Marxism and the interpretation of culture* (pp. 271–313). Urbana: University of Illinois Press.

Sum, N.-L. (2013a). A cultural political economy of financial crisis: The turn to BRIC and the subalterns in China. *Economy and Society*, *42*(4), 543–570.

Sum, N.-L. (2013b). Rethinking developmental state via cultural political economy: Neoliberal developmentalism and the case of China. In *Relocating developmental states in their transnational and local contexts*, Conference Proceedings, SNU Asia Centre, National Seoul University, South Korea, 22–23 August, 73–88. Retrieved from https://stateandregion.files.wordpress.com/2013/08/1st-workshop-on-geo-political-economies-of-east-asia-full-proceedings.pdf

Sum, N.-L., & Jessop, B. (2013). *Towards a cultural political economy*. Cheltenham: Edward Elgar.

Sun, W. (2014). *Subaltern China*. Lanham: Rowman and Littlefield.

Szablewicz, M. (2014). The 'losers' of China's Internet: Memes as 'structures of feeling' for disillusioned young netizens. *China Information*, *28*(2), 259–275.

Thomas, P. (2009). *The Gramscian Moment*. Leiden: Brill.

Tomba, L. (2009). Of quality, harmony, and community: Civilization and the middle class in urban China. *Positions*, *17*(3), 591–616.

Vahabzadeh, P. (2008). *The conditions of subalternity: Reflections on subjectivity, experience and hegemony*. Retrieved from http://socialiststudies.com/article/view/23782/17667

Wenweipo.com. (2014). *People's Daily: Diaosi concept will damage the youth spirit*. Retrieved from http://news.wenweipo.com/2014/12/02/IN1412020071.htm

Wu, F., Webster, C., He, S., & Liu, Y. (2010). *Urban poverty in China*. Cheltenham: Edward Elgar.

Wu, F., Xu, J., & Yeh, A. G. O. (2007). *Urban development in post-reform China: State, market and space*. London: Routledge.

Xiao, H. (2010). Love as a capacity: The narrative of gendered development in Chinese-style divorce. *Journal of Contemporary China*, *19*(66m), 735–753.

Xinhuanet.com. (2013). *Media report Shanghai and Beijing property prices rose by 500% and 365% respectively in a decade*. Retrieved from http://www.news.xinhuanet.com/fortune/2013-02-/25/c_124385598.htm

Yan, H. (2008). *New masters, new servants: Migration, development, and women workers in China*. Durham: Duke University Press.

Yang, L., & Lim, C. K. (2010). Three waves of nationalism in contemporary China: Sources, themes, presentations and consequences. In E. Yeoh (Ed.), *China in transition: Social change in the age of reform* (pp. 461–486). Kuala Lumpur: Institute of China Studies.

Yang, P., Tang, L., & Wang, X. (2015). Diaosi as infrapolitics: Scatological tropes, identity-making and cultural intimacy on China's Internet. *Media, Culture and Society, 37*(2), 197–214.

Yu, H. (2011). Dwelling narrowness: Chinese media and its disingenuous neoliberal logic. *Continuum: Media and Cultural Studies, 25*(1), 33–46.

Zene, C. (2011). Self-consciousness of the Dalits as 'Subalterns'. In M. Green (Ed.), *Rethinking Marxism* (pp. 90–104). London: Routledge.

Zhang, C., & Barreda, D. (2013). *Hip, young, and wired: China's 'Diaosi', in charts, Atlantic's Tea Leaf Nation.* Retrieved from http://www.theatlantic.com/china/archive/2013/06/hip-young-and-wired-chinas-diaosi-in-charts/277359/

Zhang, F. (2014). *China's urbanization and the world economy.* Aldershot: Edward Elgar.

Zhang, L. (2010). *In search of paradise: Middle-class living in a Chinese Metropolis.* Ithaca, NY: Cornell University Press.

Zhang, N. (2014). Performing identities: Women in rural–urban migration in contemporary China. *Geoforum, 54*, 17–27.

Zhang, X. (2013). *China's 'ant tribe' present social survival situation and personal financial advice.* Retrieved from http://www.ccsenet.org/journal/index.php/ass/article/viewFile/24350/15405

Zhuayoukong.com. (2014). *Volkswagen will push three cheap brands, targeting the Chinese Diaosi market and plans to sell 500,000 cars.* Retrieved from http://www.zhuayoukong.com/733454.html

The China Price: The All-China Federation of Trade Unions and the Repressed Question of International Labour Standards

ROB LAMBERT* & EDWARD WEBSTER**

**University of Western Australia, Perth, Australia*
***University of the Witwatersrand, Johannesburg, South Africa*

ABSTRACT *The focus of this paper is the character and role of the All-China Federation of Trade Unions (ACFTU) in securing and sustaining a cheap labour regime within China. This labour regime is shaping the character of neoliberal regimes across the globe with dire consequences for societies everywhere. We argue that the international labour movement has the potential to create a movement against this regime, a movement defined by the international labour standards (ILS). The rise of the Southern Initiative on Globalisation and Trade Union Rights (SIGTUR) is a southern network grounded in ILS. However, in spite of SIGTUR's commitment to independent trade unions there is division within the movement as some support the ACFTU on ideological grounds. We conclude by arguing that support for democratic unions in China can best be achieved by linking local workplace struggles to ongoing pressure on the ACFTU to apply ILS.*

In August 2010, South African government officials began closing down clothing and textile factories in the country town of Newcastle, in the province of KwaZulu-Natal. This came in the face of workers' angry protests because the owners were paying less than the statutory minimum wage of 324 Rand (US$49) a week. The factory owners said they could not pay more and survive in the face of cheap Chinese textile imports. They called it 'the China price' (Webster, 2012, p. 116).

Our paper grapples with the All-China Federation of Trade Unions' (ACFTU) role in sustaining the China price and its wider significance for democratic labour movements and the societies in which they are embedded. We examine how this role is an expression of the current marketised employment relations in China. We contend that this labour system is the cornerstone of neoliberal restructuring and that this has implications for the cost of labour everywhere. The Chinese system is a cornerstone because the political commitments to neoliberalism across the globe (the removal of all protections in trade, investment and finance) have created perfect conditions for global corporations to exploit the uneven geography of labour (Harvey, 2002, p. 31). The consequent restructuring has led to a concentration of investment in nations where international labour standards (ILS) are denied, resulting in a corresponding process of factory closures where labour rights and freedoms exist. China is a pivotal force in these transformations, attracting large-scale corporate investments into designated export processing zones (EPZs) like a magnet. These zones then trade cheap manufactured goods into world markets (Friedman & Lee, 2010). This has created a process of uneven and combined development which has proven to be socially destructive (Bieler & Morton, 2014, pp. 35–47). Harvey (2006, p. 34) views the coincidence of the United States and Britain's shift to neoliberal restructuring at the very moment when China introduced neoliberal reforms as 'a conjunctural accident of world-historical significance'. What comes into play here is the complementary role of authoritarian statism and neoliberal market forces sustaining an unending attack on ILS across the globe. Indeed, the question of ILS addresses globalisation's core contradiction between 'the race to the bottom … and the international agenda for improvement in labour conditions which aims to create "decent work" for all' (Lerche, Guerin, & Srivastava, 2012, p. 1).

We argue that reasserting ILS globally is one crucial aspect in the struggle against neoliberalism. The Global Labour University's launch in June 2015 of its online course which focuses on workers' rights in the global economy for trade unionists is a welcome innovation.[1] ILS's fundamental principles, ILO Convention 87 (freedom of association; workers' right to join organisations of their own choosing), Convention 98 (collective bargaining rights to ensure that unions are not dominated by employers), and Convention 151 (the rights of public sector workers), need to be promoted so as to inform political debate in workplaces and communities. Such an intervention provides a moral compass, distinguishing democratic unions from state and corporate organisations. In terms of this choice, our paper assesses the ACFTU by analysing the contradictions embedded in its reform process, contradictions which the international trade union movement needs to consider in their rush to endorse the ACFTU as a genuine trade union. In the context of the global logic of neoliberalism we pose the question: why is ILS not deemed applicable to the ACFTU? Apart from the International Union of Food Workers (IUF), all the other trade union internationals have endorsed and therefore legitimated the ACFTU by claiming it is becoming a genuine union movement.

Our paper is divided as follows: firstly, we show how ACFTU's actions have emboldened the international trade union movement to recognise the official Chinese union. Secondly, we dissect the ACFTU's contradictory character and highlight the federation's role in the evolution of labour law and workplace elections of union leaders. Thirdly, we briefly specify the nature of ILS preconditions. We illustrate this through the choice the Southern Initiative on Globalisation and Trade Union Rights (SIGTUR) made to build democratic unionism (SIGTUR, 1996). Fourthly, we analyse the position of Southern unions, showing how they remain divided with some who are sympathetic to the ACFTU on ideological grounds. We conclude by reflecting on the implications of this division for the international trade union movement. We argue for a profound change in the role of trade unionism confronted by neoliberal restructuring. This can best be done, we suggest, by developing closer links between local workplace organising and ongoing pressure by the international labour movement on the ACFTU to apply ILS.

Part of the data for this article is drawn from our active engagement in SIGTUR, a networked movement in the Global South formed in May 1991. Rob Lambert is one of its founders and Edward Webster has been a principal advisor since its inception. This has given us access to democratic movements across the Global South enabling us to conduct interviews with key informants and observe the changing dynamics within the international labour movement. In this we raise a vitally important issue: do democratic unions in the Global South pose a challenge to the ACFTU? Before we engage this issue, we present a critique of the ACFTU and the role of the established trade union movement in relation to the claims being advanced by the Chinese labour federation.

The ACFTU and the Repressed Question of ILS

If the question of ILS remains repressed (removed from consciousness) by the international trade union movement's leadership, then the basis for assessing the ACFTU's character is weak. In the absence of ILS it becomes easier to manipulate the contradictions by exploring only one side of the ledger and obliterating the other from consciousness. From this vantage point, the ACFTU appears under the guise of a trade union undergoing deep reforms which benefit Chinese workers. Certainly the ACFTU has gained influence in the halls of political power through its long-standing relationship with the Chinese Communist Party (CCP). Hence, the international trade union movement contends that the federation is using this power to improve the position of workers and their local enterprise unions. The ACFTU, it is argued, has demonstrated an enduring commitment to this reform process over the past 20 years. The international trade union movement therefore spotlights what they view as positive advances:

- As a result of the passage of the 1994 National Labour Law, all workers have a written labour contract with one employer with the potential to secure basic rights in the workplace.
- The flexibility of these contracts has stimulated dynamic economic growth thereby creating jobs and opportunity for Chinese workers.
- Labour law change now protects the working conditions of Chinese workers. These include an 8-hour day, a 44-hour week, overtime limitations, retirement benefits, sickness benefits, including occupational diseases, maternity leave, and unemployment benefits. Some of these provisions are regarded as an advance on those in the European Union.
- The law places constraints on subcontracting companies. Companies can only employ workers on subcontracting arrangements for 1 year. Thereafter, they are required to directly hire workers. Few countries in the world have tackled this thorny issue.
- Further constraints are applied to 1-year short-term contracts. A December 2006 draft of the labour law advanced the idea of open-ended contracts after 2-year-long fixed-term contracts had run their course.
- Conflict resolution through mediation and arbitration processes is evolving.

From the vantage point of one side of the ledger, International Trade Union Council (ITUC) and the Global Union Federations (GUFs) are impressed. They argue that if the ACFTU has achieved these progressive changes over the past 20 years, they are well positioned to advance further working class protections without impeding China's remarkable economic growth rates. Furthermore, the ACFTU is promoting the democratic elections of union leadership which will empower workers and create space for workers to express their views quite openly.

However, the situation of workers in China looks different when the contradictions are acknowledged and both sides of the ledger are considered. As Taylor and Li (2007, p. 701) argue, the ACFTU is not a legitimate union; there is no effective electoral system for union office holders; the federation is a state organ closely subordinated to the CCP. Their inability to represent workers, the authors argue, 'comes from the dual role imposed by the CCP': firstly, unions exist to intensify production and thereby compete globally in achieving the 'China price'; secondly, unions exist to represent workers. This goal is unattainable because of the centralised control imposed by the CCP (Taylor & Li, 2007, p. 709). This analysis highlights the negation of democratic trade unions and the grass-roots associational power they embrace to effectively enforce the new rights of workers under the law. Operationalising these rights is severely limited.

Tendencies within the CCP and the ACFTU to acknowledge workers' rights under the law are being applied in the present system. However, they are not ready to admit that ILS is critical to breathing life into the labour relations system. Free and independent trade unionism will have the capacity to fight for change from below, recognising that top-down gifts without a genuine trade union movement present lean pickings at best.

Dissecting ACFTU Contradictions

As we have argued, ILS distinguishes the character and the role of a genuine trade union through a value judgement reflecting a choice to build a *moral* economy grounded in giving voice to the voiceless. History demonstrates that this option is only available when workers are free to choose and construct their own unions *without previous authorisation* (ILO Convention 87).The interests of marginalised workers can never be realised, when unions are under the domination of corporations and the state. However, only one international union, the IUF, has moved against the tide by contending that the ACFTU is not a genuine trade union. Indeed, the IUF argues that the Federation unites Chinese state and corporate power in a force which intervenes to manage, control, and—when the need arises—repress freedom initiatives from below, thereby complicating and undermining emerging solidarity relations.[2]

In sharp contrast, the established international trade unions' movement, the ITUC and the GUFs, does not view the ACFTU in these terms. Over the past 7 years, all barring the IUF are deeply engaged in 'dialogue' with the official federation. International Trade Union Council's Secretary, Sharon Burrow, led a delegation in early October 2014 stating, in the presence of a leading Political Bureau member, 'I appreciate the progress China has made in seeking social development and workers' rights over the past sixty-five years' (Xinhua News Agency, 2014). National organisations such as the German trade union federation, *Deutscher Gewerkschaftsbund* (DGB), and certain global unions have met with ACFTU leaders, moving from a 'no contact' strategy to a 'more proactive and cooperative approach' which recognises that the ACFTU is developing a 'more aggressive and open policy' (Sander, 2009, p. 3). Even the powerful progressive International Transport Federation (ITF) has signed a Memorandum of Understanding calling for 'harmonious relations' between the two bodies, which would 'ensure mutual respect and the recognition of the roles of both parties' (Maritime Unions of Australia, 2014). The ITF claims that 'international solidarity' will develop out of this cooperative approach. According to Sander (2009), all of these initiatives reflect changes within the

ACFTU towards greater independence from state and party. In the view of these unions, there is credible evidence of such a change.

What is the evidence? In the minds of those promoting constructive engagement, the ACFTU is a uniquely CCP-styled trade union. Thus, political and cultural difference needs to be recognised. CCP unions differ, it is argued, from the Western model and the reform achievements realised through a close connection with the Chinese state and the CCP is a historical phenomenon which should not be moulded into Western-styled unionism since this is a product of a different history (Maritime Union of Australia, 2014). For example, notwithstanding the lack of independent workers' representation and poor enforcement of consultation outcomes, Shen and Benson argue, the widespread introduction of tripartite consultation is a first step towards more genuine collective bargaining (Shen & Benson, 2008). Furthermore, it is contended, concrete achievements should be acknowledged. An intimate relationship with party and the state has given the ACFTU status, influence, and authority in policy-making in the economy, society, and politics. This has enabled the federation to promote a reform programme in labour law, including collective bargaining, direct union elections in companies, the advancement of unionisation in foreign enterprises, legal aid to workers, and the settlement of labour disputes (Chen, 2009, p. 673). Such influence was not possible in an earlier period of history when the ACFTU had minimal influence in the party and the state. Despite being formally incorporated into the party/state structure when the communist state was formed in 1948, the Cultural Revolution between 1966 and 1976 undermined that status. Their role was reactivated in 1978 when Deng Xiaoping introduced market reforms. However, the Tiananmen repression resulted in tighter controls over the federation with the party appointing union leaders. This incorporation and subordination resulted in a bureaucratic-styled unionism where structures emerged without participation, mobilisation, and struggle for improved wages and conditions. Chen (2009, p. 663) analyses the nature of the power derived from being strategically positioned within the CCP and the state. Through this relationship the ACFTU becomes a state apparatus contradicting the provisions of ILO Convention 98.

Four new departments were set up which are responsible for collective contracts, democratic management, legal affairs, and grass-roots organising. Furthermore, it is argued that, given its official status, the ACFTU played a major role in advancing legislative change through labour law reforms in 1994: the Trade Union Law of 2001 and the Labour Contract Law of 2007. The ACFTU contends that they played a crucial role in the development of these legal rights and that their institutional status was vital to realising these changes. But what was the nature of the legal changes, which the leadership of the ACFTU claims to have played a key role in formulating?

The ACFTU and Legal Reform Contradictions

Labour law reform in China (the National Labour Law of 1994; the Trade Union Law of 2001) is integral to the post-1978 economic reforms which embraced neoliberal globalisation. Lifetime employment and job security in state-owned enterprises gave way to insecure short-term individual contracts as legal reform was shaped by free market ideology (Friedman & Lee, 2010). The 1994 National Labour Law stated that all workers in China should have a written labour contract with one employer to secure rights in the workplace. Since the mid-1990s the vast majority of labour contracts are fixed term where the length of the contract has become increasingly shortened (Gallagher & Dong, 2011, p. 7). This has now reached the extremity where the majority of corporations employ workers on the basis of a 1-year contract, and they are at liberty to end employment when the contract expires. These changes have created highly insecure employment conditions in China and have undermined workers' bargaining power. The underlying neoliberal commitment promotes the contention that the 'flexibility' of these short-term contracts has driven economic efficiency. However, the promotion of flexible labour markets and privatisation has led to accelerating social inequality and social instability reflected in a rise of strikes and conflict. As an academic involved in the legislative process publically observed, 'China's recent economic growth and success has been at the expense of its workers. They have been sacrificed' (Gallagher & Dong, 2011, p. 14).

These legal changes are beset with contradictions. They have led to considerable internal disagreement within the ACFTU and sections of the CCP on the issue of short-term contracts. This is reflected in a December 2006 draft of the labour law which advanced the idea of open-ended contracts after two fixed-term contracts had run their course to reduce workers' precarious situation (Gallagher & Dong, 2011, p. 31). The draft also included constraints on the way subcontracting companies operated. This intervention took the position that companies could only employ workers on subcontracting arrangements for a 1-year period after which workers must be hired directly (Gallagher & Dong, 2011, p. 27). In addition, key clauses on collective contracts were introduced and the ACFTU was given increased powers to establish collective contracts. A further positive dimension of labour law change is the entrenchment of notable benefits in the legal changes of 1994. These included an 8-hour day, a 44-hour week, overtime limitations, and benefits for retirement, illness, occupational disease, maternity leave, and unemployment. However, these benefits are often unenforced and/or unclaimed as local states appear not to have the capacity or political will to apply these provisions. This situation is exacerbated by the absence of legal penalties for non-enforcement of these provisions. It is further undermined by the ACFTU's subordination to the CCP and the emphasis on the primacy of economic growth which is promoted in a way which fails to properly address the need to defend workers' basic rights (Clarke, Lee, & Li, 2004). The Trade Union Law of 2001 specifies the role and essential responsibilities of the ACFTU at company level. Local enterprise branches of the federation must 'safeguard the constitution', prioritise 'economic development as the central task', and 'uphold the people's democratic dictatorship'. This statement again highlights the ACFTU's subordination to the CCP and how democratic centralism is a euphemism for party control. Crucially, enterprise-level trade unions are obliged to follow the dictates of local party and government leadership. They are primarily concerned with promoting the neoliberal model of economic growth which defines China's role as one of providing cheap manufactured products to global markets. Since local-level union leaders are employed and paid by companies, they do not promote the independent voice and needs of workers. Instead, they concentrate on the neoliberal notion of 'balancing' the interests of management and workers. The legal reforms also focus on dispute resolution processes set out in the 1994 labour laws. These include internal company mediation, compulsory arbitration, and internal court litigation. Most workers reject company-based mediation as being too close to management, preferring arbitration instead. A large number of disputes are now being resolved through arbitration. These disputes were also expressed in strike action, which can be interpreted as a failure of ACFTU enterprise unions to become involved in the resolution of strikes because of the absence of leadership and organisation in workplaces.

What can we conclude on this labour law reform front? Fundamentally at stake is the CCP's choice to place the neoliberal market model at the centre stage in 'reforming' the Chinese economy. Such a strategic move has global consequences as 'flexible' contracts (code for zero employment security) strikes fear in the hearts of Chinese workers. They recognise their precarious status. These contracts attempt to control the workforce through this fear. Further, law reforms do not alter the fact that individual contracts dominate, relegating collective agreements to the margins. Could the election of leaders in the workplace create a leadership ready to fight for security?

The ACFTU and Democratic Workplace Unionism

Democratic, participatory unionism is fundamental to building associational power (solidarity and collective action) to defend workers' conditions and job security (Silver, 2003, p. 13; Webster, Lambert, & Bezuidenhout, 2008, p. 11). In accordance with China's labour law, foreign funded enterprises (FFEs) and domestic companies are required to establish union branches within months of setting up their investment. In our view, these attempts at unionisation are stillborn because Conventions 87 and 98 are denied. This opens a pathway for a situation where candidates for shop floor leadership are most often not workers—they are drawn from management and, in many instances, they are the human resource managers (Chan, 1993, 2000; Chen, 2009). A management-manipulated shop floor structure is not in any sense a trade union as defined by ILS. Consequently, any gains the ACFTU leadership has won in negotiating within the CCP, such as collective bargaining rights, an end to short-term contracts, the regulation of working time, overtime limitations, and other worker benefits are not being monitored and applied. A fundamental conclusion can therefore be drawn: the ACFTU has no proper foundation in workplaces and therefore exists as a mere shell without capacity to transform the situation of Chinese workers. Chen's (2009, p. 681) insightful analysis distinguishes between bureaucratic and associational power where the former leads to 'unions' which exist in name only:

> Union formation in private enterprises is a top down process to meet the target of union bureaucracies (or the government), rather than developing out of the workers' initiative. Completely controlled by employers and management, such unions serve only a cosmetic purpose. It is thus not surprising that many workers in private enterprises have no interest in unions.

The fault lines in these shop floor elections exist because of the failure to commit to democratic unionism (applying ILS Conventions in China), preferring instead the iron clad controls of a Leninist democratic centralism. Consequently, the union is marginalised at all levels below the province (Chan, 2000, p. 274). In this context, how have election initiatives been experienced? We illustrate these constraints through the much publicised case of Walmart (Chen, 2009, pp. 675–676; He & Xie, 2011, pp. 421–440). Following discussions between the leadership of ACFTU and the Service Employees International Union (SEIU), the ACFTU launched a secretive organising campaign at select Walmart stores. When approached, Walmart decided to recognise ACFTU branches at all their facilities. However, instead of such a move consolidating the possibility of building branches which were independent of management, the initiative resulted in the traditional outcome of management-controlled organisation in the workplace. Further branches were set up with the assistance of junior human resource managers, many of whom were appointed chair of the union branch. Remarkably, these initiatives were taken without the workforce's knowledge. The fact that workers were not even informed gives a clear insight into just how fatally flawed the ACFTU is. These initiatives demonstrate quite conclusively that this federation is not a trade union. As Convention 98 makes clear, 'unions' which are dominated by management represent a false unionism; it is a unionism set up to control workers rather than represent and fight for their interests. In the absence of a proper trade union in the Walmart stores, poor conditions were imposed on the workforces. These included keeping wages down to the minimum rate and the imposition of flexible working hours exacerbated by pressures to do voluntary work. He and Xie conclude their analysis of Walmart's trade union by suggesting that 'the compromise and tacit agreement between Walmart and the party-state not only reflects a marriage of convenience but also indicates some deeper compatibility between China's state corporatist model and Walmart's neoliberal approach' (He & Xie, 2011, p. 422).

Other examples confirm the trend of management being directly involved in setting up and controlling the 'union' at workplace level (Howell, 2008; Seung Wook Baek, 2007). In these circumstances, the notion of 'balancing' the interests of management and workers is an obfuscation of the existence of capitalist relations of production in China—there is no balance—only an inequality of power. In such a dynamic, workers are left isolated, without proper representation, thus confirming the significance of ILS as a principled means to expose the ACFTU as a sham structure when placed under this spotlight. This assessment is confirmed by pointing to similar trends in other enterprises. For instance, concerned about adverse publicity regarding its role in China, Reebok pressurised one of its suppliers, a Hong Kong/Taiwan-owned factory in Shenzhen, to allow free trade union elections at its facilities (Chan, 2008, p. 297). The election was contested and democratic. This was the first democratic trade union election in China's FFEs. However, this lasted for less than a year. Management co-opted the trade union candidate through a salary hike. This again highlights the weakness. Leaders could not be co-opted with such ease if a strong democratic union existed in the workplace.

In another highly publicised case, strike action at a supplier to the Honda auto parts factory in Guangdong province resulted in a remarkable 33% wage increase and a commitment to organising a fair election of a union chair. Workers did not succeed in the latter, which is an indicator that the ACFTU is still wary of allowing a trend towards greater independence to grow in strength. 'The main barrier to effective workplace unionism', Chan and Hui (2012, p. 668) conclude their analysis of the dynamics of the strike,

> is the lack of external support for workers' unionisation efforts; . . . on the one hand, the lower-level local trade unions are structurally integrated into the patron-client relationship between the local state and the global capital. On the other hand, support for workers from civil society is handicapped by the party-state's opposition to independent labour organising. (Chan & Hui, 2012, p. 653)

The Honda strike was part of a wave of wage strikes in the EPZs during 2010. The strikes highlighted the contradictions which have arisen as a result of the legal reforms outlined earlier (Chang & Cooke, 2015; Traub-Merz, 2011). In certain instances, workers have acted collectively to challenge the violations of labour law where wage payments were below the legal minimum and overtime was not paid. These strikes were spontaneous and the ACFTU intervened to advance the interests of the state and the corporations, exposing the failure of the federation to organise genuine trade unions (Traub-Merz, 2011). The significance in these collective actions is the evolving social consciousness of the workforce. Many of the strikers were second-generation migrants below the age of 30 who now saw their future in the cities. This future depends on whether or not they will build the capacity to fight for their rights despite the complication of ACFTU attempting to control and preempt collective action (Van Heerden, 2012).

This context opens up a potential solidarity role for the international trade union movement if they establish closer links with what are called 'grass-roots unions', a reference to the branches of the ACFTU at workplace level (Ma, 2011, p. 155). The strike wave of 2010 is evidence of a growing pressure 'from below' and a possible new role for emerging unions (Zhu, Warner, &

Feng, 2011, p. 129; Hui, 2012, p. 72). Labour shortages and the rise of modern production techniques, such as Just-in-Time, have increased Chinese workers' structural power. The rise of labour non-governmental organisations (NGOs), social media, and the relaxation of household registration have increased the potential of associational power (Pringle, 2014).

However, the political will to commit to grass-roots leadership is unlikely to develop as an option, because the international union leaders are of the view that the Chinese state, the CCP, and the ACFTU are successfully implementing a wide-ranging reform programme which is changing Chinese workers' conditions. In sum, we argue that the international trade union movement has moved too early in removing the pressure from the CCP and the ACFTU to endorse and apply ILS, which would allow for the growth of a genuine trade union movement in China. The fulsome, unqualified recognition and legitimation of the ACFTU is a major setback for all those forces striving to challenge the logic of neoliberal globalisation. Given the key role China has, and is playing in advancing neoliberalism, strengthening Chinese civil society is a critical priority.

If the spirit of resistance is in decline in the international trade union movement, could a commitment to social change in China be driven from the Global South?

Challenging the Role of the ACFTU?

Earlier we introduced a definition of democratic unionism grounded in ILS. Here we briefly consider whether or not the emergence of such unionism has the potential to democratise the ACFTU. Our research on this issue based on interviews with key SIGTUR leaders from Argentina, Brazil, South Africa, and India leads us to draw somewhat pessimistic conclusions. We will briefly show that this failure emerges out of intertwined historical relations between these SIGTUR unions and the ACFTU. SIGTUR was founded in May 1991 as a union-based movement of democratic unions committed to building power aimed at undermining neoliberalism (Lambert & Webster, 2001; SIGTUR, 1996). The aim was to construct new forms of power to face this enormous challenge. At various moments in SIGTUR's history a hope was sustained that an alternative to neoliberalism could be sustained. However, at the time of crafting this article the situation is indeed bleak. The South African Congress of South African Trade Unions (COSATU), once a leading democratic union movement which acted on principled positions locally and globally, is now a shell of its former self. The federation is deeply split and its power and influence has declined markedly. In this final section of the paper, we review the interviews we conducted with leaders of some of the largest SIGTUR unions. This foregrounds the difficulties of adopting progressive positions and struggling for their realisation.

We begin this brief analysis with a consideration of the role played by the Centre of Indian Trade Unions (CITU). Contradictions are highlighted through the dilemmas CITU has faced over the past 23 years. On the one hand, CITU's leadership drew closer to the Chinese leadership through their involvement in a major boarder dispute China confronted. This stance has, however, spawned contradictions. On the one hand, China has featured prominently in exploiting the opportunities created by restructuring in India through the creation of Free Trade Zones. On the other, CITU mobilised widely against the imposition of neoliberalism in India in 1991. This has taken the form of mass mobilisations of society, running into millions of protesters. The most recent national strike in September 2015 mobilised an estimated 150 million workers against neoliberal change. Such a level of mass mobilisation is remarkable given the era we are living through and has potential to build CITUs credibility and capacity to push the need for an alternative to neoliberalism to the forefront of the movement agenda.

The contradictions spawned within the South African movement also limit any opposition to the ACFTU's strategy. COSATU's response to the ACFTU is a complex one and reflects divisions that go back to its origins in 1985 as a strategic compromise between the shop floor tradition of workplace trade unionism and the national democratic tradition led by an alliance between the African National Congress (ANC) and the South African Communist Party (SACP) (Lambert & Webster, 1988). These divisions spawned different approaches to the international trade union movement, which have persisted into the post-apartheid period.

These differences came to the surface during the 11th COSATU Congress in 2012 (COSATU, 2012). There were those in COSATU who wished to retain a more non-aligned position and were sympathetic to SIGTUR, and those who wished to develop a closer relationship with the ACFTU. The former had reservations over the lack of union independence in China; the latter wanted to develop closer relationships with the ACFTU as they sympathised with the CCP ideologically. The ANC and the SACP had developed deep links with the CCP over the past 60 years, particularly after the turn of the ANC/SACP alliance to armed struggle in 1961 (Naidoo, 2012). These links were sustained after the defeat of the apartheid regime. Against this backdrop, divisions emerged inside COSATU over the China question. The SACP faction inside COSATU contended that the Chinese model represented an initiative which challenged underdevelopment in the age of neoliberalism. Solly Mapaila, Second Deputy General Secretary of the SACP, suggested that it was an insult to brand the Chinese regime as authoritarian. He argued,

> we can't say there are low wages in China. There is a social wage. There is free education, free housing and subsidies on transport, food and water. Chinese earn more if you consider the social wage than in hard cash.[3]

As the general secretary of the SACP, Blade Nzimande, observed, 'perhaps the single most important weakness of 20th century socialism (including the then actually existing socialism and its communist theory and strategy), was its primary focus on the transformation of relations of production (in this case the overthrow of capitalism and its exploitative relations), often at the expense of adequate and simultaneous focus on how to grow the productive forces; . . . the Chinese path is a particular model of building productive forces for socialism in an underdeveloped country and in the context of a unipolar world, dominated by neoliberal capitalism' (Nzimande, 2015).

These arguments from within the SACP imply that the CCP is the guardian of socialism in China. This is a position which fails to acknowledge that the CCP is committed to advancing continuous work restructuring based on the neoliberal market model which imposes the China price on workforces across the globe. As we will argue in the conclusion, this political stance does not address the social and psychological impacts on the massive workforce in China which is impacting dramatically on workforces across the globe.

In the 1980s the formation of COSATU was grounded in ILS democratic unionism. There were similar developments in Brazil with the formation of the *Central Unica Dos Trabalhadores*, which was abbreviated to CUT Brazil. The new federation evolved a close relationship with the Brazilian Workers' Party (PT) in government and this relationship forged through a similar political position shaped by social democracy influenced their response to the ACFTU. A senior leader in CUT's International Department argued that 'CUT does not have a deep relationship with ACFTU. Our impression of the ACFTU is they are a different kind of union—they are a state-run union. Therefore they have an enormous financial capacity.'[4] He elaborated:

> They are very active in self-promotion through annual international trade union conferences on globalisation which take place in Beijing. At these events they have a particular way of doing politics through organising large banquets. The size of their International Department is amazing. The ACFTU has high level support from ITUC and WFTU. Everything is carefully organised at these banquets and the seating is allocated to ensure that Chinese ACFTU leaders have access to union leaders from a wide range of countries. This is complemented by carefully organised programs where leaders are taken to industrial areas outside of Beijing where they meet union representatives. When we talked to them about collective bargaining and strikes their answers were unreal. They said that they had no need of strikes because they had the means to negotiate. When we asked about union membership they told us this was at one hundred percent density.

The progressive union CTA Argentina (Central de Trabajadores de la Argentina) has adopted a similar position to CUT Brazil. An international leader from CTA assessed the situation in this way:[5]

> There is not a debate on the ACFTU in Argentina. CTA has a very formal relationship with the ACFTU. The ACFTU does not seem to be heavily engaged with Latin America, other than through the Brazil, Russia, India, China and South Africa (BRICSA) relationship. We do not think that the ACFTU is really a trade union. The situation is similar to Cuba where the left engages with the Cuban unions even though they are not independent of the Cuban state.

There is a problem in that the Latin American left does not view China as playing an imperial role in Latin America that is similar to the US role. However, there is a debate which contends that China trades in cheap industrial products, whilst importing minerals from Latin America. Argentina tried to put up barriers to Chinese exports but the government was then hit with a cancellation of a shipment of soya bean oil exports from Argentina—so it is very tricky. There are demands that the Argentina government defend the interests of local producers. This is a hidden debate and politicians and union leaders are not willing to bring this out into the open. What is trade union autonomy in these debates?

What conclusions can be drawn from these positions taken by leading SIGTUR unions which carry the banner of ILS committed unionism? The overall picture is bleak. These unions do not have a uniform position. They do not have the vision or political will to challenge the logic of party-driven state unionism.

Conclusion: Navigating between the Local and the Global

We have suggested in this paper that the combination of an authoritarian state in China and neoliberal market forces has led to a relentless global attack on ILS unionism (Li, 2012; Lee, 2014). This 'race to the bottom' has shifted the balance of power within the international labour movement leading to a pragmatic approach to the lack of independence in the ACFTU. Similarly, as we identified above, SIGTUR's unions are divided in their response to the ACFTU, with some maintaining an ideologically sympathetic approach to China.

As pressure mounts from the struggles of Chinese workers, these contradictions are coming to the fore with parts of the ACFTU aspiring to become a real union. But this is unlikely in the near future. State policy is likely to direct which way the ACFTU should go. Importantly, the state has not yet decided what this direction will be. The driving force for change will be the militancy of ordinary workers. Linking these struggles to real pressure from the international labour movement on the ACFTU is likely to be a more effective strategy than 'normalising' relations with China.[6]

Being in practical, engaged solidarity with the emerging struggles of Chinese workers is a challenge to the international labour movement which needs to contribute to the eventual liberation of all workers from the twenty-first-century despotism imposed on the global working class by the free market. As this paper highlights, the corrosive insecurity of the neoliberal labour market creates a fearful working class driven by intense 12-hour shifts, desperately hoping to survive. But we have also seen opportunities emerging for a new kind of labour internationalism, taking advantage of information technology to connect workers directly across the globe. Whether the international labour movement, and SIGTUR in particular, is able to navigate between the local and the global in a way that revitalises the international labour movement remains to be seen. Meanwhile the China price will continue to wreak havoc on the lives of workers worldwide. Recognition of this fact should inspire the building of a new kind of movement with new forms of logistical interventions which aim to humanise work as we move through the twenty-first century. Boundless insecure work is destroying individuals and communities worldwide. The creation of secure work should stand at the centre of working-class struggle. Battles to transform ACFTU are central to these hopes and aspirations aimed at forging an alternative to neoliberalism.[7]

Disclosure Statement

No potential conflict of interest was reported by the authors.

Notes

1 This certified course consists of six modules. It is designed for unionists to understand global workers' rights and the institutional structure of the international labour organisation (ILO) as the key player in setting ILS. It is aimed at deepening unionists' understanding of the concepts behind the fundamental rights of freedom of association and collective bargaining.
2 Interview with Dan Gallin (2013), previously long-time General Secretary of the International Union of Foodworkers (IUF), 25 September 2014, Geneva. Gallin is founder of the Global Labour Institute.
3 Interview with Solly Mapaila, Second Deputy General Secretary of the SACP, 2 August 2014, Johannesburg, South Africa.
4 Skype interview with senior CUT official, 4 August 2014.
5 Skype interview with senior CTA official, 12 August 2014.
6 Skype interview with Dan Gallin, Director, Global Labour Studies Centre, 26 August 2014.
7 Interviewed by Rob Lambert, 25th September 2014.

References

Bieler, A., & Morton, A. (2014). Uneven and combined development and unequal exchange. *Globalizations*, *11*(1), 35–45.

Chan, A. (1993). Revolution or corporatism? Workers and trade unions in Post-Mao China. *The Australian Journal of Chinese Affairs*, *29*, 31–61.

Chan, A. (2000). Globalization, China's free (read bonded) labour market, and the Chinese trade unions. *Asia Pacific Business Review*, *6*(3–4), 260–281.

Chan, A. (2008). Challenges and possibilities for democratic grass roots union elections in China: A case study of two factory-level elections and their aftermath. *Labor Studies Journal*, *34*(3), 293–316.

Chan, C., & Hui, E. (2012). The dynamics and dilemma of workplace trade union reform in China: The case of the Honda workers' strike. *Journal of Industrial Relations*, *54*(5), 653–668.

Chang, K., & Cooke, F. L. (2015). Legislating the right to strike in China: Historical development and prospects. *Journal of Industrial Relations*, *57*(3), 440–455.

Chen, F. (2009). Union power in China: Source, operation and constraints. *Modern China*, *35*(6), 662–689.

Clarke, S., Lee, C. H., & Li, Q. (2004). Collective consultation and industrial relations in China. *British Journal of Industrial Relations, 42*(2), 235–254.

COSATU. (2012). International Policy: The meaning and practice of international working class solidarity in the 21st century, adopted at the 11th Congress of COSATU, September 2012.

Friedman, E., & Lee, C. K. (2010). Remaking the world of Chinese labour: A 30-year retrospective. *British Journal of Industrial Relations, 48*(3), 507–533.

Gallagher, M. E., & Dong, B. (2011). Legislating harmony: Labor law reform in contemporary China. In S. Kuruvilla, C. K. Lee, & M. E. Gallagher (Eds.), *From iron rice bowl to informalization: Markets, workers, and the state in a changing China* (Chap. 3, pp. 36–60). Ithaca, NY: Cornell University Press.

Gallin, D. (2013). The WFTU-hydroponic Stalinism. *Global Labour Journal, 4*(1), 78–87.

Harvey, D. (2002). *Spaces of hope.* Edinburgh: Edinburgh University Press.

Harvey, D. (2006). *Spaces of global capitalism: Towards a theory of uneven geographical development.* London: Verso.

He, B., & Xie, Y. (2011). Wal-Mart's trade union in China. *Economic and Industrial Democracy, 33*(3), 421–440.

Howell, J. (2008). All-China federation of trade unions beyond Reform? The slow march of direct elections. *The China Quarterly, 196*(12), 845–863.

Hui, E. (2012). Trade Union reform and labour legislation in China: An interview with two labour activities. In N. Pons-Vignon & P. Ncube (Eds.), *Confronting finance: Mobilizing the 99% for economic and social progress* (pp. 72–77). Geneva: ILO.

Lambert, R., & Webster, E. (1988). The re-emergence of political unionism in contemporary South Africa. In W. Cobbet & R. Cohen (Eds.), *Popular struggles in South Africa* (pp. 20–41). Trenton, NJ: Africa World Press.

Lambert, R., & Webster, E. (2001). Southern unions and the new labour internationalism. *Antipode, 33*(3), 337–362.

Lee, C. K. (2014). The spectre of global China. *New Left Review, 89*, 29–65.

Lerche, J., Guerin, I., & Srivastava, R. (2012). Guest editors' introduction. *Global Labour Journal, 3*(1), 1–4.

Li, J. (2012). Fight silently: Everyday resistance in surviving state owned enterprises in contemporary China. *Global Labour Journal, 3*(2), 194–216.

Ma, Z. (2011). Industrial relations in China: A review based on a six-party model. *International Labour Review, 150*(1–2), 145–162.

Maritime Unions of Australia. (2014). Memorandum of understanding between the All China Federation of Trade Unions (ACFTU) and the International Transport Workers' Federation (ITF), signed in Beijing, April 2014. Retrieved from the private archive of Robert Lambert, email rob.lambert@uwa.edu.au.

Naidoo, N. (2012). The 'Indian chap': Reflections of a South African underground trainee in Mao's China. *South African Historical Journal, 64*(3), 707–736.

Nzimande, B. (2015, July 23). The People's Republic of China: An opportunity for delinking from imperialism? Reflections from Beijing. *Umsebenzi Online*, 11(25). Retrieved from http://www.sacp.org.za/main.php?ID=4830

Pringle, T. (2014). Regulation of labour conflict in South East Asia. Conference on Collective labour conflicts in Russia and Foreign countries. Presentation at National Research University, Higher School of Economics, Moscow (14 November).

Sander, A. (2009). *German trade unions & China: From non-interference to cooperation?* Berlin: Hintergrundinformationen.

Seung Wook Baek. (2007). The changing trade unions in China. *Journal of Contemporary Asia, 30*(1), 46–66.

Shen, J., & Benson, J. (2008). Tripartite consultation in China: A first step towards collective bargaining. *International Labour Review, 147*(2–3), 231–248.

SIGTUR. (1996). Principles for participation: 13–14 August 1996. Johannesburg, South Africa.

Silver, B. (2003). *Forces of labor: Workers' movements and globalization since 1870.* Cambridge: Cambridge University Press.

Taylor, B., & Li, Q. (2007). Is the ACFTU a union and does it matter? *Journal of Industrial Relations, 49*(5), 701–715.

Traub-Merz, R. (2011). *Wage strikes and trade unions in China—End of the low wage policy?* Bonn: Friedrich Ebert Stiftung.

Van Heerden, A. (2012). FLA Investigation of Foxconn in China. *Global Labour Journal, 3*(2), 278–281.

Webster, E. (2012). The dilemma of job creation and decent work. In N. Pons-Vignon & P. Ncube (Eds.), *Confronting finance: Mobilizing the 99% for economic and social progress* (pp. 115–118). Geneva: ILO.

Webster, E., Lambert, R., & Bezuidenhout, A. (2008). *Grounding globalization: Labour in the age of insecurity.* Oxford: Blackwell & Wiley.

Xinhua News Agency. (2014, October 8). *Senior CPC official meets ITUC delegation.* [press release]. Retrieved September 2, 2014, from http://news.xinhuanet.com/english/china/2014-10/08/c_133700107.htm

Zhu, Y., Warner, M., & Feng, T. (2011). Employment relations 'with Chinese characteristics'. *International Labour Review, 150*(1–2), 127–143.

What Future for Chinese Labour and Transnational Solidarity?

ANDREAS BIELER & CHUN-YI LEE

University of Nottingham, Nottingham, UK

ABSTRACT *In this article we argue that class struggle is central to the future of Chinese workers and the improvement of their situation. Technological upgrading in itself will not automatically result in better working conditions. Moreover, we point out that Chinese workers have a number of old and new sources of power to draw on. What is, however, most problematic in this respect is the role of the All-China Federation of Trade Unions, operating as an official mediator rather than an independent trade union, and the resulting lack of associational power. Hence, informal labour NGOs have an important role to play in supporting social justice for China's workers.*

This volume is based on the workshop *Chinese Labour in the Global Economy*, held at the University of Nottingham, UK on 11 and 12 September 2014. It concluded our ESRC research project 'Globalisation, national transformation and workers' rights: An analysis of Chinese labour within the global economy' (£275k, RES-062-23-2777). In the period from when our project was first conceived in 2009 and the final workshop in 2014, the question of labour supply became increasingly important. The initially abundant cheap labour, so essential to the Chinese development model, was increasingly in doubt. Since 2003, comments and reports about labour shortages have emerged especially in coastal areas such as Guangdong and Shenzhen (Huang, 2004). From 2004 onwards, many factories in coastal areas could not find sufficient or suitable workers (Knight, Quheng, & Shi, 2011, pp. 585–588). Cai argued that China has indeed faced labour shortages due to demographic change and declining fertility as well as because the official minimum wage had not kept pace with fast-increasing living costs in coastal cities (Cai, 2008, pp. 7–10). Others, however, maintained that China still has abundant unskilled low-wage labour in rural areas as a resource to draw on (Golley & Meng, 2011).

The debate on a potential labour shortage echoes, in fact, what we are partially concerned with in this volume: the changing nature of migrant workers in China, the so-called second- or third-generation migrant workers, who entered the labour market in the mid-2000s, and their role in industrial disputes. This generation of migrant workers is different from their parents: most of them grew up under the 'one-child policy' and reform era; they care more about a decent working environment, not just a bowl of rice (Pun & Lu, 2010, p. 495; see also Chan and Selden in this volume). The changed perspective of second-generation migrant workers was certainly influenced by the grand societal changes in China brought about through economic reform, and the strength of migrant workers was arguably reinforced by the implementation of the labour contract law in 2008 (Wang, Appelbaum, & Degiuli, 2009, pp. 497–498). The fast-increasing number of industrial disputes after the late 2000s was not only because of the promulgation of the labour contract law, however, but also because, following the financial crisis in 2008, many export-oriented factories in the coastal areas, facing a sharp drop in international orders, were forced to close down (Schmalz & Ebenau, 2012, pp. 496–497).

As Jane Hardy mentions in her article in this volume, the Chinese development model is based on significant contradictions. Most importantly, the drive to raise domestic consumption at the same time as maintaining comparative advantages based on low wages undermines current attempts at finding ways out of the crisis. Capitalist development is characterised by processes of uneven and combined development and China is no exception in this respect. Unsurprisingly, the rising inequality in China along the rapid relocation of capital under the state-led Go West developmental initiatives has resulted in widespread industrial unrest. The main focus of this volume has been on how to understand the dynamics underlying the Chinese model based on super-exploitation of workers and their resistance to it. In this article, we will first highlight the centrality of class struggle in obtaining gains for workers, before we examine the various power resources available to Chinese labour.

Chinese Workers and the Centrality of Class Struggle

Pringle (2013) argues that migrant workers have emerged as the main agent of class struggle in China. This observation is confirmed by the contributions to this volume. Especially, the article by Chan and Selden focuses on the role of second-generation migrant workers and their emphasis on improving their lives in the cities of their workplace rather than returning home. The decline in available cheap labour, they argue, has increased the bargaining power of these migrant workers. As companies struggle to find replacement, they have to improve wages and working conditions to entice workers to stay. In fact, the Chinese government has taken this demographic change into account. The 'second child' policy announced in October 2015 is proof that the need for a young workforce is of pressing concern to the nation (*BBC News*, 29 October 2015).

Nevertheless, it is not only the young generation of migrant workers, which has been involved in strike action. As the article by Schmalz, Sommer and Xu in this volume makes clear, older migrant workers are prepared to take action, if their retirement payments are endangered. A total of 40,000 workers went on all-out strike at the Yue Yuen shoe factory in Dongguan in 2014, when it had become apparent that their employer had not kept up with paying the legally required social insurance contributions.

How then can the situation of Chinese workers be improved? At the end of the 2000s, the Chinese government started to emphasise industrial upgrading, as was reflected in the slogan of Guangdong's then-party secretary Wang Yang: 'empty the cage to exchange the birds' (Miller, 2009). The government's strategy of industrial upgrading followed the arguments of scholars of supply chain studies (Gereffi, 2009, pp. 46–48). China should gradually develop her own capacity for research and design (R&D) into different supply chain clusters, led by foreign and domestic Chinese capital. In other words, technological upgrading has to be made towards production in higher value-added industrial sectors for social upgrading to occur. And indeed, as Bieler and Lee demonstrate in their comparative assessment of the electronics sector and the higher value-added IT sector, working conditions and pay are better and the relations between employer and employees more consensual in the latter, as stability and skills are necessary in this particular sector to ensure competitiveness. There has also been some technological upgrading in the electronics sector in the Pearl River Delta, as Butollo and Lüthje outline in their contribution to this volume. Low value-added electronics manufacturing did not simply engage in a 'race to the bottom' or move to cheaper production sites. Rather, in conjunction with finding cheaper production sites further in-land in China or drawing on 'student interns' as a new source of cheap labour—Foxconn, for example, employs as many as 150,000 'student interns' on the assembly lines to undermine labour solidarity and to cut costs during the peak production months in the summer (Chan, Pun, & Selden, 2015)—factory owners also made efforts at upgrading production facilities. However, as these authors argue, the upgrading of production sites has done little to improve workers' situation. Technological upgrading does not automatically lead to social upgrading (Butollo, 2014).

Instead, as several of the contributions to this volume make clear, it is class struggle by workers, which may ultimately lead to an improvement in their conditions. As Chan and Hui indicate, when the economy started to recover from 2010 onwards, workers reasserted their demands. The main class struggle in China takes place between internal migrant workers and global capital around the issues of wage levels, pensions and other labour regulations. In the end, after industrial action had spread widely, the Chinese state, understood as a field and condensation of class struggle, endowed with relative autonomy, had to step in supporting some of the workers' demands to ensure stability and, thus, to secure the general viability of capitalist accumulation in China. Tim Pringle, in his analysis of class struggle in China, reaches a similar conclusion. Migrant workers, he argues, have emerged as a class against capital in Guangdong changing the balance of class forces. Hence, they succeeded in pushing capital and state into forms of collective bargaining, which resulted in gains for striking workers. Xuebing Cao and Quan Meng's analysis of the Yantian International Containers Terminal (YICT) strike also confirms that only taking strike action forced management to the negotiations table and secured gains for workers.

Nevertheless, these successes and gains of workers should not be regarded as automatic, nor should they be taken for granted. As Ngai-Ling Sum's article in this volume indicates, capital attempts to co-opt dissatisfied, highly exploited workers, the so-called Diaosi, into capitalism by developing new forms of consumption patterns to which this group of workers has specific access. Class struggle is always open-ended and can go either way, working class gains or a reassertion of capital's power. In relation to the latter, as Sum also shows, the state often plays a crucial role in supporting capital. This is reflected in recent events in China. From October 2015, several labour activities, including the actions of labour lawyers, had been closely monitored by the government. Eventually, the government tightened its net and arrested six labour NGO activists in the Guangdong area on 3 December 2015 (Friedman, Halegua, & Cohen, 2016). International scholars launched a petition campaign to ask the government to release the detainees in mid-December 2015, but at this moment in time, those activists are still in detention.

When assessing the possibilities of workers to resist conditions of super-exploitation, it is important to reflect on their potential sources of power. We will look at this issue in relation to Chinese workers in more detail in the next section.

Chinese Workers and Sources of Power

Beverly Silver, drawing on the work of Erik Olin Wright, identified two main sources of workers' power: (1) associational power depending on collective organisations such as trade unions and political parties; and (2) structural power sub-divided into two subtypes.

> The first subtype of structural power (which we shall call marketplace bargaining power) is the power that results directly from tight labor markets. The second subtype of structural power (which we shall call workplace bargaining power) is the power that results from the strategic location of a particular group of workers within a key industrial sector. (Silver, 2003, p. 13)

And these sources of power are also visible in the case studies investigated in this volume. As Chan and Selden point out, the declining birth rate has increased the marketplace bargaining power of Chinese workers. As there are fewer young workers entering the workforce, the cheap labour development model is under pressure and workers are in a stronger position, when they demand wage increases, better working conditions and social benefits.

The second noticeable source of power is workplace bargaining power. In tightly integrated global commodity chains (GCC), the disruption in one segment of such a chain can result in huge losses for capital. Again, as Chan and Selden indicate, even cheap labour workers in Foxconn production sites potentially enjoy this type of power, as their stoppage disrupts the complete production process of the highly coveted Apple products. The workplace bargaining power is even more visible in the case of the YICT strike. Dockworkers enjoy a unique location in global production. The moment they are on strike, whole GCC break down as parts and finished products are no longer moved along. Equally, it is very difficult for capital to replace one port with another. Spatial fixes of this type are not really feasible in transport. Additionally, dockworkers had workplace bargaining power due to the introduction of modern technology in ports. They are highly skilled and cannot be replaced easily.

Furthermore, there are also new sources of power, logistical and symbolic/societal, available to workers (Webster, 2015). Societal power involves 'the struggle of "right" against "wrong", providing a basis for an appeal both to the public and politicians, as well as to allies in civil society' (Webster, Lambert, & Beziudenhout, 2008, p. 12). Cao and Meng, in their analysis of the YICT strike, identify this type of power in the discourse about endangered health as a result of the way work in ports is organised. Logistical power, finally, was available to the dockworkers in the form of social media, allowing them to organise collectively even though the workplace trade union was not the initiator of strike action. At the Yue Yuen strike too, social media played a crucial role in the collective organisation of large-scale industrial action (Mason, 2014). In short, both old and new forms of power resources have proved vital in the case of Chinese workers' struggle for better working conditions and social justice.

At the same time, capital has also responded flexibly to this pressure, partly by moving production to other countries with available cheap labour such as Vietnam (see Schmalz, Sommer and Xu on the employer's response to the Yue Yuen shoe factory strike), and partly by introducing new technology to automate the production process needing fewer workers (see Butollo and Lüthje in this volume). Capital, moreover, attempts to integrate disadvantaged workers through specifically devised consumption strategies—see the assessment by Sum in this volume on attempts to co-opt the Diaosi. Equally important is the general state of the economy. As Chan and Hui assert in their contribution, only once the economy started to recover in China from 2010 onwards, did the state feel pushed to intervene on behalf of striking workers. During the economic crisis in 2008 and 2009, fewer workers were needed anyway and marketplace bargaining power evaporated. Finally, while the state at times intervenes on behalf of workers to ensure stability, it has increasingly also clamped down on striking workers and informal labour NGOs, which had supported them in their struggles.

This issue of state repression turns our attention to the issue of associational power and the potential role of trade unions and here in particular, the All-China Federation of Trade Unions (ACFTU). As the various contributions have made clear, the ACFTU has played at best a mediating role between workers and the government, but it has not functioned as an independent organisation representing the interests of workers. On the one hand, it speaks for the state to mobilise workers for more production; on the other, it collects workers' views to report back to the state. These two functions are contradictory in themselves and, unsurprisingly, the latter function is rather superficial and less developed (Chan, 1993, pp. 36–37). From an international trade union perspective, Lambert and Webster argue in their contribution to this special issue that the ACFTU has several contradictions as a 'functional' trade union. To date, the ACFTU has refused to accept the ILO international labour standards. Thus, it serves more as a 'transmission belt' for state policies. It is still institutionally affiliated to the Chinese Communist Party, the union's leaders are not elected by shop floor workers, and, more importantly, the ACFTU does not have workers' support and hence does not and cannot represent the workforce in China. At times, often in response to labour militancy, the ACFTU mediates conflict on behalf of the state and protects workers' legal rights, but it is not an independent workers organisation. Informal labour NGOs, on the other hand, either focus on supporting workers through after work, cultural programmes as, for example, several NGOs in the Yangtse River Delta or they are increasingly repressed as the informal labour NGOs in the Pearl River Delta, which had represented directly the individual and collective interests of workers (see Bieler and Lee in this volume). In short, associational power on a more permanent institutional basis is extremely little developed in China. At times, workers creatively overcome these limits through logistical power as represented in the possibilities of social media (see above), but overall, there is the danger that Chinese workers cannot fully use their structural power, as long as they are institutionally so weakly organised. This also provides a challenge to the global labour movement, which may need to engage more with non-conventional institutions relevant to Chinese workers' struggles against globalised capital. As Lambert and Webster suggest in their article, rather than engaging with the ACFTU and being blended by its large membership, the focus should be on strengthening Chinese civil society and the support for those informal labour NGOs, which have been attacked in the past as well as in the present.

Acknowledgements

We are grateful to the contributors to this special issue and Barry Gills for their comments on an earlier draft of this concluding article.

Disclosure Statement

No potential conflict of interest was reported by the authors.

References

Butollo, F. (2014). *The end of cheap labour in China? Industrial transformation and social upgrading in China*. Frankfurt am Main: Campus.

Cai, F. (2008). *Approaching a triumphal span: How far is China towards its Lewisian turning point* (UNU-WIDER Working Paper, 9). Retrieved from https://www.wider.unu.edu/publication/approaching-triumphal-span.

Chan, A. (1993). Revolution or corporatism? Workers and trade union in post-Mao China. *The Australian Journal of Chinese Affairs*, *29*, 31–61.

Chan, J., Pun, N., & Selden, M. (2015). Interns or workers? China's student labor regime. *Asian Studies (Official Journal of the Asian Studies Association of Hong Kong)*, *1*(1), 69–98.

China to end one-child policy and allow two. (2015, October 29). *BBC News*. Retrieved from http://www.bbc.co.uk/news/world-asia-34665539

Friedman, E., Halegua, A., & Cohen, J. A. (2016, January 2). Cruel irony: China's Communists are stamping out labor activism. *The Washington Post*. Retrieved from https://www.washingtonpost.com/opinions/cruel-irony-chinas-communists-are-stamping-out-labor-activism/2016/01/03/99e986f2-b0bb-11e5-b820-eea4d64be2a1_story.html

Gereffi, G. (2009). Development models and industrial upgrading in China and Mexico. *European Sociological Review*, *25*(1), 37–51.

Golley, J., & Meng, X. (2011). Has china run out of surplus labour. *China Economic Review*, *22*, 555–572.

Huang, Y. P. (2004, August 6). A labour shortage in China. *The Wall Street Journal*. Retrieved from http://www.wsj.com/articles/SB109174691909084454

Knight, J., Quheng, D., & Shi, L. (2011). The puzzle of migrant labour shortage and rural labour surplus in China. *China Economic Review*, *22*, 585–600.

Mason, P. (2014). China's workers are turning from analogue slaves into digital rebels. *The Guardian*. Retrieved from http://www.theguardian.com/commentisfree/2014/sep/14/china-analogue-slaves-digital-rebellion

Miller, T. (2009, June 10). China's plan to empty the bird cage. *Financial Times*. Retrieved from http://www.ft.com/cms/s/0/4accc3bc-5556-11de-b5d4-00144feabdc0.html#axzz3w7GMTBfT

Pringle, T. (2013). Reflections on labor in China: From a moment to a movement. *The South Atlantic Quarterly*, *112*(1), 191–202.

Pun, N., & Lu, H. (2010). Unfinished proletarianization: Self, anger, and class action among the second generation of migrant workers in present-day China. *Modern China*, *36*(5), 493–519.

Schmalz, S., & Ebenau, M. (2012). After neoliberalism? Brazil, India and China in the global economic crisis. *Globalization*, *9*(4), 487–501.

Silver, B. J. (2003). *Forces of labor: Workers' movements and globalization since 1870*. Cambridge: Cambridge University Press.

Wang, H., Appelbaum, R. P., & Degiuli, F. (2009). China's new labour contract law: Is China moving towards increasing power for workers? *Third World Quarterly*, *30*(3), 485–501.

Webster, E. (2015). Labour after globalization: Old and new sources of power. In A. Bieler, R. Erne, D. Golden, I. Helle, K. Kjeldstadli, T. Matos, & S. Stan (Eds.), *Labour and transnational action in times of crisis* (pp. 115–27). London: Rowman & Littlefield International.

Webster, E., Lambert, R., & Beziudenhout, A. (2008). *Grounding globalization: Labour in the age of insecurity*. Oxford: Wiley-Blackwell.

Corrigendum

"Forum: Beyond Business as Usual: COP21 and the Future of Climate Change Strategy", *Globalizations*, Vol 13, No. 6, December 2016, pp. 928–969.

The Editor of the above special Forum was Barry K. Gills. His name was mistakenly omitted when the Forum was published.

Index

Note: page numbers in italic type refer to figures; those in bold type refer to tables.

For Product Safety Concerns and Information please contact our EU
representative GPSR@taylorandfrancis.com
Taylor & Francis Verlag GmbH, Kaufingerstraße 24, 80331 München, Germany

www.ingramcontent.com/pod-product-compliance
Ingram Content Group UK Ltd.
Pitfield, Milton Keynes, MK11 3LW, UK
UKHW050755180926
475701UK00007B/1070

* 9 7 8 0 3 6 7 2 2 0 4 7 1 *